Addie

Addie

Mary Lee Settle

University of South Carolina Press

© 1998 University of South Carolina

Published in Columbia, South Carolina, by the
University of South Carolina Press

Manufactured in the United States of America

02 01 00 99   5 4 3
Library of Congress Cataloging-in-Publication Data

Settle, Mary Lee.
   Addie : a memoir / Mary Lee Settle.
   p. cm.
  ISBN 1-57003-284-X
  1. Settle, Mary Lee—Family. 2. Women novelists, American—20th
century—Family relationships. 3. Grandmothers—West
Virginia—Biography. 4. Family—West Virginia—History. I. Title.
  PS3569.E84 Z463 1998
  813'.54—ddc21
   [B]   98-25487

To my beloved cousin, Roger Tompkins

Beginning

An autobiography that begins with one's birth begins too late,
in the middle of the story, sometimes at the end.

To wait for a story is to wait for a way of telling that can be
no other.

I was formed by riverrun, east from Virginia, where the mountains
cut us off from our past but not our memory, west to the Ohio,
the Mississippi.

I was formed by eons of earthquake, and the rise of the mountains
and the crushing of swamps into coal as surely as by timid human
copulation.

Old choices, not my own, set me down in one place and not
another.

Old habits I had not made clung to me.

Old decisions, old quarrels, old disguises were my inheritance.

To honor them, recall them, present them, and to admit my love,
is to cast them off at last.

*I*n 1927, when the Florida boom burst, we went home in a Model T Ford with what was left packed in orange crates tied to the running boards. We went to Cedar Grove, Kanawha County, West Virginia, the only place my mother ever called home in her life.

So that was why, on an early summer afternoon when I was eight years old, I was lying in the same hammock where my mother had lain in her Peter Thompson suit with her high-buttoned shoes in 1908, smiling at a camera. The hammock had a design of flowers and leaves, vaguely oriental. Fringe hung down, even though it was pretty ratty by 1927. It had always been suspended catty-cornered at the foot of the back stairs, between the old, thin wooden columns of the back porch, shaded by a huge trumpet vine that made a mat which kept the sun away.

I was half asleep, weighed down with heat that stuck my dress to my stomach. There was only the creak of the hammock, and then silence, and then again the creak of the hammock when I put a foot down to move it. I remember especially the silence that seemed blessed since it was such a rare thing in that house where there were so many people.

There was always talk at Cedar Grove, oceans of it, afternoons of it, evenings of it. But I never in all the time I was growing up saw one of the aunts, uncles, or in-laws touch another, ever, in love or sympathy or anger, except when Addie, my grandmother, smoothed my hair as she passed by, or broke a switch off her favorite tree, swished it to test it, and said, "If you won't listen, you'll have to feel."

From the corner where I lay I could see the place where she had had the breezeway between the dining room and the kitchen filled in with brick. In that magic time Before the War, it had been open, and slaves had brought the food through the open air from the kitchen. My mother said that it was wrong to change things like that in a lovely old historic place. Not house. Place. She had said that ever since I could remember, as if she were seeing the house that once was, or could be, but never as it was at the time.

My grandmother, Addie, hadn't changed the back porch, though. She said that suited her. So it remained what it had been since the house was built in 1844. The well was under the roof at the long side of an ell. It was table height so you could hike yourself up on the stone ledge, lean over when there were no grownups around, look down a long way and see yourself, a little scared face in the black water. Beside the well, the smoke house and the milk house were built into the brick ell behind the main house, both of them dark and cool even in the hottest days of summer. The breezeway between them and the kitchen which had matched the one between the kitchen and the dining room had been left open. Addie said she had a use for that, an easy way to get to the corncrib and the hog pen to slop the huge sow with her evil eyes and her squealing piglets. My nastiest cousin said that if I fell into the pigpen, the old sow would eat me. There would be nothing left. The pen and the corncrib were in a row away on the east side of the backyard with the chicken house which had once been my mother's playhouse.

I didn't hear her walk onto the porch. Like many heavy women, Addie had silent feet. I did not know she was close to me until she spoke. "The Catholic Church is the Whore of Babylon in the Book of Revelation," she said to wake me up. She wanted to talk. She said she thought I ought to know that about the Catholics, in case.

I was still half asleep, and I saw the Whore of Babylon on the Great Beast, riding astraddle, as Miss Addie put it, across the hot white summer sky beyond the back porch, and I heard again the creak of the hammock.

If she had found any of the other ten grandchildren, she would have routed them out for a chore, made up on the spur of the moment to get them moving. Then we would hear her voice of thunder, "Shame on you! A great big thing like you asettin down," or, if she caught them smoking, "You put out them coffin-nails! You'll stunt your growth," or, worst of all, "Quit that, you little HESSIAN!"

But I was privileged. Because she had lifted me up and taken me to Serena's breast when I was, she said, just laying there waiting to die at a month old, she still thought when I was eight that my mother wouldn't raise me. She would say, "You rest, honey. You never can tell when the knell will sound."

I heard the creak of Miss Addie's rocker when she settled herself to talk. I opened my eyes. She was wearing the blue and white checked poke bonnet that made wings down both of her cheeks and partly hid her face, red from working in the summer heat. It had a frill at the back to protect her neck from the sun when she bent over. She made the bonnets for herself, and she wore them when she went into the garden, no matter how much it embarrassed the girls. She didn't refer to her daughters any other way. "My girls," she would say, glancing over her shoulder at them whenever they were gathered at the center of the house, the huge kitchen table, discussing their troubles, "have not got one iota of gumption." Then she would add, "except for your mother." It was the only nice thing, at least I suppose it was nice, that she ever said about my mother. "Not one iota" was a favorite size with her. She could use that diminishment like a club.

She sat there on the back porch foursquare upon her hams, with her legs apart, leaning on a hoe. I recognized that stance later when I saw statues of Athena that seemed to grow out of the ground. I never thought of Miss Addie as fat, but she had a thick body like the trunk of an old tree.

There she is, as alive for me as she was that afternoon, an old woman in summer, looking in memory like the goddess of justice, timeless and chthonic, in the shade of the porch, in her straight-backed rocker nobody else dared sit in, keeping a rocking rhythm on the stone floor. The shadows of afternoon filtered through the trumpet vines and swayed over the stone sides of the well, the flagstones of the floor, fluttered across the wall of bricks behind her that had been made by slaves, and time had changed to soft pink.

The places where she sat became, when she was there, the center of the house, and when she left them, and walked away, always alone, into the garden, or up the hollow to the tenant houses that had once been slave cabins, the ever-present voices of the "girls," her daughters, my mother and aunts, rose in volume as if they had been released and flew as they called to each other from floor to floor and room to room, from the upstairs back veranda rail, from the wide front lawn or the spreading front porch.

Addie's voice, that day, drifted in and out of dreams and summer until I was awake and watching her, which was what she had waited for. Then, out of some thought deep within herself that she made into words, she decided for the first time to tell me her version of the always whispered about but never admitted family scandal.

"Let me tell you something," she began, as she often did, to draw us to her whenever she caught us drifting. She talked mostly to her grandchildren. Her daughters had stopped listening. "I been thinking about this in the garden. My Lord, it's hot out there." The acre of formal garden that had been laid out when the house was built Before the War in patterns of herbs and peonies and roses and tiny English boxwood had long since been turned by her into a vegetable garden. Little wisps of its neglected and ignored past still showed forlornly in the spring. She said nobody but a fool would have too many flowers and too few vegetables, with things the way they were. "Things the way they are" was another one of her choruses.

"Well, this is how it was. I was no more than fifteen years old when I married that devil Chris Morris. By the time I was eighteen years old I already had three daughters. Chris Morris was mean to me." She settled back into her story, still grasping the hoe like a spear. A bandanna rose slowly and she wiped her forehead under the poke bonnet and began, as she did whenever she rested, to talk about Jesus. "You can't tell Him a thing," she complained. "You just have to set there and listen." She was completely familiar with Jesus, and her conversations with him were on as equal terms as she could manage.

Once, being smart aleck, I asked her what Jesus sounded like, and, instead of punishing me for taking the Lord's name in vain, she thought for a long time, and then she said, "Near as I can explain, real quiet, a little bit like your grandfather."

Her language was a mixture of Bible, fairy tale, ghost story, coal operator, and hillbilly. At any time, out of the house of her own recall and contemplation, one of the days or nights of life would come forth for me, from some kind of darkness that she lit with words. So much of it was legend, legend that now she believed and stated as facts.

"One Saturday night I heared Christopher Morris a'comin home from the saloon and I knowed he was drunk. He was always drunk on a Saturday night. He was a'comin up that road hell-bent for election, mutterin to hisself, and I knowed what that meant. I clumb a tree to get away from him. And there I was a'settin in that tree, no more than eighteen years old, and already married three years to that devil, and I looked down through the branches and there was Chris Morris mean drunk and lurchin around down there a'lookin for me."

Her voice changed, quieted. "Right there up that tree I heard the voice of Jesus." She began to sway and use her witness-bearing voice. "Jesus said unto me, Addie, you are nuthin but a damn fool. Ain't you ever heard of divorce?"

That was the way she remembered her Christian holy past, a victim up a tree, with Jesus to give her courage to act, a battered woman among so many battered women.

Nobody had ever said directly what had happened; we gathered around it later, picking up fragments, some malicious, some true, I suppose, but when I found the court records, I found the pathos and violence she had replaced with Jesus.

All the time I had known her I thought of her as Miss Addie. I would not have dared to do otherwise. But when I began to glimpse the woman she had been, she became, for me, Addie, more familiar and more mysterious than she was in life, Addie young, Addie hurt and proud, Addie beautiful, and finally, again, an old woman, sitting that day on the back porch, looking as she did when she entered my own childhood memory and stayed there and still does, as strongly as if she has just left the room I am in now, having shaken the curtains because somebody had been smoking coffin nails.

She had not been eighteen, she had been twenty-six when she filed for divorce, and she had already met my grandfather. It had been one of the first divorces in West Virginia, but the facts are misty, the legends crossed, and I saw more truth if not more fact in the way Addie told it that day.

The records of the divorce, the births, the marriage to my grandfather had remained ever since in the County Courthouse. When I finally saw them, they were less believable than the story of the voice of Jesus. The courage that she had shown was almost unbearable.

Christopher Morris said he wanted to get rid of her anyway. He didn't like being married and his mamma couldn't stand her. He had already left her three times in the course of their eleven-year marriage. She had made her living and fed her children by being a seamstress. They had lived in one of those board and batten houses, with inch-thick walls, three or four rooms, and a front stoop. Later, when the coal companies built housing for their miners, such dwellings were called "Jenny Lind houses" after the cheap method of building used at the Jenny Lind mine in Colorado. But they had long been built that way in West Virginia. The farmers used board and batten to cover the logs of their cabins as a sign that they were moving up in the world. The next stage toward gentility was broad clapboard, overlapping and painted white.

Addie had been a beautiful woman, the most beautiful, they said, in the valley. There are no pictures of her then, only people's memories, and in memory, beauty grows. She was of her time—the chestnut hair she could sit on, the tiny waist, even after three daughters born in the single bedroom of that poor house on the south bank of the river. If she screamed it was to a local midwife, and when the third daughter came the other two watched from the doorway. "There wasn't nobody to make them scat," she said. "Chris Morris was off drunk somewheres." Her birth stories were not calculated. She would have scorned calculation. They were simply facts of life, often too strong for the blood of her daughters and granddaughters.

She sued for divorce on the grounds of cruelty and desertion. She was represented by the leading law firm in the city of Charleston, twenty miles downriver, where, because of the new coal business, lawyers had gathered like a plague of locusts. My grandfather had hired the law firm that had been there years longer than the "new people," and whom she never would have heard of or been able to pay for.

It was obvious from the court records that they were prepared to do a favor for the old friend who had "kicked the end out of the same cradle" and who they sat with on the porch of the Ruffner Hotel, looking at the river, drinking juleps, and talking politics.

In the legal layer presented of past events, her husband had "deserted" her three times. The last time, in 1889, he did not return. She said she saw him sometimes across the road in the town at the foot of the hollow in a wide place in the valley, where a ferry plied across the Kanawha River.

The Kanawha runs west to the Ohio. Its direction has dictated industry, economies, marriages, and mores ever since the valley was settled in 1775. Its direction has formed the longings and lies of so many of its people—dreams of gentility east of the Alleghenies in Virginia, dreams of fortunes west along the Ohio at Cincinnati. It has flowed past coal companies with their shack towns, narrow bottomland, and knife-cut hollows between steep hills on its south side. It passed large old farms with several small towns grown up around on the north side until, a few miles east of Charleston, beyond the lush beautiful farmland and virgin forests on the hills, the land had once been blackened and denuded of trees when the salt business had been the first of the exploitive industries in the valley. Upriver, the cultural banks were farther apart than the mere fact of a hundred or so feet of deep water.

According to Addie's testimony, the river had held for her a terrible way out. She had tried twice to drown herself in it. The first time, she said, had been in the first two years of the marriage, the second within the year of her statement. She had tried to kill herself by taking a bottle of laudanum when she was eight months pregnant. She had bought it at the Company Store. She said she had tried to go to the station to catch the train to see her mother, and Chris Morris had followed her and forced her home by pulling a knife on her. She said her mother had died without Addie being able to visit her.

Her first witness was her housekeeper, who had looked after the children while Addie earned her living after the desertion. In her testimony she said that she had seen Addie jump into the river, had seen Addie's husband beat her. She added that he was a mean drunk and that the children weren't safe with him. Addie's oldest daughter,

Minnie, was put on the stand to testify that her father beat her mother. She was eleven years old.

It had been Chris Morris, though, who came back to the house after threatening Addie with the knife and found her insensible on the bed, with the empty bottle of laudanum beside her. He called the family doctor. The doctor testified that he nearly lost her that time.

Jesus and the legal evidence were only the first two layers of the event. The third consisted of rumor, memory, facts let slip, a patchwork of events that had to be put together like a quilt, the kind that Addie and her friends stretched across two big trestles and quilted all through the winter. Some of the gossip came from daughters-in-law who didn't like her, some from my mother when her memories of "home" slipped into reality without her being aware that she had spoken. My mother tended literally to speak her mind, let out in words the secret scenes that she was seeing.

All the memories are real. Of course they are, like dreams are real, like old wounds that insist until they heal and leave a twinge of memory in the scars.

Chris Morris did pull a knife on Addie, not because she wanted to visit her mother, but because he knew she was pregnant with another man's child. She did try to go to the station, where the trains then ran several times a day and made the whole valley into one railroad town, a forty-mile corridor down the south side of the river. But she was not going to meet her mother who had been dead for years, but her lover, my grandfather.

By the time of the trial she was buried in scandal, unable to breathe. The doctor told the truth until he said he knew nothing against her reputation. He must have pitied her, he, nearly eighty, too old for judgment, she still young, still lovely.

She had seen a way out, a way that was taboo. She took it and then, for too long, had the door slammed in her face. Her dreams while she worked at her sewing machine, over the washtub, calling the children, patching, darning, quilting, cooking, became nightmares. The laudanum was real. The bottle was empty.

She was surrounded by catcalls and rumors, that Chris Morris was paid off, that my grandfather had bought her from him for a sack of corn.

Chris Morris and his buddies played sandlot baseball on a Saturday afternoon, got drunk at the saloon on Saturday night, and threw five sticks of dynamite from the mine on the front porch of her stepfather's house, where she had gone to wait for the divorce to be final. Addie ran out, stamped on the long fuse, picked up the bound sticks and threw them into the woods. She saved her children's and her stepfather's lives, and her own, which by then wasn't worth a plugged nickel. No wonder that, in those days, when she heard the voice of Jesus, he must have sounded like Mr. Tompkins, my grandfather.

*W*hat Addie called her home in heaven was as sensuous as a Moslem's. One morning she caught me sulking on the front porch with my legs hanging over the porch floor. I was kicking rambler roses. To cheer me up she told me, "Oh, honey, last night I had the most wonderful dream. I dreamed that I passed over at last and I went to heaven, and when them great gold gates parted, there in front of me was a big table laden with golden dishes and every dish was full of beautiful food, and there was flowers and silks and satins and purple for the kings and blue for the saints, and there was all my relatives that had gone before all waiting to welcome me at the great table, and all their relatives and friends that had gone before, a great host at the banquet . . . "

She stopped; she had heard me make a small sound, a humph, and she said, "What's the matter with you?"

I said that didn't sound much like heaven to me, that I lived with too many people already who didn't understand me and I certainly didn't want to get stuck with them forever in heaven when I got there.

"All right," she said. "Go on to hell where you don't know nobody."

All her life she loved Jesus, ghosts, my grandfather, and food. Her dinner table was always laden with food, and she looked at it as if it might disappear.

Much of Virginia beyond the mountains had been Confederate in sentiment during the occupation of Federal troops in western Virginia, which became West Virginia in 1863. The army took the people's mules and their livestock. Secretly the southern sympathizers called the new state the bastard son of political rape.

In 1865 men from both armies were straggling home. Some had given up and lit out for the territories. Some were simply never heard of again—dead or missing. Addie said her real father had been a Confederate spy and had been hanged when he was caught. She was ashamed of that. My grandfather told her that it was braver to be a spy than a soldier, but she never quite believed it.

She had been taken up by a family called either Ross or Elswick. None of her children knew whether her father had been called Ross and her stepfather Elswick, or the other way round. No mention had ever been made of her mother, who had not survived the starving time. All that was known was her mother's last name—Martin.

Sometimes Addie said she was descended from Pocahontas. Pocahontas's only child has been accused of having a million descendants in Virginia. But sometimes Addie just told us that her great-great-grandmother was a squaw. In the early days of the Virginia colony, women were rounded up and sent over from England to be wives. Up to the early eighteenth century the saying in the colony was "Better a clean squaw than a London whore." By the mid-eighteenth century, of course, many of the settlers were younger sons of peers, according to their descendants, but Addie scorned what she called that piece of foolishness. The shape of Addie's face and her eyes hinted at the truth of the squaw.

During the Civil War (the greatest of all historic oxymorons) there were only the old people and the children to work the steep fields of the small farms. They gathered wild greens in the woods when the spring came to cure the cabin fever and the scurvy that came from eating only jerky, the dried meat that had been put up for winter, after the dried beans and yarbs and corn and the vegetables in the root cellar had long since run out. They lived as people on the frontier had always lived, long after the frontier had passed them by.

Gradually the young men straggled back and the fields were plowed again. A mule was a luxury few could afford. Addie remembered how the women steered while the men were hitched to the ancient plows their grandparents had brought over the mountains. She followed with corn seed, and stinking fish, three seeds for the hole—one for the critters, one to rot, and one to grow. She laid a piece of rotten fish in the hole for fertilizer. She still planted corn that way when she was an old woman, but she said the three seeds were the Father, the Son, and the Holy Ghost.

When Addie was nine years old, her world changed more profoundly than we can fathom. The coming of the railroads and the opening of the coal mines in the Kanawha Valley were as violent a change to the farmers of Addie's childhood as the great industrial revolutions were to earlier Americans. We are seeing something like it in our own lives, and are now once again in a frightening economic upheaval, this time requiring intelligence, a new language, more delicate skills, instead of the once-proud working man's muscular strength.

John Henry has been replaced by a fourteen-year-old computer genius in a garage. The newly honored intelligence that was once derided when muscle was needed at the coal face is leaving bitterness, as the men Addie grew up with became embittered when their mules were "commandeered" by war and their farm skills were no longer needed. Some retired deeper into the hollows, like animals after a flood has passed, then, as now, leaving dangerous residues that turned into hatred of what had passed them by.

In 1873 the Chesapeake and Ohio railroad was completed on the south side of the river, and later the Kanawha and Michigan railroad on the north. Coal barges plied the river below Cedar Grove in the months when the river was navigable, following the way of the salt barges, on their way to Cincinnati in the salt boom of the early 1800s.

The new boom was coal. Cash money poured into the valley with the opening of the great coal seams. A farmer who had had sense enough not to sell his mineral rights could (and did) become a millionaire overnight. Coal had names as overblown as the hopes that came with it—black diamonds, black gold, King Coal. Later F. Scott Fitzgerald, who was at Princeton with coal baron heirs, was to call a coal fortune "The Diamond as Big as the Ritz." Most of the money went to stockholders who didn't know or care about how people were living in West Virginia. The saying on "the street" was "dividends don't make demands."

In the next five years of Addie's growing up, the soil darkened with coal dust. Spurs of the railroad snaked up the hollows. Rich men came in their private railroad cars. The train engines belched long lines of smoke. If you traveled on the train you could smell coal dust, clean linen, furniture polish, good whiskey, and fat cigars. It was the smell of new money. My father told me that the first time he ever saw a grapefruit was through the window of a diner on the C&O.

The hillbillies watched the trains go by and made up songs. "Here she comes, look at her roll, there she goes eatin' that coal." Billy Richardson of Hinton became immortal when a song told about how he was beheaded by a projecting signal on the water tower but brought the train to a halt in the station anyway. John Henry challenged a mechanical pile driver in the digging of No. 9 tunnel under Gauley Mountain on the C&O. Casey Jones died at the throttle when he lost his average on a three-mile grade. At the railroad town of Thurmond on the New River, new kinds of men gathered, glamorous men—coal operators, railroad men, speculators. A poker game in the Dunglen Hotel went on for thirty-four years.

Life, for a while, was good. Local men had work that paid cash or the scrip that meant they could buy, but only at the Company Store. There were things at the Company Store that they would have had to go all the way to Charleston for in the past, if they had the cash, which they usually didn't. It stocked gingham and shoes and clothes, and overalls that the women didn't have to make.

There were barrels of dill pickles, huge wheels of store-bought cheese, white bread, drugs and whiskey, and mangles for the washtub. At Christmastime there were oranges from Florida and Skookam apples all the way from the West Coast. There was sheet music from New York. They could order pianos, upright and player and even baby grand. There were cans of fruit and vegetables the women didn't have to put up, the essence of luxury. When my grandfather asked a miner who had ten children how he was managing to feed them, he answered, "Well, Mr. Tompkins, we don't eat no canned peaches."

They came down out of the hills, from the farms, off the immigrant boats from Europe. An Italian consulate opened at Montgomery, a few miles upriver from Addie's home. There was no English spoken at some of the new mines. It was a new "volunteer" fashion for ladies from Charleston to go upriver to teach the Italian women to speak English, to cook (when they had been cooking Italian food all their lives), and to be "American."

Then, as it has ever since, in a kind of systaltic, diastaltic progression, the bottom dropped out of the coal business. For the first of many times, people who had come to work in the mines were thrown out of the shacks the companies had built. The United Mine Workers began to grow on the rocky soil, now poisoned by acid from the slag.

Addie had married at fifteen into the Morris family, who were victims of a change that had been going on since 1812, when the salt wells were dug north of the river at Burning Springs, a few miles east of Charleston. Christopher Morris, her husband, like the most of the men, had gone into the new mines. He was a drunkard, but then so many of them were. He did beat her, but in that world of coal mining, day long, night long, where petrified tree trunks called kettles could loosen and kill, where the white bones of ancient fish in the coal caught the light from the miners' head lamps, and the crystal skeletons of plants were known as flowers of darkness, where accidents waited for millennia when the earth was disturbed, the men were all edged with fear, like people in a perpetual war who go about their business as best they can.

There were too many shootings on Saturday nights. From the new language of machinery and the railroad they took the phrase "letting off steam." In winter, when he had work, Chris Morris left home before dawn with his carbide lamp lit on his miner's hard hat to show him the way; he made the daily trip by mule-drawn tram into the mine, sometimes as far as two or three miles. When he returned, long after dark, with his lamp lit to show him the way home, Addie heated water on the kitchen range and tried to scrub off the black gold while he sat in the washtub.

You could tell a coal miner by his eyes, and it was still so when I was a child there. They were darkened around the rims with coal dust that never came off—Nefertiti eyes. Yes, he beat her. Yes, he drank. Men then lived hard, died early, carried guns, gambled, and, being so on the tether of some decision made someplace else by men who didn't know their names, they swaggered even more. Those with brains fought their way downriver, to college, but carried the scars of the coal business, and still do. The feudalism. The exploiting of earth and men. Owner and worker, each far from the other, were threatened by the same diseases of danger and indifference, recognized each other as brothers who don't claim kin.

We are all marked, who have lived and been blooded by the coal fields. We never get away because it is deep in us, whether our fathers have worked the coal face, or bought our clothes and our college educations with money that was as black as the rims of coal miners' eyes. We have all been formed long before human ancestry or our culture or kindness or hatred or lack of money has affected us. These are all personal. And they can twist and stunt, or lie fallow in us, or help us grow strong.

But the coal mines, the darkness, like the mark of Cain, are as deep within us as the eons that formed us both, slowly and inexorably, millions of years ago, where patient time has crushed and dried ancient seas, swamps, forests, animals into something mysterious that seduced the world we lived in, made us rich, made us poor, broke the health of some of us, made some of us refugees. Like people who have been deserted by a lover, we may hate it, but we never forget it.

We who have the stigma recognize each other. Sometimes the recognition goes unrealized for years. At least ten years after I grew close to a fine singer, Bobby Short, I found out that his father had been mashed in a mine in Kentucky. Ann Beattie, who is a writer of Mozartean prose, told me after I had known her for twenty years that her mother was brought up in a coal town. An Englishman I nearly married and whom I knew only as an RAF pilot turned out to be the heir to a coal fortune. What is it that is between us, deeper than country, race, or sex? Is it a residue of genetic fear, the fear of the exploited depths?

Even if we have lived far from it, maybe we inherit a residue, too, daily and unnoticed, the awareness of darkness, listening and not listening for accidents, for boom and bust, for failure, for wild success, all from the earth-stabbing we are born into. Mining, the boring for oil, gas, minerals, unlike farming or the making of things, is the taking of something that only more eons can give back. It informs politics, too. The ones who do the dangerous work produce paper profit for people without names or responsibility or care.

Almost directly across the river from where Addie was born was the house my great-grandfather had built with money from salt. It was one of the three largest farms in the valley, a place that must have seemed a mirage to her in the starving time. On early mornings as a child in linsey-woolsey, she would have seen the horses and the cattle, and a few black people who had stayed and were getting wages of a sort and enough to eat, all like shadows, moving too far away for her ever to reach.

Then, when Addie was twenty-three or -four, there was a moment so short, so far-reaching, that it still haunts my dreams and my habits as it did my mother's. It fashioned our bones. My mother was brittle with imitations of some faraway gentility, always thin, always upright, always watchful, and yet, within, she carried the voice of Addie, mocking her as she mocked herself. The moment was the meeting of my grandparents.

There has always been a mystery to how Addie and my grandfather met and what they could have had in common. Maybe they shared the immediacy of memory of a better, richer earth before the black change came in their lifetime. Was the meeting on the ferry that plied between her town and his?

Or was it on a country road? I like to think so. Make it a hot morning and sandy bottom at the mouth of one of the hollows. The althea is in bloom, and scraggly roses crawl over a stump in the sandy front yard—a hot morning that smells of grass and sand and the wet wash that flaps on the line.

I see Addie standing by the fence, as if she is resting for a minute from too much work. The sweat, the glow, as Mr. Tompkins would have called it, stands out on her lovely forehead. She is small and lithe and beautiful. One of her daughters clings to her skirt. The two older girls are playing in the yard, but quietly, watching her from time to time as if they don't know which way the cat will jump. Behind her is the small whitewashed house with a stoop. Two rocking chairs stand still beside a corrugated tin washtub with a hand wringer clamped to it. On the other corner of the stoop, where it can catch the sun, is an incongruously elegant wire stand that holds a huge blooming lily.

She had whitewashed the house herself. She never in her life, she told me when she was an old woman, could get a man to do a damned thing. I think that just at the moment he passed by, she leaned forward on the fence and sighed and he could see the sun glistening on the hair at the nape of her neck.

He was driving downriver. Maybe. Addie made her legends come true by lodging them with us. There were our own legends and hers, elusive and ponderous, and there behind them all, deep within the heavy old woman, was Addie when she was young, slim, beautiful, on a sand road by the river in the summertime, the valley lush around her, as it is still, so lush that it hides its scars and its sins every summer until the leaves fall on the slag heaps and the forgotten shacks and the car graveyards and the piles of old tires.

She told me that the first time she saw him, he wore a flaring red tie, a poet's tie, she called it when she told the story, and he drove the fastest four-in-hand, the lord of the valley, she said, when he got his hands on those reins. She said he cut a dash. He had been the valley's eligible bachelor as long as anybody could remember and still was what they called a great catch.

The tools Miss Addie had to change the only life she could have chosen as the wife of a coal miner, were, first, her imperious eyes. She had, too, hidden maybe even from herself, a will, a passion as strong and as inevitable as the river's current.

But on that morning her life was confined by the huddled coal town, the Company Store, her stepparents' house, the little church, Church of God Holy Roller, the washtub that sat on a bench on the stoop. The sun behind her made a halo around her head of glossy hair. That was what I think he saw at that moment, at that place or at another place, a glance and then a look, and the lives of so many would spin out from it, including her children's, my cousins,' my brother's, and my own.

After they met, did she dream at the washtub, in the privy, in the tumbled bed where she had to do her marital duty, calling the children, wandering down to the riverbank and watching the river flow toward where he might be? A whole new life opened up, a dream come true and turning terrible. All she knew was passion. It was all that her life had taught her, that and work, passion and work, and for herself, all her life afterwards, an imagination the people around her never had, except for my mother, the only child out of all of them who inherited it, and was teased, it being the time when women were derided for such things. It terrified her. She threw the talent away. I picked it up—a hidden gauntlet, grandmother to mother to child—as carelessly as if I had found it in an alley and wondered what it was. I was punished for years for picking up something that might be dirty.

I guess that the year they met was 1887. I think the passion caught fire so that perhaps neither of them, certainly not Addie, could ever have withstood it. He, in his mid-forties, may have been more calculating in his watching as he passed, judging as he would have judged a dog, a horse, another man. He was the favorite son. Whatever he wanted, he got, or took with all the charm that was so famous. He wanted her. At last he had found somebody who could give him a family, which was the only thing in human relations he hadn't tasted, one way or another.

And Addie, who had never been in a house that had an upstairs? She watched across the river that had nearly taken her life and saw far-away, wide green fields and slow-moving horses feeding, and in the distance, almost out of sight, nestled in the hills beyond the river, a tiny red brick house. Its many windows caught the sun, and she knew that it was not tiny, but huge, bigger than any house she had ever seen. But the river was between her and my grandfather, impossible. She must have stood there, as she had when she was a child, long before she met my grandfather, and gazed across to the north side, the far, far side of the river.

"Across the river," the house where Addie's lover lived, was as far from the coal dust she knew as the moon. It rose above the river mist as unattainable as Paradise, and as near as the ferry that ran between East Bank and Cedar Grove. But what she saw in the distance was more a mirage than just green hills, rolling fields, and calm. She saw feudal divisions of money, property, and power in what had been, such a short time ago, a frontier valley.

*O*ver forty years ago I was allowed into the basement storage section of the British Museum, which must be the most valuable junk heap in the world.

In order to be allowed into such a secret place, I had, of course, to prove that I was an "expert." Expertmanship is one of the British Museum's great protections. You can't go in and just say, "I want to see what my grandfather gave to the museum of the Indian artifacts that he found on his property somewhere around the turn of the century so I can hold it in my hand and maybe it will take me to what my ancestors called the Endless Mountains. You see, I'm upstairs in the round room of the library writing a book about eighteenth-century America, and I'm far from home."

So I knocked on the door of the American Indian curator's office. I said I wanted to see the artifacts of American Indians which were not on display. He look toward me down a haughty nose. He knew how to get rid of Americans, and the famous Museum nuts, the eccentrics who had been in the Reading Room for years, searching for ancestors and warmth.

"Tribes?" he said, as if the word were new, or worse, incorrect. It was the first test.

"Eastern United States." I was, I hoped, prepared.

It wasn't enough. "I suppose," the nose slid the words down toward me, "you mean the Nez Percé?"

The examination before his pearly gates was as primitive as what I was looking for.

The final test. I said a resounding, "No." Louder than I meant to. "The Nez Percé are about three hundred miles west of the tribes that I am researching"—academic word. It pleased him. "The Eastern Woodland Indians . . ." I had rehearsed the private language. I knew it.

I had been living with the traces of the Indians in the Museum for ten months, in books published in the eighteenth century, story after story to feed the fascination in London with the new glamorous red men. Some of the books had been uncut since the time they had been lodged there. I read everything I could find that was contemporary with the eighteenth century before 1775. The American language changed so radically after 1775 that I read for language that had not changed. I read for mores, for fashions, for what people thought was happening at the time. I read without taking any notes in order to grow an organic memory instead of a file of four-by-six cards.

There was still so much missing. I needed to touch something, a blanket, an arrowhead, a breechclout, a headdress, anything that would give me the vision of a Beulah Land that was two centuries and three thousand miles away. I did not mention my grandfather.

The curator's nose relaxed. He smiled. I had spoken his language. We took an elevator, a lift, and went down farther than I had intended. Down, down, down, basements down. Corridor after corridor, as far as I could see, or hoped I was seeing, faded away into the unreflecting whitewashed darkness. There must have been miles of hallways, with cave rooms opening off them like the ancient shops in Pompeii. We walked past Roman statues, covered and ghostly—an exposed hand, a dusty marble toga, a head with stone curls, the furniture of the past, the shadowy hints of the loot of Empire—deeper into the vaulted corridors.

We came to a whitewashed cave, open to the corridor, where Indian artifacts were piled high, all hand-numbered years before on little faded tags. I had expected feathers, tools, arrowheads. We had picked up so many when we were children, down where the Indians had camped in spring when the water ran high, to build canoes at the mouth of Kelly's Creek where it ran into the Kanawha.

A superb yellow and orange matchcoat, made of the underfeathers from behind the ears of birds, hung across one wall. There were piles of tomahawks, breechclouts, feathers, pelts. He let me wander, picking up things. I forgot grandfathers and property. My hands were learning, as a blind person learns a face, learning the long winters it took to carve the tools, the arrowheads, the matchcoat that was made so strong that it had survived at least two centuries, softer to the touch than any down I had ever felt.

The matchcoats, like great capes, that the braves wore in winter, disappeared when the Hudson Bay Company began to distribute guns to bring in more beaver pelts to feed the fashion for beaver hats in London. They paid for pelts with thick blankets, wool coats. Still, if you look at a Hudson Bay blanket, you will find a few short black lines woven into the cloth. They stand for the number of beaver pelts the blanket cost. At the sound of guns in the woods, the bright, shy birds were harder to catch; only the old women, and then, eventually, nobody, could make a matchcoat of feathers.

At the back of the room, in the corner, there were two large tea chests, piled high with round leather pieces tied to willow hoops that looked like the darning hoops Addie used to use. They were as thin and frail as fine parchment; delicately painted—yellow and black and white and red—with designs in their centers. I picked one up, a yellow one with a painting of a tomahawk. A hank of blond hair fell nearly to the floor. Both tea chests were full of scalps.

The curator could tell me nothing. They had simply been there, for a long time, forgotten. It has taken me over forty years to find out where they came from. I found the answer when I began to search for some clue to my great-grandfather's life that would bring him near to me out of so dim and unknown a past.

All I had were two portraits, one a daguerreotype of him, his face watercolored, probably by one of his daughters; girls were taught those things then. He looks boyish, the kind of boyishness that has nothing to do with age, but with a way to look, as if the world were new every day. In the other he sits beside a wife who looks older, in control, but she is not older and she is not in control. She is sitting like a strict Presbyterian, which she is. She is nearly twenty years younger than he.

My great-grandfather was William Tompkins. His wife was Rachel Grant, from Maysville, Kentucky, on the Ohio River. It was easier and closer to go courting west downriver than it was to face the hard mountain journey "back east."

Only his eyes seem as if they had ever been alive. They still pierce through the years, ice-blue. I have hung the picture on the wall of my workroom. The eyes have followed me wherever I have moved or left a shadow, until I have begun to live with him, to take him for granted, with his secret, kindly, certainly quiet, intelligent face. The person who so carefully colored his eyes had known him for a long time.

Now I know that behind the eyes, deep into the secrets men carry and do not share, behind the quiet-seeming, secure face that he has constructed through the years of his success, he kept one of the bloodiest wars in America history, a forgotten war. It was in searching for that secret western war that I found the answer to the contents of the tea chest.

The isolated farms that were west of the Endless Mountains, in the part of Virginia known then as Kentucky, the frontier from 1775 to 1782, had been almost entirely wiped out by the Indian-British alliance during the American Revolution–an episode still festering as a deep horror in adults around him when my great-grandfather was a boy, a genetic fear that cut down trees, invented protections, told stories in the night about a time that nobody could forget.

"Wiped out" is such a generic phrase for what happened. I found a letter. It is a military report written, as one of so many military reports that are left after wars, impersonally, businesslike, revealing more than it is meant to. It was written by a Major Crawford to Governor Haldimand of Quebec and is dated January 3, 1782.

May it please your excellency: at the request of the Seneca chiefs, I send herewith to your excellency under the care of James Boyd eight packs of scalps cured, dried, hooped and painted with all the Indian triumphal marks of which the following is an invoice and explanation.

No 1: Containing 43 scalps of congress soldiers, killed in different skirmishes; these are stretched on black hoops, 4 inches in diameter; the inside of the skin painted red with a small black spot to denote their being killed with bullets; also 62 farmers killed in their houses, the hoops red, the skin painted brown and marked with a hoe, a black circle all around to denote their being surprised in the night and a black hatchet in the middle to denote their being killed with that weapon.

No 2: Containing 93 farmers killed in their houses . . . white circles and suns to show that WE surprised in daytime. Black bullets in some, hatchets in others. [The capital letters are mine.]

No 3: 97 farmers, hoops green to show working in fields.

No 4: 102 farmers, 18 marked with yellow flame to show that they were burned alive after being scalped. Most farmers appear by hair to be young or middle aged.

No 5: 81 women, long hair; those braided to show they were mothers.

No 6: 93 boys scalps various ages, white ground on the skin red tear in the middle.

No 7: 211 girls scalps big and little small yellow hoops marked hatchet, club, knife, etc.

No 8: Mixture 122 with box of birch bark containing 29 infant scalps small white hoops. Only little black knife in middle to show they were ripped out of mother's body.

Note of Seneca to Governor Haldimond

Father: We wish to send these over the water to the great king that he may regard them and see our faithfulness in destroying his enemies, and know that his presents have not been made to an ungrateful people.

Father: The king's enemies were formerly like young panthers, they could neither bite nor scratch; we could play with them safely, we feared nothing they could do to us. But now their bodies are becoming as the elk, and strong as the buffalo; they have also got great and sharp claws. They have driven us out of our country for taking part in your quarrel. We expect the great king to give us another country.

It was that promised country where my great-grandfather fought as a young man in 1812. On the other side were the Indian alliance led by the great warrior Tecumseh and the well-disciplined and war-blooded British Army, some of whom had fought under Wellington against Napoleon in Spain.

By the early 1800s the Kanawha Valley had already been "taken up" for twenty-five years, since the border had moved to the Ohio. It existed mostly as a passage west—for Virginians looking for new farms in the new state of Kentucky. Their goal was the blue-grass country. Only twenty years after the terrible raids, Kentucky was already being resettled and was becoming civilized enough to live in, in the way they had been accustomed to in eastern Virginia.

One of the new settlers in Kentucky was Mary Michie of Albemarle County, Virginia, who had been born in the Michie Tavern when it was on the James River at Scottsville. She had married William Tompkins's father when she was sixteen, long before the Revolution. They had a place in Louisa County, near Richmond. When Mr. Tompkins died in 1800, she married again and moved with her new husband, Mr. McArthur, children, slaves, livestock, English furniture, domestic truck, pots, kettles, pans, a whisky still, farm tackle, blooded horses, all that was left of Mr. Tompkins's movable property, in a long, slow wagon train to Scott County, Kentucky. She and the children's stepfather rode in the family carriage with the youngest boy. The rest of them, including my great-grandfather, aged seven, were walking to Kentucky.

Kanawha Falls, with its great lake, was, and still is, hauntingly beautiful. It was the first place the family saw, as the long line of carts, drays, wagons was eased down the steep grade of Gauley Mountain, the slaves yelling "Ho, hey, ho" at the oxen, over and over, echoing through the mountain trees, holding the teams back with ropes through the wheel spokes to keep them from slithering hundreds of feet down the rocky slopes in the mud. Gauley was the last of the mountain barriers between the Kanawha Valley in the west and the Shenandoah in the east, mile after mile, wave after wave of barrier ridges that not long before had been called the Endless Mountains, hard to cross, exhausting, and dangerous.

The beautiful valley that opened up beyond the mountains must have looked like heaven. The New River, one of the oldest rivers in the world, flowed north and west from the Carolinas, and the Gauley flowed down from the north. They met and ran west, side by side, one brown, one green, until they mingled in the air over the falls that were the source of the Kanawha, flowing from east to west as one river to the Ohio.

It was William's first view of the valley. It was also the oldest daughter, Elizabeth's, first sight of the place she would spend the rest of her life. But the bottomland didn't even begin to widen enough for another thirty miles to make what they thought of in eastern Virginia as a decent size farm. Oh, the Kanawha Valley was beautiful and romantic in 1802;

romantic scenery was very fashionable. But the land was poor, and who could live on romantic scenery?

None of the family was to see it again until Colonel Aaron Stockton turned up in Kentucky in 1807 and married Elizabeth. He came from New Jersey, the proud grandson of one of the signers of the Declaration of Independence. He, like so many others, must have chosen the almost unknown valley of the Kanawha as an investment, the place for an empire, no matter how obscure.

He chose the land around the great falls and brought his new wife back to a place she had never forgotten. It had been over forty years since the valley had begun to be inhabited and farmed, when the land-hungry stopped at the last safe narrow bottom, leveled Indian burial mounds, some thousands of years old, and burned the bones for lime, girdled the trees to kill them so they could till the new fields. Much of the valley had been bounty land for Revolutionary soldiers.

It was safe from Indian raids. But new invaders came, not scalping from the west but from the east. It was one of the first of the migrations west of businessmen looking for investment. They paid ready money for the acres of hill and hollow land the settlers couldn't pasture a goat on. Most of the poor dirt farmers were only too willing to sell for real money and move on west.

As soon as the west opened up beyond the Ohio, Cincinnati grew into the western center for meat production. Red Kanawha salt was found around Burning Springs, about five miles east of the confluence of the Elk and the Kanawha Rivers. It was considered to be the best salt to use to cure meat before sending it downriver to the markets that stretched from the Deep South all the way up the Atlantic coast. Winter jerky. Salt meat for the long voyages of ships going out whaling for months. Supplies to back up meat that could be readied for the wagons going west. Rations for the peace-time army, which wasn't much, but needed to be fed.

The salt business had begun as early as 1805. By 1812, instead of log houses, dark satanic mills were built of the trees in the valley, and acre after acre was stripped and burned to dry the salt from the wells that were dug near the Burning Springs that Mary Inglis had seen across the great river, lighting frightening figures of men in the night. She had been captured by the Shawnee at her home at Draper's Meadow near what is now Blacksburg, Virginia, east of the mountains. She had escaped in 1756 and struggled though the valley east to safety.

With the new owners of vast acres, even acres underground, the valley became a fiefdom, not a warpath or a romantic vision. Black smoke from the salt furnaces darkened the land and made a pall of the sky. Anne Royall, the traveler and journalist, called that part of the valley a dismal place, with "bare, unhospitable looking mountains from which all timber has been cut." She accused the men who had gathered around the salt industry of "total disregard of shame, honor, and justice," In other words, she found the kind of wild, disreputable new frontier, industrial instead of territorial, which was already being established in pockets across the new country.

Forty miles east of the dirt and waste, overlooking Kanawha Falls, and the idyllic scene, which he dubbed the American Switzerland, Aaron Stockton had built his mansion, which is still there, much changed. He turned it into an inn as fine as any in Virginia. It was good business. There was also good company. It was the first place the new army of industrial hopefuls could see as they came down the steep grade off Gauley Mountain. Colonel Stockton was the man at the gate to guide them across his veranda into the wide hall, and warn them about the land vultures downriver.

He also, being no fool as far as business was concerned, took advantage of the Virginia law that said there should be either an "Ordinary" or a night's lodging in the house every thirty miles, a day's journey apart, for the travelers in the nearly vacant land. It was an ancient idea for the relief of travelers. Thirty miles downriver from the falls, he bought the White House Inn, which had been owned and run by the Morris family, and the several thousand acres of bottomland and hills that made up their property on Kelly's Creek, where the first fort had been built beyond the last mountains to the west. Mr. Morris said he was tired of talking, there were too many people in the valley, and he was going to Missouri.

Aaron Stockton was foreseeing what now would be a hotel chain. He had also, of course, invested in the salt business, which interested him less.

In Scott County, Kentucky, William Tompkins had already had several years of schooling. His family said that he could fix anything broken, he was good at mathematics, and he could draw. All of these were the talents that masters of the most elite clan of artisans in Kentucky and Pennsylvania were looking for in apprentices. William was carefully interviewed, his family paid a fee, legal papers were signed. At twelve or so he was apprenticed to Captain West, a gunsmith in Georgetown, Scott County.

He was to learn delicate wood carving, brass etching and inlay, forging for the iron gun barrels, the intricate work of "rifling" barrels, to make the Kentucky long rifle, known on the frontier only as the Kentucky, the most formidable weapon for accuracy at one hundred yards known at the time. The Kentucky was hand made, with long and detailed discussions of the chasing, the barrel length, the bore of the rifling, between the gunsmith and the customer. The gleaming brass-trimmed wood stock was fitted to the shoulder as carefully as if the gunsmith had been a tailor.

When the fears of the alliance between the Indians and the British became real again within the lifetimes of the older people in the state, at the beginning of the War of 1812, the Kentucky militia was mustered under William Henry Harrison. John Randolph coined the name "warhawk" for the young, eloquent Henry Clay, the senator from Kentucky.

The seaboard cities in the north didn't even want the war. It interfered with their trade with both warring nations, England and France. What were a few sailors, taken off American ships and pressed into British service, compared to the fine boom in commerce? The New England coastal states kept on trading, even exporting to Canada and the British Army while the United States Army was fighting them, almost entirely in the west.

In Kentucky, the men took their own rifles, dressed in their own buckskin hunting clothes, and went, once again, to protect settlements from the Indians, who by then they so resembled in their fighting style that they were known in the east as white Indians. Six of the Kentucky delegation to Congress went back home to join the militia, one as a major general, one to raise a company himself, and the rest to join up as privates. William and his master gunsmith, Captain West, joined the militia together. They took with them Kentuckys they had made themselves, with shiny brass inlays and stocks sanded to silk. They all thought they would be back at home in a few weeks; they were as naive as fawns.

The Kentuckians walked across Ohio to years of border battle, massacre, hunger. Instead of the pride they felt in themselves as citizen militia, they were treated with contempt by regular army officers. They ran into delays so long that they had to fight in two feet of snow, commanding officers so incompetent that they were both court-martialed, and one, Hull, dropped from the army list. They faced Proctor, a sadist, as the British commander they had to fight, who was later court-martialed in England for misconduct.

Of all the men killed in the War of 1812, which lasted three years, sixty-four percent were from the new and sparsely settled state of Kentucky

When the war was over, William found that the art of making hand-made guns was no longer needed. Factories had opened during the war and had taken over their manufacture. Only the rich could afford the hand-made Kentucky, and only a few of the most famous gunsmiths stayed in business.

So William and his older brother, Henry, went back east to the Kanawha Valley their family had once scorned to seek their fortunes with their brother-in-law, Aaron Stockton.

William, who was younger, and trained in working with iron to make gun barrels, was taken on as a blacksmith at Aaron Stockton's salt wells at Burning Springs. Henry, called Colonel Henry, was hired to run the White House Inn on the old Morris property. Until Aaron Stockton had built his own fine, red brick house by the falls, it had been the only painted inn west of the mountains.

The White House Inn was three stories high, set on a hillside, lording it over the valley. Travelers stopped there on the way up the Mississippi, to the Ohio, and then to the Kanawha on the great water highway to Virginia. At the White House Inn they took carriages across the mountains to the fashionable White, Blue, and Red Sulphur Springs.

Henry Tompkins' guest book, where he marked down the destinations of, and sometimes the looks of, his guests, was a small history of the toing and froing between the west and Washington. Mr. Sam Houston, Mr. Henry Clay, Mr. John C. Calhoun, and the English traveler Captain Marryat, the author of *Midshipman Ready*, were in the registry. Families from what Colonel Henry called the New South were registered, with comments about their politics, their looks, and their worth.

My cousin and my aunt and uncle lived there in the 1930s, long after it had been turned into a Victorian house by my great-uncle, John, with a front veranda and gingerbread carving. Only the kitchen and the loft were left of the old inn. The old coal mine had been turned into a wine cellar, but there was nothing in it in the summers then but a lawn mower and hidden moonshine, which my cousin and I always found. We slept in the loft sometimes to scare ourselves—lay there listening to the ghosts turning over in their perpetual sleep, snoring faintly, like the wind or the squirrels and doves in the roof.

The first year William worked for Aaron Stockton, he was paid three hundred dollars, the second year he was paid six hundred. The third year he and Aaron Stockton had become partners. Together they already owned over 17,000 acres of Kanawha bottom land. The holdings ran in huge plots for over thirty miles from Gauley Bridge to six miles from the Ohio River. They owned it by law *ad coelum ad infernum*—from heaven to hell. So their descendants later were able to sell or lease hell and live in what they thought was heaven.

By the time he was thirty-seven, William Tompkins was becoming the man in the portrait that haunts my workroom wall. He owned salt wells. He was a partner in one of the first "trusts" formed by a group of salt manufacturers to control prices. He was amassing money, property, and salt leases hand over fist in the salt boom.

The boom didn't last long. Salt prices fluctuated. There was another barrier to profit as well. For a long time, oil and natural gas, found in the same geological pockets as salt, was siphoned into the river before the salt could be cured. William Tompkins invented a way to burn it in the salt furnaces, long after they had cut down all the trees and denuded the lower valley. But for a while there was ready money, a lot of it, and he and his family spent it like it was as never ending as the water that flowed down the great Kanawha, known by 1812 as Old Greasy around Burning Springs because of pollution.

Henry Ruffner, the ecclesiastical member of the Ruffner family, who were also in the salt business, making money hand over fist, was one of the bravest men ever born in the valley, an abolitionist among slave owners, who wrote what may have been the first American novel about the treatment of minorities. He also wrote that the salt makers had amassed "boundless wealth," and that most of the families had already become "recklessly expensive in their habits." Among the reckless new rich families was my great-grandfather's.

As cotton built the fine houses on the Mississippi that we visit as "the old South," salt built the first layer of grand houses, following the old American tradition of forming an aristocracy as quickly as possible, imitating the tobacco barons of Virginia a hundred years before, who imitated the English barons, who for centuries had danced for their titles and imitated the ones who had danced, served the state, and intrigued before them. The new houses in the Kanawha Valley were copies of Virginia plantation houses built fifty years before in the Shenandoah Valley, far from the English imitations in the Tidewater.

William Tompkins bought all of Aaron Stockton's land on Kelly's Creek that had belonged to the Morris family, who had settled it and built the first fort. It included thousands of acres of hill land, bottom land and the White House Inn.

So sensibly, in 1844, he moved his growing family away from the industry-torn lower valley to his cleaner and fairer holdings upriver and built them a fine house surrounded by hills in an idyllic setting. He chose the little valley where Kelly's Creek ran down to the river and formed a harbor for river barges so that it was easier at the right time of year to get supplies. Like other farms at the time, he made it not only self-sufficient, a closed world, but he put industries there that would bring in a little cash. He was no stranger to land-poor years, and money was welcome, always, walking-around money, ready money. So there was the horse mill and the boat yard, which had been there since the Indians carved canoes. Maybe. There is always a maybe for those hand-me-down realities, but we did, when we were little, find arrowheads and rotten baskets that we didn't know at the time were Indian, down by the creek when we went swimming.

The house was built of brick "made on the place"—a euphemism for slave labor that like all the other euphemisms for slavery in the South stayed in the language long afterwards, and still remains in cusps and niches of denied memory.

He chose the spot for his house in a half-circle of surrounding hills, and had it built in a grove of cedar trees, thought then to be "salubrious." Two great cedars stood like sentinels on either side of the front walk, with little knolls to sit on at their bases and their trunks whitewashed against insects for seven feet or so. He named the new house and its farm Cedar Grove.

On the right side of the house an acre of formal garden was laid out. Rose bushes were sent from Woods in Richmond, and little boxwoods lined the brick walks. In the back of the garden Mr. Tompkins built a small house for his office, with a bedroom for a house slave to live in. Under the office slaves dug a large stone-walled wine cellar.

On the left side of the house a lawn sloped gently down to Kelly's Creek, a stroll away in the distance. It was kept cropped by a small flock of Merino sheep that were family pets. Kelly's Creek had been named for the first settler in the three-mile cup of a valley, who had been scalped and left in the water to bleed to death seventy years before. The creek was almost hidden behind a large stand of cedars. From the hollow behind the house, a little mill run flowed from deep within the hills into the creek, and at the mouth of Kelly's Creek, nearly a mile away, ran the Kanawha beyond horse fields and meadows where earlier farmers had left a few single virgin trees as shelter for the cows from the sun and the rain.

William Tompkins didn't like to use his slaves in the salt furnaces. He said they were too valuable, like using good riding horses to plow a field. Some of the men had been trained as carpenters and brick makers for surface jobs at the salt works, so when time came to move the family upriver, away from the industrial grime and dirty water of the salt industry where much of the money came from, he was rich enough to hire whites, and take his "people" with him to Cedar Grove.

It was a large, classic Virginia farm house with four twelve-paned windows across the front in the days when wealth was measured in windows, and most houses had only two, with eight panes. On the outside hung long shutters painted dark green. There was a fine fanlight over the large front door, and classic glass panels down its sides. In front was a portico with columns, and its own small upstairs veranda, with a French door to balance the large door below. Two twelve-paned windows in each of the twin parlors were set in alcoves where heavy dark red silk curtains fell to the floor. Between the windows of the left-hand parlor a huge gilt mirror reached from floor to ceiling.

On the first floor the fireplaces were marble with classic grooved Doric columns and mantles. On the second floor wooden fireplaces of the same carved design kept the bedrooms warm. The wide central hall was traditionally Virginian. Its design and function had grown out of the old dog run, or possum trot, the way to keep a two-roomed cabin cool.

The woodwork of its arches, the finely carved banisters, all the mantles of wood or marble, two primitive urns of stone for flowers outside in the front garden, and two fine tall stone gateposts with pointed tops like Egyptian obelisks were carved by Italians who came and lived at the building site until they were finished. They also carved an underground burial vault. It was in the little cemetery where people had been buried since 1775. I saw the same kind of houses for the dead in the Etruscan cemetery in Orvieto. The Italian stonemasons had built what they had known for centuries.

The furniture, which was bought new for the mansion, came upriver from Cincinnati on a returning salt barge—the huge dining room table, the sideboard almost as long as the wall, sixteen dining room chairs, twin drop-leaf card tables, fine beds. Silk for the curtains and fine linen came from Richmond. The flat silver, the tea set, the coffee pot, the condiment stand, and the serving dishes were designed by one of the daughters and made in Cincinnati from silver coins earned by salt deliveries.

All of the rooms had ten-foot ceilings. The front parlor was on one side of the hall, the library on the other. Behind the right-hand parlor was the dining room, and behind the left-hand parlor was a room called the ladies' retiring room but used as a downstairs bedroom for the cousins who came and stayed, sometimes as long as several years. Later it would be the bachelor bedroom, and later still, the room to die in.

The carved stairway ran to the upper floors. The second floor had four bedrooms, and a "bathroom" with a slave to bring hot water for baths, and to empty the slops every morning into Kelly's Creek. In the back a long upstairs veranda, where the family sat in the shade of the evening, ran the width of the house. Back stairs descended to the kitchen porch, where there was a hammock soon half hidden by trumpet vines at the foot of the stairs. My grandfather, born a year after the house was built, hid there when he was a little boy with his slave, who was his own age, Obediah, called Obe, who he always told my mother was his best friend. She said he gave Obe half of his apple instead of just the core like his older brothers did their slaves.

A well surrounded by a stone wall was dug on the back porch, which had a blue slate floor. Beside the well, the brick milk house and the smoke house were built with foot-thick stone inner walls in the long kitchen ell, and behind the house a wide, sloped back yard ran out toward the hollow made by Horse Mill Creek. It ran past the wide side lawn where the sheep gathered on hot days. Beyond the creek there was a fine stable for the blooded carriage and riding horses, and a large barn. Behind it the bull was kept in a fenced bull-field and beyond it, all the way up the wider hollow made by Kelly's Creek, was field after field of corn, grazing meadow. In the summer there was the smell of cedar, honeysuckle, and clean water.

At the entrance to the hollow between the hills behind the house, the overseer's house was built where the hills fanned out into tiny creek-side fields. Behind it the horsemill stood, where a horse trudged round and round, grinding the huge millstones together. For half a mile up the narrow hollow there were one-room log slave cabins with big mud and rock chimneys, like those the original settlers of the valley had built.

In the new house the family began to live as they wished always to have lived, high but stern. Mr. and Mrs. Tompkins were, after all, strict Presbyterians.

That house, changed, its tap root grown deeper into the land, was the house of my childhood, and, still, of my home dreams. What I learned of its past, the way of living, was filtered, altered, edited, lied about, diminished, censored, and enlarged into the fairy tales of Before the War, told to me by my mother, and to her by her father, Mr. Tompkins of the red tie, the perfume, the rake's reputation, and the four-in-hand, who was fifteen when the Civil War began.

*H*enry Preston, known as Pressy until long after he grew up, who was born the year after the family moved into the fine new house, never knew another. William Tompkins, his father, lived for thirteen years at his fine new property. When he died in 1857, he was buried in the underground vault made by the Italian carvers. He was sixty-four years old, and he had managed to acquire a fortune that today would be worth two and a half million dollars in money, industry, slaves, and land speculation.

He left the whole fortune to his wife, who was in her late forties when she became a widow. He entrusted her in his will to make all decisions for his children, who he felt were too young to decide for themselves. This was to happen three times in my family. The family joke has been that the Tompkins men come from a long line of bachelors. The men married and bred late. My mother was a hundred and seven years younger than her own grandfather.

So the stories handed down to me of the world Before the War are more immediate than most, even if they are tilted toward romantic visions. Much of the reality of the days came through my filtering and checking the stories that my mother's father told her.

Rachel Mary Grant Tompkins, William's widow, ruled with a rod of iron and a hand on the purse strings. The Presbyterian vein was as deep and hard as the coal that ran under the valley and into the mountains behind Cedar Grove, and which was not yet worth a red cent.

She had insisted on the Grant name as part of her own heritage, even though she said her brother in Kentucky wasn't worth a hill of beans. He had moved to Ohio because he said he didn't want to live in a slave state when he couldn't afford slaves. She was fond of her nephew, Hiram Ulysses, though, and she invited him to the valley in the summer, upriver from Cincinnati on the salt barge. When it was time, she sent him to the West Point on the cars and gave him a little money to "gwie upon."

"God knows," her voice echoes down through the years and the family memories, "his papa couldn't do it." They called him Hiram (the S in Ulysses S. Grant was a mistake made at West Point that nobody corrected).

That was the roost that great-grandmother Rachel Grant Tompkins ruled. It was never recognized that she did more. Women didn't do such things, at least so that they would be noticed, but among the women, the frequent widows, they all knew what they really did behind the habits and the traditions, the politeness and the legends of blood, all so quickly acquired in what was still new country. They ran businesses, plantations, bought and sold land, "kept things going" after their husbands died.

There was a family joke that Mrs. Tompkins went to law so often that she sued her son, Beverly, for taking a ten-gallon apple-butter kettle off the back porch and not bringing it back when she wanted it. I found the copper half buried in the back yard last year, where somebody had put flowers in it, but the flowers were long dead.

The joke covered the fact that she took over the salt business, along with a family and its "people," and protected the investment so well that in 1860 she had added to the fortune in land, slaves, livestock, salt works. Her lawsuits were against men, including her own Grant relatives, who had asked Mr. Tompkins in the old gentlemanly way to "go on their paper" or to lend them money. She collected it all. Fortunately for herself and her family she was not a gentleman. There were no such rules for ladies.

Then the war came. She was an impassioned Confederate. She wrote to her niece, "If you are with the occursed Lincolnites, the ties of consanguinity shall be forever severed." But she did keep the letter that General Grant sent her in case it came in handy. It did. When, in the western campaign, the house was taken over by Northern troops, the letter saved it from being burned when they left. There were military orders to burn houses where there had been headquarters to be sure that papers didn't fall into the hands of the "enemy." Her heart may have been with the South but when either the Northern or the Confederate troops came through the valley she had the livestock hidden a mile up Horse Mill hollow.

When the war was over, new laws for land tenure meant that prewar land grants had to be resurveyed and reassessed. Rachel Tompkins added at least twenty thousand more acres to the property. She was only afraid of one thing. To her shame, which she covered with pride that can be seen in the only portrait of her when she was old, she was terrified of horses. Her carriage when she came down to the city of Charleston was drawn by four snow-white mules.

*I*t was the winter of 1867. For ten years Rachel Tompkins had taken care of the property and the children, years when she had to fight more battles than the Civil War, battles with people who tried to bamboozle her because she was a woman, battles with lawyers over property lines, battles with her grown children, which she always won but which left her shaking and exhausted so that she looked forward with dread to some of their visits. During the war, there had been constant battles with the soldiers from the North and the South who occupied the house when there were no servants left.

For the first time in their lives, she and the girls had had to change beds and empty slops for the soldiers. Often the sheets they had embroidered were ripped and torn by the men when they went to bed drunk with their boots and spurs on, or needed a bit of rag to clean their gun barrels. She had to keep watch day and night over the girls. She had lain awake night after night listening, when the soldiers were drinking down in the dining room, to the breaking of her fine glass. The whole thing was nonsense. The war was nonsense. The awful killing was nonsense. She had been too angry all through it to be really afraid, that was, until it was over, and then she came down with neuralgia.

All that time there had only been Pressy to be the man of the family and he was just a boy of fifteen when it began, twenty when it ended. She had made him promise on the Bible he wouldn't run off to war; she needed somebody. He had done his best to run the farm when most of their people had hightailed off to Ohio. He tried to hire white men, but what few there were had never worked for anybody before but themselves. They would rather see their families starve than do "nigger work."

Some of "their people" had stayed, mostly children and their mamas, without any place to go. They worked for wages, but none of them would live in the house like they used to. They wanted to live in the field hands' places up the Horse Mill hollow. Every Saturday they all made a ceremony of collecting their pay.

Rachel Tompkins was dogtired of having the whole lot of them tied to her apron strings. She was tired of trying to hold things together. She was sixty-one years old and she'd been through a war the fool men had seen as going off marching and then bragging and not doing a lick when they got home at last. Women's war was day after day after day, never knowing, always listening for some news that didn't come that she wouldn't have named. William had gone to war. Charley had gone to war, too, and what going east to college hadn't ruined, the war had. That was war to her, that and seeing people she had borned with her own hands, while the midwife held the mother's head, valuable people, just prance off like they owned the damned earth. I don't think my great-grandmother would have admitted any of this to a living soul, including herself.

I see her in the master bedroom I know so well. I think she lay there at night after the house had calmed down, the only time a woman could think without being interrupted by a thousand things. She had lain alone in the big four-poster mahogany bed where she had had all of her children and where Mr. Tompkins had warmed her feet with his for twenty-three years, and in time she had grown to think of it as a haven and not a loneliness.

Maybe it was February, a hard month to survive anyway, and I think she planned that night, which was her way of worrying. It was all personal. Everything was personal, after all. Men never understood that. Men, she told the ceiling where light from the full moon reflected in the night, and the shadows of the skeletons of tree branches floated and fell in the moonlight, just didn't understand daily things. They never had had to.

The wind was rising, whipping the frozen branches so that they sounded like bones breaking. The snow glare under the moon made it seem like some haunted day. The boys were asleep in the cyclone room, and the little night creaks and whispers were a comfort. Ellen, the only one of her girls that was left at home, was making little wiffly noises like a dog in her sleep across the hall in the front bedroom the oldest girl always had. It made her feel less like she was lying wide awake in a house that had been empty since the dawn of time. She was methodical, even in her worrying.

She started with William, the oldest. He had come back from war as sane and sensible as he had left, but after all he had a family, so he had had to give up practicing much medicine and move down to Malden to run the salt business. There was nobody else, and it was, in that bad year, all that was bringing in ready cash. Not that the cash was worth much. Even the fortune that she had been left, to which she had added nearly a million dollars in land during the war when it was easy to acquire, was worth a lot more on paper than it was in her pocket.

Charley was hightailing it around the lobby of the Mayflower Hotel in Washington, jumping from one financial crisis to another. He was a rabbit, a babe in the woods, a damned fool up there among the tough men who were making their own fortunes out of the postwar, and he was trying to use his kinship to General Grant in a way which shamed her. It seemed like every month since he had been back from war and had been so eager to take the oath that she found it hard to say a word to him, he had "floated," as he called it, one big scheme after another and lost money so quickly that she thought he had "floated" an open sewer in Washington and was pouring the money down it. Almost every letter threatened that "the drop will fall" if he wasn't bailed out. She was tired of bailing, and bailing, and bailing.

A large branch fell with a gunshot crash, and she jumped under the pile of quilts. It made her want to. She hated doing that in the middle of the night because her piss smelled old, and she hated that. But she dragged herself out of bed for the third time since she had tried to go to sleep and lifted the mahogany cover of the commode chair beside the bed, rested her arms on the carved commode arms and listened to her own tinkle into the china chamber pot. She had always loved it. It had belonged to her mother. It was English china with hand-painted forget-me-nots. There had been one of the commodes in every bedroom and in the daytime they were just chairs, after the chamber pots had been slid out of their niches, cleaned and put back. But two of them had been broken by the soldiers who didn't know what they were.

She moved across to the dying fire, huddled in her own arms, and threw some coal from the fine brass coal bucket on the embers and jiggled them with the poker. A little while after she got back into bed and found the still slightly warm hot water bottle with her feet, the fire caught and danced on the ceiling with the moonlight and the branches.

The night in February grew as long as a life, and the moon went down and still she could not sleep. Beverly, the third boy, was a constant worry, with a family and in debt all over the valley. He had already run through nearly a quarter of a million dollars of family money, and there had seemed to be no end to it until she set her foot down at last. He was another one of those embittered men. He sat down at the St. Albans farm half frozen with disappointment that things weren't the same anymore, refused to do a lick of honest work because he was an officer and a gentleman. It made her kick the hot water bottle and hurt her toe against the earthenware. His puny little old wife waited on him hand and foot and fully expected it to be that way.

She didn't like Beverly much. Never had. Of course this was something she only admitted in the night. She loved her children of course, but love and like were different and she just plain didn't like Beverly. He was always taking things from the house and never bringing them back, until she decided to stop it and sued him. All she got back was the old apple-butter kettle, but at least she made him mad enough so that he let her alone.

She was fair to the girls, all three of them, even if she didn't like their husbands very much. Colonel this and Colonel that, and Virginia's husband a preacher, even if he was Presbyterian. She liked John but she loved Pressy. Liked and loved. He had been so strong all during the war when she knew he wanted to go be a soldier but had kept his promise to stay and help her. There was always one in a family, a big family like that, who was a favorite, and with her it was Pressy.

Everybody loved Pressy. The girls certainly did. At twenty-two he was as handsome as paint, and witty, and he had the Grant eyes, the only one who did. You could draw a line under them straight across his face like hers, dagger eyes when they wanted them to be, but sheathed most of the time.

John had worked too, God knows, she couldn't fault that, and she had done her best with everything else to keep their school work going when the tutor left to go back up north. But John was still only twenty and wild as a rooster. Pressy was wild, too, but in a different way—he rode hard and courted hard, and, she had to admit, he drank hard, but somehow, it was different with Pressy. The wildness was—she looked for a word—kindly. There wasn't a mean bone in Pressy's body.

It was lifting toward dawn when she knew what she was going to do. "Now let's see," she said aloud to the dawn, and as soon as it was light enough, she got out of her bed, put on her quilted winter dishabille, fed the fire again, and with her hair still braided down her back, she sat at her little desk, stirred the ink in its crystal ink bottle, poured a little in the well that matched it, and began to divide thousands of acres and what money was left between herself and her children. There was not an acre she didn't know as if she'd walked over it.

It only took her an hour, until Aunt Manny came in to look at the fire and found her awake and fussed at her. But it took the children and the lawyers all the way to April to agree to do what she had had in mind in the first place.

The land that fronted on the north side of the Kanawha River for five miles, and which ran back in two huge tracts in the hills, was divided between Pressy and John. Pressy was given Cedar Grove, John the land around and behind the old White House Tavern, which had been empty since her brother-in-law's death Before the War. Since Rachel didn't consider the tavern in good enough repair to live in, John got a lot more acres in the hills.

Rachel obviously considered two things as carefully as she could, in all fairness, as she would have said. She stipulated for her own lifetime share that she would inhabit Cedar Grove, with its garden, its outbuildings, and several acres of fields. Since it was legally Pressy's, he was expected to run his inheritance, of course.

So my grandfather, as the favorite and the member of the family who could do no wrong, was locked into a prison of bachelorhood. It was as recognized as marriage itself in Southern families. One of the boys would stay at home as surely as one would become a priest in large Catholic families.

The only thing his mother demanded was that there would not be any sale to coal companies, who had already begun to range beyond the navigable Kanawha with the promise of a railroad, to buy up the hell rights to the land. So the farm stayed as clean of coal as it had of salt. Rachel still ruled the roost, and Pressy took to spending a lot more time in Charleston where his sisters lived.

He had satisfied them all by assuming the role of the valley's eligible bachelor, who provided his strait-laced sisters and their husbands with enough exploits to lighten their gossip by the parlor lamps with the small roses on them. Genteel roses were small. And pale. That was what they had been taught to like.

All but Pressy. He loved red and he loved perfume, so that when he dressed he put perfume from France on his luxuriant mustaches. He saw no reason to wear the scents he loved where he couldn't smell them himself. His mustaches were no little brush at the upper lip, but fine shining auburn double wings across his face. There is a photograph of him when he was in his early thirties. For years it hung on the wall at Cedar Grove. Now it hangs beside his father on the wall of my workroom, and I can see that the descriptions of him were true. He wears a white bow tie and a winged collar. His shoulders are tailored perfectly, a handsome dandy who looked so like John Wilkes Booth that years later when there was a television documentary about the assassination of Lincoln, my Uncle Bado called my mother and said he was embarrassed.

For a few years until his mama died, he had the world by the tail. He drove the most famous four-in-hand in the valley. He raced a filly in the Kentucky Derby. He courted all the women he could unlace. His brother John had married Miss Amelia from Maysville, Kentucky, where his mother had come from. She was his cousin. She "brought money." Pressy made having to stay with his mother, and having his heart broken because Miss Amelia chose John instead of him, the excuse to raise some fine horses and some very fashionable hell.

He went to the White Sulphur Springs. He went to Louisville. He went to Saratoga. John and Miss Amelia stayed home with Rachel while they were making the old White House Tavern into Melrose. It was made into a fine modern house built with part of Miss Amelia's dowry.

The new house had the latest long-paned windows; the panes of the front door were of tinted glass with designs of ferns. My cousin and I used to put paper over the etched ferns and make crayon rubbings. The parlor had rosewood paneling; the stairs were walnut with a red carpet and the newel post was crowned with a pineapple for good luck. There was a handsome small porch with the same ornate carving as the interior fireplaces. In the thirty years since Cedar Grove had been built marble flowers and vines had come to replace Greek columns and swags.

Rachel Grant Tompkins was not cold in the Etruscan vault beside William before her two sons, Preston and John, sold over a thousand acres of the mineral rights under hill land, ad infernum, to the Supply Coal and Iron Company from New York. After all, the river was still not navigable, and the new railroad was south of the river. Anyway, the firm made a fine offer for land so far up the hollows that John and Miss Amelia were convinced that the coal would never soil their inheritance. The drift mine would be underground inside the hills, a long way inside the hills. After all, the New York company was willing to pay the equivalent of four hundred thousand dollars.

The tipple was to be built downriver nearly a mile from Preston's fine fields and his horses. The boat yard was the only business at Cedar Grove and that was all the way down at the mouth of Kelly's Creek. It wasn't all that hard to persuade Preston anyway. He could see that the mine would never infringe on the farm, and that he could even carry on his fall hunt. Friends came upriver from Charleston, and across the mountains from Richmond for fox chasing where the men sat around a campfire deep in the hills and let their dogs range around for miles while they talked and drank and listened to the music of the hounds, bugle mouths, bay mouths, treble mouths. All the dogs had their own voices.

There had been a cabin up on the hill for a long time, even in his father William's day. Preston had it rebuilt and enlarged so that it was a fine small log hunting lodge. Obe went up days ahead of time and got it ready for the gentlemen.

Preston Tompkins was spending money too fast, and enjoying it too much. He must have mourned his strict mother and sighed with relief at the same time. He had never been asked to grow up. His mother had insisted on providing in the deed of division that John sell him five hundred or so acres at three dollars an acre if he required it, because she thought that the division of land was unfair. John had argued that there wasn't a decent place for him to live on the upriver farm, except for the old inn that had been neglected since the war, and that the added acres balanced losing Cedar Grove to his brother.

Instead of selling to Preston, John bought the Cedar Grove land from Kelly's Creek east to his own line for five dollars an acre. The five hundred acres were put in the name of Miss Amelia, and Preston agreed to become her trustee. He was an agreeable man. Another parcel, from beyond the last orchard up Kelly's Creek, was sold to Mr. Ward. Preston liked Mr. Ward. They spent a lot of time together. Preston was gregarious and lonely and unmarried.

Then he sold the rest of the Kelly's Creek land to John, with land for a tipple at the mouth of Kelly's Creek which would be visible from the house. After all, he couldn't refuse his brother. He never had. The Cedar Grove coal seam was proving too valuable. Gradually, deed by deed, offer by offer, the holdings that Preston controlled shrank. The years tolled out in sold land, while Preston's inheritance was turned into money. After all, there were still thousands of acres. John was a "good business man," far better than Preston. It was one of those family truths that was not questioned.

Preston was drinking a lot. Not that he couldn't hold it. I once asked my mother if she had ever seen her father drunk. It offended her. "I never saw my father drunk in his life," she said. And then she grinned, memory sweeter than lying. "And I never saw him sober."

In the manic depressive coal industry, land changed hands long before a single tipple was built, or a shovel of coal taken from the seam. There is no record that the New York company ever opened their mine. But John and Preston at last gave in to the pressures of the booming industry that was taking over the upper valley, just as the salt works had blighted the valley above Charleston. They tried to open a mine themselves, selling shares locally, some for a dollar to the men who were going to work the coal face. The first name for the mine was the Cedar Grove Cooperative Coal Company. It was only the first of many names for the mine that was gradually taking over the farm and building a town where the stock had grazed.

Jenny Lind houses were put up. A company store, its facade a replica of the house at Cedar Grove, was built of brick beside the tipple. Kelly's Creek Coal and Coke, Cedar Grove Collieries: by the late 1880s the coal land had already had several names. The brothers ran it for a while, and then leased again to a firm based in Ohio. By the late 1880s the farm called Cedar Grove that Addie had watched from across the river was named in deeds, "a tract of coal land."

*A*s soon as he heard of the attempt to kill Addie with the dynamite, Mr. Tompkins pulled up with a carriage, a wagon and several men from his own mine across the river, and moved a heavily pregnant woman, her children, her housekeeper, her sewing machine, and the button-hole scissors and the little stitch pick-out she had nearly forgotten and run back for. His men kept watch, handed her up into his own open carriage, and off they drove to the safety of Charleston, where he owned a house on Broad Street.

He had always been spoiled by the women, his mother, the ones he had made love to, his older sisters, and the rulers of the houses in the growing river town of Charleston where he had spent much of his bachelor time. Postwar Charleston still had a hard, withered core of pride and defeat, where prejudices changed with county lines, and the signs of "who you were" were read constantly.

Most of the land-owning prewar families had gone with the South. They formed a thin hard line socially, and they influenced Democratic politics so that office seekers had to court them, even though some of them had been what the new people thought of as ruined.

They were guardians of money and legitimacy. Their pasts were known from uneasy forays into "genealogy," the science of faking it. English genealogists in the nineteenth century had found a gold mine of naivete. Irish names were connected to Tara, Scottish names to the Stuarts, and English names to a plethora of peers. New rich only forty years before, by the 1880s the Tompkins family were old rich. They owned land for literally miles along the narrow valley of the Kanawha

River. The children of William Tompkins, apprentice gunsmith, saw themselves as gentry—poorhouse Tories, because they still had dinner at three o'clock and scorned new rich Yankee ways.

There were no lace curtains and ice-water like the despised "Tennessee genteel," no drink but tea served when ladies were present like the gentry did east of the mountains, no dinner at night like the new coal people putting on airs. I inherited the residue, as we all do, of habits, gestures, genes, hopes, fears, and lies which are called Family.

My grandfather took for granted, as such men do, that the women of his family would give him whatever he wanted as they always had. He had not reckoned on their envy and their perpetual hopes for him. Preston Tompkins's two older sisters, who lived in Charleston, ran a ridge of mountain gentility of their own. It did not include divorce, and even more, it did not include marrying somebody they didn't know.

They, who had so long ago been belles, had married ex-Confederate officers. Their own first cousin once removed, Sally, had been called the Florence Nightingale of the Confederacy, even though they had to admit that their other first cousin was General Grant, but after all, he had become president and that was something.

By 1889, they had had their own disappointments, had grown middle-aged, and were living through Preston a youth they considered they had been robbed of by the war. They fastened for new life onto the entrancing scandal. They refused to receive the woman who wasn't like any woman they had ever admitted to knowing. Their envy, their hard-shelled Presbyterian religion, and their own dead-center certainty of "who they were" were all their pride. Pressy's Addie rattled their gentility of iron, and they protected themselves from her as they fed on her existence, their barriers mounted to keep their small town pride, their barricade after the late unpleasantness.

The house on Broad Street was a fine, new four-story brick house then, darkened by huge trees on the main street that ran between the river and the railroad station. Addie had known nothing larger in her life than the railroad station upriver, and once or twice, she never said how often, and she seemed aloof from her memories of that, she had come down the river in the paddle steamer. She had never lived in a house that had more than one story.

So my grandfather was left with Addie, and a family of three growing stepdaughters and a child on the way that kept Addie out of pry-
ing eyes so that she didn't even take walks under the trees. Addie
was queen of the house on Broad Street, and queen of nothing. Poli-
ticians and lawyers came and went and were over-polite to her, but
not one woman in the town who had known my grandfather all his
life recognized her existence. They invited their beloved Preston to
Sunday dinners, balls, and socials as they always had. He went alone.
Miss Addie told me years later that she made him do it. "He was easy
bored," she said, to explain.

For a long time she tried. She must have been so lonely there trying
and having it all rejected, the new manners other people took for granted,
changes from the language she spoke, which, had they known it, was
more like that of an eighteenth century duchess than theirs, so she
wouldn't shame my grandfather, in a house where only men came to
visit.

She was as lonesome as a child, this young country woman, suddenly cast into a role that shamed her in a pitiless town. She hung up
her favorite picture of Jesus and built, from those days, her own wall of
safety that protected her all the rest of her life.

Charleston had not changed so much in the forty years from Addie's
time there to when I first knew it. It was a pretty river town then. The
branches of huge trees met over the paved streets. The coal-baron-Gothic
and the salt-baron-Federal houses lined the river, with their huge columns like bank buildings, new in Addie's time, but when I was a child
weathered and full of old events. I had my first real kiss, not peck, in
the attic of the four-story house across the street from the house he took
her to.

The ice wagon still came by. An old woman drove an electric
brougham. There was still sawdust spread on the street outside of houses
where people were very ill. The church I went to was the same building, the new Romanesque First Presbyterian Church, that had been
built not long before she lived in the town. The northern Presbyterians had split from the southern Presbyterians and built their own
new Gothic church. But the leisure of the streets where I walked was
much the same.

I passed the house my mother had been born in (but had never admitted) for years before I learned that Addie had come there as a faulted mistress and stayed summer and winter in the rich coldness of that place. By the time I knew the house, it looked more dark and forbidding than it must have when there were children in it—a place that had long since been turned into the kind of boarding house with drooped curtains where traveling men spent as little time as they could in their rooms.

Mr. Tompkins sat with men he had known all his life on the porch of the then new Ruffner Hotel, which had replaced the fine old Hale House that had burned a few years before, watched the river traffic, read the paper, drank juleps, and talked politics.

Miss Addie told little about those years. So I have a shadow figure, remarks, a Joseph coat, a death, belligerent love, belligerent hate, to make a man of, who had so much to do with the lives of all of us who came after him. What was taught me consciously about him was not a clear mirror of his real existence. I had to learn that the few times that protective forgetfulness was broached.

My grandfather was the kind of man who excited passions, of protection from his men friends, love or hate from women who were either kin or lovers. He left destroyed and destroying hopes to mirror a past that only partly happened, dreads that we inherited as fears of sex and passion, both of these seen as scandal.

As for Addie—or the Miss Addie she became—who told about him later, there were only hints, dropped remarks, once in a while a story that was like opening a closed door, letting light in, and then closing it before there was anything more than a glimpse.

Last year I found a pile of blackened photographs that opened a time that had been legend and secret, and there they were, my grandfather Preston, Addie, my mother and my aunts and uncles as children, as young girls and men. They had been there all the time, hidden under neglected papers in a drawer, so black that they were shadows of people in the night. I must have picked up the album when my mother died and then forgotten it.

I could not see their faces, but they haunted me. I took them to computer imaging, and they came out to meet me, the sun shining, the water glistening, the dead young, the scandal new but hidden by their straight backs, their smiles, their wide skirts, the completely direct gazes of liars. Leading them all, as she had in life, was Addie, when she was Addie young, Addie hurt and proud, Addie again, until my wild card grandmother, Miss Addie, entered my own childhood.

One picture was not blackened by time. It was of a five- or six-month-old baby in a carriage, a child old enough to be watchful, to have a face of her own. It was not a faded Kodak print but a studio picture made in Charleston. The baby carriage is covered by a parasol with a white lace fringe. There is lace around the pillows, lace around the sides of the carriage and falling over the front. The baby rests against a fur-covered pillow. It is my mother. She is already quite recognizable. She looks, as I have seen her look so often, sad and a little adrift, as if she already knew the secret of her birth that she would hide for the rest of her life, maybe even consciously from herself, within her frail cage of bone. She holds a little black doll. If I had no other proof that it was my mother, the doll would tell me. My own first doll was chosen by her, and it was black, as hers had been.

Addie's divorce was finally granted in April of 1892. She had waited for three years. She and my grandfather were married in the same month. She was twenty-nine. He was forty-eight. They were alone. None of his family, or hers, came to what must have been a sad little wedding. In many ways it was a disaster that they have never been forgiven, in many ways a love which was the deepest one that many of us ever knew.

When my grandfather finally took my grandmother to her house of mist, great-grandmother's daffodils littered the lawn as if they had been broadcast to welcome her. It was said—maybe another legend—that Addie, still tiny-waisted and lithe as a colt, didn't wait for my grandfather to open the gate. She vaulted the picket fence in her joy, and from that time on until she died she was the queen of what she called "a piece of property" she could understand. She took to the rule of the valley a lot better, they said, than those who had been born to it and didn't give a damn anymore.

Grandfather, at forty-seven, was already on the road to the kind of quiet gentle drunkenness that was called with some pride "holding your licker."

"She kept your grandfather," was the echo, part of the legend, part of the truth, "from going to hell in a handcart."

It had taken just fifteen years since my great-grandmother had died for a coal town to grow up around Cedar Grove. There were horses tethered to the iron rings on the porch of the company store. Two small brick houses had been built for superintendents on either side of it, so that it formed a little red brick town center. Mr. Calderwood's store had opened, too. Its second-floor assembly room was used by everybody in the town from the local people who put on plays there, to the church members who had socials, to the local union who met there whether the lessees of the mine liked it or not. Mr. Calderwood said it was all the same to him. They were all customers.

Further along, where the railroad from Mr. Ward's mine already cut the town in half, there were rows of coal company shacks going down to the river where the mill and the boat yard still ran. The town had grown quickly, a mixture of old slave-made red brick, white trim, Roman dentils on the big house and the company store, and the wild west—mud, saloons, and Jenny Lind houses.

A few cottages with gingerbread carved porches had been built Before the War along what was still called the James and Kanawha turnpike. Several tall large wooden houses were up long steps on the opposite hill where the superintendents from Ward and other coal companies lived. There were two churches, but the children still went by ferry to school on Addie's side of the river. The roads were already dark with coal dust, ground in by the weather. The raindrops on the windowsills were black.

The people of the little coal town all knew Mr. Preston. They were fond of him in an adopted way, and they commiserated with him when his brother John, who they didn't like as much, insisted on leasing out the coal company again. It had been under Preston's leadership, probably the only time he did lead, when in 1880 they had tried to make a cooperative of the mine with the men on the coal face as part owners at a dollar a share, but it hadn't pulled in as much money as John thought they ought to make with the big out-of-state corporations.

So Preston went back to his horses and his farm, new people ran the company store, and when he drove Addie up to the gate of the Big House, it looked to him like failure. Sale after sale for quick money had let the miners' houses be built almost up to the back of the barn. The bull field was the only large piece of land left along Kelly's Creek. The horses and the cattle were kept in hillside fields behind the house where there were still a few acres where he had managed to keep control.

At least the coal town had not crossed the turnpike and besieged the lawn of the Big House in the front. The barn, the fine stable, great-grandmother's neglected formal garden, and the vista of the river half a mile away over the low buildings and the mill were as they had always been. The whitewashed outbuildings still ran along the side of the back lawn by the Horse Mill Creek, so that when they were inside the gate it was almost as it had been all his life. Uncle Obe had tried to keep it that way even though there was nobody there. Mr. Preston had lived down at Charleston most of the time.

Obediah, the same age as my grandfather, had come back after years in Ohio. He said he got homesick. After all, Mr. Preston had been his best friend since he was a little boy. He told the children that more and more often as he got older. He said he knew Mr. Preston didn't have the right kind of sense to look after himself. That was his conscious reason for coming back and appearing one day at the gate of the house in 1878. There hadn't been anybody there. So he carried his few belongings to the room in the little office. When my grandfather came back three days later from Saratoga, he had lit the fires and cleaned the place.

"I was never as glad to see anybody in all my born days," my grandfather told my mother, a phrase he never used for any other event.

Obediah, now Uncle Obe, his title given him as formally as if it were the law when he reached the age of forty-five and his hair turned white, had been watching for them all day. The furniture wagon from downriver had come, and he had put most of it where he thought it ought to go.

If Mr. Tompkins drove through what he thought was failure, Mrs. Tompkins was driving through heaven. By the time she saw the house for the first time, close enough to touch and take possession, it was early evening and the old cedars with their high white-washed trunks cast long barriers of shadow across the front lawn. The lowered sun touched the glass of the doorway through the fine portico and it glowed as if it had been lit by fire.

Uncle Obe had lit the lamps, two in the hall, and one on the table in the drawing room. The first floor of the house was nearly empty. It had, as it would have later when it was again neglected, a frailty about it, large as it was, a whisper of loss in the wide halls, the unused rooms, the overgrown gardens.

Some of the finery had been left in the sharing out of the inheritance. The great dining room table was still there, too large to move. It seated sixteen in a house that later became so crowded that my mother said she was sixteen herself before she sat at the "first table." The card tables from Cincinnati, the marble mantels, the huge carpet that covered the whole of the parlor, were still in their old places. The great gold framed mirror with the water line across it at five feet where the water had come into the room during the great flood of 1860 still covered the space between the front windows. The once fine silk curtains from Richmond that the daughters hadn't wanted for their houses, not when lace-trimmed voile was all the rage, sagged at the windows.

The kitchen table had been scrubbed for years until it was white, and the chairs that went with it had been caned and caned again by Uncle Obe. The rocking chair his mama had died in, at least he told the children that, was still in place in front of the iron fireplace. Above it was the heating cupboard. Its patterned wrought-iron doors were inlaid with china medallions of a woman's head in profile, ivory-colored. I used to stare at the woman when I was a child, thinking, as I'm sure others did when they sat and watched the space before their eyes, of other things.

Uncle Obe had been stoking the big iron range all afternoon to keep warm the succotash and the biscuits he had made for them. Obviously it was the room that Uncle Obe had lived in most. It felt alive, used. He had put the heavy, authoritarian bedroom suite that had come upriver from Charleston in the master bedroom, the high bed with a mahogany back, a needlepoint-covered armchair on springs that made it into a rocking chair, and a fine mahogany dresser. Several mahogany armchairs with gros-point covered upholstery and a spindled rocker had been moved into the parlor. The upright piano that my Aunt Bertha, Addie's second daughter, had begun to learn to play was put against the wall where the grand piano had been.

The house may have looked betrayed and desolate to my grandfather, but it looked like a palace to Addie and the daughters she had brought with her, now four. My mother was being carried by my grandfather, her long handkerchief-linen and lace dress that Addie had made trailing almost to his ankles.

Addie had entered into her kingdom. She walked into the wide hallway. Maybe she stood there. It had been a long journey. She had had her life threatened, had suffered through the worst of genteel brutalities. She had been treated as if she did not exist. In the Soviet Union it was to be the name for a state punishment, to become a non-person. She had been, and still was, to her husband's family, a non-person, one of the oldest and cruelest punishments, not for what she did (had there been enough coal money she would have gotten by with it) but who she was. But in that house she was Mrs. Tompkins. Her husband called her that all his life, and he, to her, was Mr. Tompkins. They had fought for those titles of respect and they used them always.

She walked slowly through the drawing room, the wide hall, across the brick floor of the open archway from the old kitchen to the dining-room. She inspected the walled well on the back porch, the ell of the kitchen where the smoke house and the milk house were a part of the kitchen wing. Behind her, all through the house, her three daughters roamed and nosed and laughed. The eldest, Minnie, was fourteen, only a year younger than Addie had been when she married. Mr. Tompkins warned Mrs. Tompkins that the girl had to be trained on a rubber bit; she was so wild she would lunge herself to death on a curb.

Bertha and Myrtle were younger—ten and seven. Bertha was show-ing talent that everybody praised for the piano. Myrtle, the shy one, whose legs were already bowed from early rickets nobody recognized, carried one doll. She had named it Mine. Only Mr. Tompkins suspected that she would never, except for a few mistaken years, leave the house until she had to, as an old woman. He said that she ran into the house first, as if something in her knew that her inheritance of blood and val-ley was deeper than his.

Her own father was a descendant of the Morris who had built the log fort, the White House Inn, whose family had lived on the property until Aaron Stockton had come to him with cash money to buy his land. Did Myrtle, like a small dog who smelled familiar smells, simply take it into her body and soul that she was home?

Mr. and Mrs. Tompkins had come to the end of something, both of them. They began that day to lead the life that intrudes in my dreams, my memories, that formed my mother and bent my aunts to their own futures. Those two, the lovers, had replaced the love by a marriage that they had hoped would redeem them. It did not. There was a core of suffering that Addie had been handed and she handed it on to her chil-dren as surely as if it were part of their genes.

But on that first evening Mr. and Mrs. Tompkins strolled through her new kingdom. They walked among the scents of shade and dew, brick and roses from Woods in Richmond, so old that they straggled across the grass. Addie's silk skirts and petticoats trailed along the great sweep of the front lawn toward the last of the grove of cedars, virgin and enormous, down in the corner of the lawn that made a sky-high canopy of shade, dark and mysterious, by the creek that had run for more than a hundred years to cleanse itself after Kelly had been scalped, and urged by the water against a large stone that made a miniature cliff where it was deep enough for a swimming hole for children.

My grandfather told my mother she still hadn't said a word. They stood there together watching the creek beyond the trees, and then they turned and stood for a long time, looking beyond the wide lawn at the house, and all they surveyed, in the distance; the barn, the stable, the bull field, the corncrib, the distant pigsties, the chicken house. There must have been, even for her, a moment anyway of calm and of acceptance.

"Mr. Tompkins," she said at last, "this house don't have no porch."

*S*o, barricaded, and within her kingdom, Addie had come to rule, first the charming, feckless new husband she had fought so hard for, and then, in the big high bed that had been moved into the master bedroom, the three more children who were born in it, as women did then, writhing on the bed while the midwife kept the men and the children out in the downstairs hall, listening to the sounds of it, and then the new cry.

Maybe, for a while, she thought the bad days were over. Then Mr. Tompkins's brothers and sisters demanded that their parents be moved from the Etruscan vault. They were reburied in Charleston, with fine new marble monuments. The vault was left empty.

Addie never forgave them. She said later that Mr. Tompkins died a little bit then. She didn't say a word to him nor he to her, but she never got over the abandonment, even by the dead. But she did not, for one moment, give in to the demands of that silence. She had tried for a time to imitate them to please Mr. Tompkins, by giving up everything that had made him fall in love with her. But after the removal of the bodies of his parents, as if they thought her presence defiled even the dead, she finally turned and faced her tormentors.

She went back to her own religion and her own way of talking and her own opinions. Instead of imitating their brutal politeness, as cold as charity, which is the way such behavior has been perpetuated for centuries, Addie gathered her habits and her way of being around her again, like something she had lost and regained. She became once again a Church of God Holy Roller, and she rubbed the family noses in it whenever she could, so maybe my mother was right when she said Addie did it for revenge. But through the years it grew beyond revenge into a way of living in the world that contained passion and mystery instead of the straight-backed, cold-hearted Presbyterianism of her enemies.

Addie's religion ruled her life—and often everybody else's. She even rejected the family church. She would have none of it. She made Mr. Tompkins deed her a little piece of property in the town and built her own church. It was board and batten, with a wooden steeple, and windows with Gothic points at the top, a wooden edition of the little brick church the family still called Virginia's chapel. Every year she made her congregation climb up and paint it pure white. She chose the preachers. She kept a key to the church and she locked it when they didn't do right.

But my mother never changed her mind. She would say, out of Addie's hearing, "We had a perfectly good church already." She added, "It was built for Aunt Virginia, Presbyterian of course. Mother never set foot in it," which was not true. She sat, when she felt she had to, for weddings and funerals, bolted to the front family pew.

Gradually Addie began to change the house into her own image; it had been too much a reminder. She never moved the stiff daguerreotype portrait of his mother and father from over the parlor mantel, but she swathed the offending marble fireplace and its Greek columns in striped silk. The silk curtains which she would have said "wasn't worth a hill of beans" were replaced with fine voile with lace trim, the latest thing, the girls told her after they had all been driven down to Charleston, eighteen miles away, to go to the store. She had wide swathes of flowers papered at the picture rail, and a fine bright green wall paper over the old dim maroon canvas of the walls. She set one of the mahogany card tables in the middle of the room, with a lace cloth and a kerosene lamp with two large globes covered with roses. She left the great mirror to reflect it all.

She splashed color wherever she could, on the walls, in the embroidery around the linen, in the quilts that covered the beds. She grew red roses. She papered her bedroom wall with red roses larger than any that ever grew on this earth. She and my grandfather surrounded themselves with a riot of red, roses, ties, dresses, ungenteel and glorious red. Lavender and roses replaced the smell of neglect and emptiness. Addie wore lavender water. Mr. Tompkins put the scent of roses on his luxuriant mustache.

She went back to wearing a poke bonnet. She made them herself, and they were of farm-woman blue-and-white gingham. I used to put one on and play like I was crossing the Alleghenies in a wagon. I see her now in the blue-and-white gingham poke bonnet, a new one every year, strengthened around her still pretty, angry face, the bonnet stiffened with buckram, with a long ruffle to protect her neck from the sun. Her daughters looked the other way.

Within months an open porch grew across the front of the house. There were slim wooden columns that ended in cupolas that circled around the ends of the brick walls. In the left-hand cupola a swing hung from the ceiling; at the other end, a hammock. My mother said that it was unsaid but understood that the left-hand swing was for gentlemen who came to talk to Mr. Tompkins, and the hammock was for everybody. It was still that way when I was a child. When my uncles went and sat in the swing, so intent on what they were discussing that the swing didn't creak, we knew to stay away.

A line of wicker rocking chairs, the latest thing, the girls said, was placed along the front. They were seldom without someone rocking, and the crinkcrank of wood against wood, and the faint creak of the wicker, was one of the sounds of my childhood. Addie planted red rambler roses on tall trellises, and they gradually shaded the porch even on the hottest days. I remember it as the main meeting and gossip place always when the weather was good. I spent a lot of time sitting on the porch floor with my legs hanging over, kicking at the roses and eavesdropping on the grownups, who tended to treat all the cousins as if we couldn't hear, which has made this book easier to write.

In the first picture I resurrected of the family, Addie sits there with two of the children and my grandfather, his mustache grown longer, a little straggly, his shirt ruffled. They are in the hammock in the cupola nearest the creek. My mother sits between them, clinging to her father. She seems to be trying to burrow behind him, the fear that was hers when she was a baby still in her face. They both are looking at the camera. She looks about four, which means that they have been at Cedar Grove less than five years. Big Brother perches at the end of the hammock, a little away from the others, watching something or nothing in the front yard beyond the camera. Addie sits as straight as a soldier in a dark (red?) dress that looks as if it were made of taffeta, with leg-o'-mutton sleeves. She watches with him. Nobody is smiling. For the first fourteen years of my mother's life, that would be the pattern of their affections.

Addie enclosed half of the graceful second-floor veranda that had run along the back of the house outside the bedrooms, and made a sewing and quilting room when nobody had ever made a quilt there before. The old carpets were brightened with new Persian throw rugs.

She thought that the open passage between the kitchen and the dining room was a piece of foolishness, especially in the fall and winter. She had it enclosed with brick she found on the property that had been made at the same time as the house brick, and covered the cold stone floor with wood. She made half of it into a large walk-in larder. Mr. Tompkins said Mrs. Tompkins could have anything she wanted. What she wanted was to be where she was.

Then she decided that the old-fashioned carved marble fireplaces were too chipped and should be removed and nice brick with coal grates put in their place, reminding Mr. Tompkins that it was more practical. What she really liked was a fire made of bright cannel coal, the most valuable, that could be brought down from the mine that Mr. Tompkins and the family still had the "right" to, even though the mine was leased.

She attacked the acre of formal garden, blowsy with old roses, and almost buried stone paths, after the eight years of neglect. It was where Mr. Tompkins and his brothers and sisters had strolled and courted when they were young Before the War. She planted a fine Catawba grapevine that covered a twenty-foot-long grape arbor. It made a shady covered walk she paved with brick, where she could stroll and pick grapes over her head. Until she died the arbor stayed there, and every year the fine Catawba grapes hung down like gifts, she said, from Jesus.

She decided that to keep a whole acre of garden in flowers was, in the words she used for such things until her death, "a piece of foolishness." So she had it plowed up, moved the altheas and the sunflowers down beyond the fence along the back walk to the road that nobody ever used but her. She put whitewashed wooden shelves by the side gate; she said it was for indoor plants to be outdoors in the summer time, but it was really a private mail and parcel drop for her. The new plants made a bowered path to the growing town beyond. She lined the path with her jonquils, and carnations that Mr. Tompkins cared for. They were his favorites, strongly scented carnations that he wore to town in his button hole.

In the place of the flowers in the garden, she planted and cared for vegetables—potatoes, squash, onions, house corn as opposed to field corn, tomatoes that she called love apples, peppers, teepee after teepee of green beans, peas—that made the right side of the garden beyond the grape arbor look like the Indians were once again camping where they had camped so often in the early years, only a hundred and thirty years before. At the end, behind the brick office, she put a new chicken run, and began to raise her favorites, white Leghorns, some guinea fowl, a few bantams, and white turkeys. When she lay in the back porch hammock in the cool of the afternoon, where I lay so many years later, she could hear them churtling and grumbling. Her rooster woke her in the mornings.

Cedar Grove was becoming a place of comfort where Addie's older daughters were not taught to sit upright and to make conversation and never to let a silence fall, which was a prime social sin for genteel women, one of the sins that my grandfather taught my mother. The rocking chairs in the drawing room were on runners so that they slid back and forth with a slight consenting murmur as she rocked.

Relatives came and stayed for months, but they were her relatives, not his. His men friends from the city came and stayed and honored the madam, as they called her. They seemed to be trying to make up for the treatment she had had and was having; they were courtly with her, because of their old friend. And they, too, stayed and stayed, so that the walls of the house began to sound again with the voices of children and men.

She saw to it with Uncle Obe that grandfather kept up all his bachelor hospitality. When it was time for the fall hunt, men came and took their dogs for miles into the hollows and the hidden valleys that had not yet been sacrificed to coal and money. Mr. Tompkins sent Uncle Obe and Aunt Liddy, who had been added to the household to cook, away up into the hills to stay at the hunting cabin and make food for them, and cook their birds and venison.

In the evening they lit a bonfire in a stone pit, and the men sat around it and drank, and listened to the fox chase, the music of the hounds. Mr. Tompkins's hospitality, his miles of hunting land, and the tenderness men have for each other when the women have abdicated time, a conspiracy of kindness, and a tongue that lashed with wit were Mr. Tompkins's yearly gift to the friends he had known all his life.

When Governor McCorkle caught laryngitis on the fall hunt, he had to stay in bed for several weeks, so that much of the state business was moved up to Cedar Grove. Once again, for a little while, the house changed its sounds, its footsteps: men's voices, men's jokes, men's drinking on the new front porch in the lines of rocking chairs as they talked about money, coal, and politics.

Finally the governor was able to leave for downriver, and Mr. Tompkins stood to watch him go, with my five-year-old mother beside him, his pet, his confidant. "You know, sissy," he said as to a grownup, "I haven't got a close friend I dislike as much as I do that man."

Businessmen stayed there and gave him the companionship he missed, except when he went for long business trips into town. The land—there was still so much of it—gave him money; he hardly noticed that it was less and less money, and that he was becoming a victim, like the miners, of the Golden Age of Spencer's Social Darwinism. He would have scorned knowing what Social Darwinism was, he who didn't even believe in free schools.

He made a close friend of Mr. Cabot from Boston. (He taught my mother that there were only two cities north of the Mason-Dixon line— Philadelphia and Boston.) Mr. Cabot spent the whole summer there, and he and Mr. Tompkins shared their passion for carnations. They wrote a small book together and illustrated it and had it bound in white leather. There were only two copies.

He and Mr. Cabot got along so well that there was no problem when Mr. Cabot bought the mineral rights to the natural gas that flowed under the land. They even put a clause in the lease that stated that the

Tompkins house should have free natural gas as long as any descendant lived there. That was when the gas lamps were put in, the gas wall sconces, the gas logs, the flat lacy white fire clay that turned first red and then a faint fine blue, shapes to stare at, and dream in new ways, not the popping of logs or the smell of coal, that bright peace, but the faint live hiss of blue.

But when Mr. Tompkins went to Boston to try and sell more leases *ad infernum* when things were bad in the valley, Mr. Cabot put him up in a hotel instead of his house. The carnation book was shunted away, then played with by the children, then lost. Only the hiss of the gas fires remained of the friendship when Mr. Cabot spent the summer and wrote a book with him. Nobody saw anything wrong with it. It was, in the last decade of the century, Good Business, and nobody questioned it, but my mother never forgave or forgot that her father had to stay in a hotel when he went to Boston.

Anger still whispered at any reminder of what was out there someplace, ready to invade from an alien world when they had such a precarious peace. Anger hid like dust and waited, and when it exploded, no one who heard it ever forgot it.

One morning my mother leaned on the railing of what was left of the back upstairs veranda and watched her mother cross the back yard below to her father's office. She remembered that it was Monday because Essie, white, somebody Addie could talk to, came and did the laundry on the back porch where the sheets were boiled in the great washtubs, sheets for ten beds at least. The washing waved and billowed where the breeze from up the back hollow caught it and it smelled as only laundry in the sun smells, as if it had caught the sun like scent itself.

That was the morning Addie found the letter from "Uncle Charlie." Uncle Charlie was still leaking family money in Washington where, in Mr. Tompkins's words, he was still floating big schemes. Forming companies was his passion. At one point he formed a company with shareholders and all the trimmings of big business, and included the boat yard, the horse mill, the coal mine, everything at Cedar Grove that he could see turned into money, none of which belonged to him anymore. His favorite place to rare back and smoke cigars among the rich and ruthless was still the Mayflower Hotel. He was his own Horatio Alger, as ruthless as a rabbit. But he did retain something of the family tradition. He was a dandy and a snob.

The letter asked Mr. Tompkins if he could come to Cedar Grove and spend the summer, pointing out that it was his boyhood home, and he missed it. He added, "I want to come back, but I must have your assurance that I won't have to speak to that woman."

Addie seized the letter and crushed it in her fist. She ran out of Mr. Tompkins's office and knelt among the flowing sheets. She raised her arms, the letter still clutched in her hand.

"Lord!" she called out to the sky, "you promised me that you would make my enemies my footstool. WHEN?"

*M*ost of my mother's memories of her early childhood were etched in light. She decided almost before my brother and I could talk that our favorite stories began, "When I was a little girl . . ." All the journeys with her father, one to White Sulphur Springs, one to Kentucky, all the rules of gentility, all the secrets, the conversations, the pleasure, were told and told, whenever she wanted to relive them, so that there only seemed to be one childhood, hers. She relived her childhood so often that it is a brighter memory for me than my own.

She told of an almost belligerent happiness. Much of it was spun into a whole cloth more acceptable to her. Maybe some of it was not true, but she was remembering it as truth, truth protected by her own armor against sadness and anger as deep as her soul. But sometimes the armor slipped and she told a balder truth. I have had to question all of this, but as far as the recall is concerned, I trust both her truths and her lies, which so often are grown out of what happened—colored, changed, purged, reformed. As in stories. Fictions. Not lies. She covered over what to her were dreads that shaped her life and almost shaped mine, towering tiny fears she kept always in her rigid body.

But when she spoke of her father, her recall was immediate. She was there with him, so happy that I could tell from her face and her voice that she was trusting the recall as you would trust clear and yearning reliving with one who has been your lover, whose gestures, remarks, turn of head, smile, touch, come back as clearly as if they were still happening, especially in dreams. I could tell sometimes when she had dreamed of him; she was gentler in the mornings, less withdrawn, but I never, when I was growing up at arm's length from her, questioned why.

She was, after all, her father's child, as her mother said over and over. When he, half drunk, put her at five years of age on a wild horse, her mother called, "Don't. Don't do that!" And then as she had learned to do with them, since they seemed not to hear her, gave up. "Go ahead. Kill her. She's your child, not mine."

To please him, my mother did as he expected her to, rode any horse, at first sidesaddle, and then, when she begged, presenting it as a challenge, what they called astraddle, a little safer. "She can ride anything," he bragged, patted the horse's wild ears and neck, saying "Gently gently," as the horse reared. Uncle Obe called out, "Gently as hell, Mr. Preston. Don't do that!"

But it was too late. He let go of the harness. She walked the horse around the back of the barn and out again, soft hands for the rubber bit which her father told her was all the horse would stand for. Her father was pleased, forever pleased with her. He took the terror in her still face after that ride as ladylike control. She no longer recognized the terror, only the praise.

Under the stories, I can see that she had little childhood. She was her father's companion, and he told her everything, as he would have a brother, a friend, a drinking companion. She was the one he needed, always there. She did not cling. He would have frowned on that. But she pleased him, always. She became, for a lonely man, surrounded by all the exuberant alien dramatic lives of "the girls," the boon companion that he needed and formed for himself. If he wanted to talk politics, he talked them to her. If he wanted to read, he read to her, all the Waverly Novels, the *Idylls of the King*, stories about Before the War.

If he wanted somebody to accompany him, she went with him in his carriage, on the train, on the river boat. He took her with him when he went downriver, dressed up as he used to dress all the time, he told her, in the old days. His mustache was trimmed. He smelled nice. He seemed to know everybody on the train. "Everybody loved my daddy," she told us.

She sat with her father in the lawyer's office, at the bank, on the porch of the Ruffner Hotel, taking it all in. She missed nothing while he negotiated, borrowed, paid back, floated loans, signed deeds, formed corporations that never lasted. She knew seams of coal, troubles and taste, bond issues, payrolls, and money whisper.

In Charleston they always stopped to see his sisters. It was where she picked up unwritten rules among the tea cups. The aunts, as they say, were quite comfortably off. (They were still rich but didn't like to show it.) They still had dinner in the middle of the day, and scorned the new people who had come in the coal business, who had dinner at night.

"Lunch," they taught her with a sneer, polite as always so the sneer was faint, was for people who went to offices, beyond some pale she was beginning to recognize. They were poor house Tories, not new rich, a sin in their eyes who had been new rich such a short time ago. They said that she should not forget that there are more important things than money. Nothing was more important than money and she already knew it. Money whispered in all the corners of the houses she knew—money, land, coal, gas, and one became the others, over and over.

It was in those visits that she learned duplicity, a split in her loyalties between her father and mother, masked as, "Don't mention our visits to 'the family.' They might upset your mother."

Her father took her with him to the bank to borrow money. Mr. J. Q. Dickenson sat in judgment over the wilder men of the valley at the bank in Charleston, the priest of their money or their lack of it. She made sure her back was straight all the time she waited for the men to finish, being quiet, holding her skirt and her petticoats down. Mr. Dickenson told her father in front of her what a fine businesswoman she would make, which was the only compliment he knew. He knew where his own money had come from, out of the ground, and he never shut down his salt wells until long after the other men who had made their quick fortunes in salt had given it up for the will-o'-the-wisps of gas and oil and coal, digging deeper into their Gehennas.

Mr. Dickenson had proved the Bible wrong by not spending the talents he and his family had earned from the salt business, but burying them in a bank of their own and letting them multiply, while Mr. Tompkins had used his talents all up and down the valley and all the way to Kentucky, Boston, White Sulphur, had flung away his fortune with historic glee—the famous four-in-hands, both tie and horses, the women who still greeted him when he walked with my mother on the street newly called Capitol Street, twirling their parasols and acting like they weren't old.

He reminisced about the Derby, how he ran a filly and bet on the nose because a gentleman never bet any other way. Of course, like the mine and the gas and the mill and the rest, the filly lost. My mother said many times, "Daddy had all the charm in the world, but no luck."

When his friends came to see him, she was allowed to linger close enough to listen. She knew more about the new West Virginia politics than most grownups.

I have more than her memories of this time. One of the photographs I found is of the children sitting on the little porch of my mother's play-house, five of them, and on the back of the picture is written *Pressy's children*, as if their mother, Addie, and their older half sisters did not exist. It was sent to my mother when she was old from one Tompkins relative to another, who had once known Cedar Grove, and forever longed for it again.

My mother sits cradling a doll. She has dressed it and fixed its hair to look like her. Her face is adult; she is acting at being a beautiful little girl for her daddy. She sits with her back straight, as he has told her ladies sit. Imperious and graceful at eight or nine, her birth date smudged by secrecy, she is a girl child of her time. Her father has taught her to be a lady and she looks like one, posed to show her fine profile. Beside her, far from her, is her brother, Preston, Addie's beloved pride and joy, intelligent, handsome. Addie has long since informed him that he will be governor some day. The children are already completely recognizable, small forecasts of themselves in later years. Aunt Helen, a year old, sits in front of him on the little stoop. Behind her, my Uncle Bado, still in dresses, stands close to my Uncle Roger.

But some of my mother's memories still held her on a knifepoint of her hurt, so that she had to tell them, too, over and over, to, as she said, get them out of her system. But she never did. They, too, were told as if she were reliving them. There was the day she lived and told over and over, when her aunts actually came to Cedar Grove, where they had grown up, and had not set foot since their beloved younger brother's marriage.

I was told it so often that I think I can remember her words, and beyond her words the parlor, where Addie had changed the furniture around. That would have been the first thing the two ladies noticed, that and the awful porch spread across the front of their dignified house, obscuring its shuttered windows, and the lovely old Georgian molding of the dentils, the fanlight of the door, as everything had been obscured, changed since that marriage.

They had withstood the War, but this was near, this took courage for them both, but for Pressy, the beloved bachelor, they would have done almost anything—almost.

My mother saw them get out of their carriage, slowly, as ladies did then, corsetted as they were for visiting, lift their parasols, all in black because a relative had died such a short time ago that they were still in deep mourning and had not yet formally changed to purple. She never told who had died, only that they were in mourning. Her father had asked Addie to wear black, too.

"He had brought Mother a box of chocolates with a big red ribbon, so I think it was Valentine's Day. They both just loved red, red and lavender perfume that my daddy called Florida water; he wouldn't deign to call it perfume, he said that was tacky. Whenever we went downriver he always brought mother something. Candy or fruit or Florida water, something she would like, and that time it was candy. I knew why the ladies had come. They were going to offer to take me down to Charleston to live with them and go to dancing school and be educated. He had told me the secret, and I didn't breathe it to a soul, but I dressed up, too, only in white, not black, because he said white was the right mourning color for children. His mother had taught him that.

"We sat there in the parlor, one of my aunts in the mahogany rocking chair, but she didn't rock, just sat there, the other in the chair that matched it. I heard their very low voices but not what they said. I stared at the lovely old card table that Mother had put in the middle of the room when she knew perfectly well that it belonged with its leaf up against the wall.

"I just sat there, we all did, waiting, and we heard mother coming slowly down the stairs. I could see her hand on the railing and her black skirt, and I thought everything was going to be all right, I just prayed, and then she came into view. She had pinned the big red bow from the chocolate box to her belt, and I knew then that it was all over"; and then, every time she told it, almost a cry: "It wasn't apropos!"

*M*r. Tompkins had always been a lover of women. He loved them as he had always seen them, ready and dressed for courting, compliments, and secret assignations, for which he was whispered to be famous. For years he collected them, the lovely ones, secretly and decorously, and old women for years smiled when they heard him mentioned. But when real love came with all its brutality, its terrible reality, the veins and arteries of it, the awful clarity, he had had nothing in his life to prepare him.

From the time of his marriage until his death, he was drowned in women as they were in the mornings, or moaning in the night, or boiling their sanitary towels in the great boiler where the laundry was done in the back yard and where he had to cross a field of the scent of blood to get to his office.

That, too, is caught in a photograph that my mother kept hidden for years. There they are, in the drawing room which already has its own new history. Addie stands, arms akimbo, in an apron, obviously taken away from whatever she was doing, her hair dragged up and forced into the six-inch-long tortoise-shell hairpins that she wore all her life, not to make it beautiful, but to get it up off her neck so she wouldn't sweat into it. There is studied patience in her face. She is annoyed, not angry. I can almost hear her say, "This is all a piece of foolishness."

By the clothes of the older half sisters, you know it is morning, the wrong time for all of this. There have obviously been no preparations for the photographer's visit. They are wearing clothes for work. Bertha sits at the upright piano that she, they said, could play so well she could have been a concert pianist. Could have, could have, was already a family legend for them all. On the piano is sheet music—"In the Shade of the Old Apple Tree," "Down on the Farm," "The Valley of Kentucky." Myrtle, maybe sixteen, stands behind her as she did all her life. She looks sad in the long pose the photographer must have required.

He had waited until the faces were in their familiar repose before he came out from under his black hood and flashed the camera. On the wall above the piano is a hand-colored photograph of the oldest sister, Minnie, already married, already troubled, beautiful, but not there, seldom there. In one of the truths my mother let slip, she said that Minnie and the man Minnie called Mr. Tompkins, always with a sneer, hated each other, then denied it, because, she said, he never hated anybody in his whole life, he was too much of a gentleman for that. She followed that with another bald truth, that when Minnie came home from one of her marriages, making verbal quotes around the word, she could tell she was there all the way from the front gate when she came home from school, because the house seemed cold and forbidding to her. I did not know for years what she meant until my own brother retreated from constant criticism into adolescent alcoholism, which was denigrated as weakness. There was the same withdrawal, the same coldness in our house.

Minnie was a morphine addict, and my mother knew it from the time she was a child. She would, my mother said, when she finally realized that I knew, drive the hypodermic through her dress into her hip as she sat beating egg whites in a china platter with a wire whisk and not even stopping. Then she added, "She was a marvelous pastry cook."

In the photograph of an old daguerreotype in the place of honor over the mantle are the great-grandparents who began it all, the new rich money, the pride in their Richmond connections, their Kentucky connections, their stark Presbyterian religion, and their descent from the clan Grant. The marble mantle is covered with a striped silk shawl, draped, and there is a spindled occasional table in front of it where Addie rests her hand on a pile of papers that have not been moved.

The two youngest sisters, Mr. Tompkins's children, sit in rocking chairs. Helen, the baby, is not three years old, so it must have been 1902 or 1903. She is pouting, which she was told was cute, and which she did for the rest of her life. She has been told not to move. Both rocking chairs are on platforms, one, Helen's, spindled. The other, fine mahogany, is covered in velvet, but that is obscured by my mother's silk dress with a fine lace collar that reaches beyond her shoulders. Her hair is combed back and tied with a large ribbon. Her arms almost clutch the arms of the chair. She looks straight at the camera, daring it.

Behind the stern watchfulness, imitation, although she does not know it, of the grandmother she is named for, in the picture above the mantle, is the same judgment in her face, the same strait-laced posture, the same anger she would show when she was seventy and found the picture for the first time in years, and went back to that morning. "My daddy wanted a picture of the girls, that's what he called us all, his girls, he was so good to them, and they didn't even bother to dress up."

These are the women he had taken to raise, had sired, and the woman he fought to marry, two families and two ways of being. My grandfather and my mother lived their own private lives in the same house with the others, but alone together. In the mornings they were relegated to the new porch that ran across the front of the house, while the older "girls" were marshaled by Addie to sweep and dust and scrub so that the house shone.

In five years the rambler roses Addie planted had grown up like shields of thorny green with clusters of red roses that bloomed, always, by Decoration Day. There, in summer, my grandfather read aloud all the books that had been his favorites, as if he were passing down to her his own childhood, and so, from her, to me, who received it kicking and screaming. The rose trellis, she said, became a prison or a castle, whether he was reading *Kenilworth* or *Ivanhoe*. She was led into seeing herself as someone out of Walter Scott. She lived the Waverley Novels with him, the lovely Rowena, or the abandoned woman at Kenilworth. He read about the Highlanders, the fiery cross, the signals across hills that could have been the hills she could see beyond the rose trellis. When I was nine, she told me she could still hear him sometimes, the way he read, making it all alive.

When she wasn't the bride in Kenilworth, she was seeing herself as Elsie Dinsmore with dear papa. Years later I, ten years old, at the dangerous age for that obscene book, would find Elsie Dinsmore in the attic with my mother's name child-written on the fly leaf. When she found me reading it, her face softened, and she sighed. She said, "Imagine finding that of all things."

The noises of the other family impinged on their reading and on his stories, belles and beaus before the War, when he was a boy, reliving for her a time made more glamorous by his missing it.

But unlike the lovely Rowena in *Ivanhoe,* my mother's anger had frozen her face into an aloofness she hardly ever let go, a shield. You would be tempted, seeing her, to pity and fear her if she did not, even at eight or nine, reject such weakness.

Weakness, to her, was already her half sisters, growing up, ranging around the big house, crying over men, washing their flowing hair and drying it over the upstairs balcony while they giggled and gossiped, peeking at each other from under the mass that gleamed in the sunlight. They washed it in water from the rain barrel and rinsed it in vinegar. I know that because my mother washed my auburn hair the same way, and her hands were hard and the vinegar stung my eyes.

*I*n the late fall of 1901, an old woman, who looked, every-body said, like butter wouldn't melt in her mouth until she opened it, stepped off the train in East Bank on Addie's side of the river. She was a pretty woman, with white curls around her face, pink cheeks, bright blue eyes. She was dressed in black with an embroidered jabot she had made herself. She wore a nice-lady black pot hat. She had been a trained seamstress, like Addie, and in her time she had dressed some of the nicest rich ladies in Chicago. She had also been a Normal School teacher.

It was nearly dark. Fallen leaves skittered along in front of her. The men who stood around the train station had all gone home to supper. Nobody saw her. She was familiar with the town. She walked through the new darkness, carrying her belongings wrapped in a shawl, and knocked on the door of a miner's house that was the same kind of house Addie had lived in the same town. A man let her into the light. That night she slept in the children's room on a pallet on the floor.

Mother Jones was seventy-one years old that year. She had learned to speak softly like a lady for her rich patrons in Chicago when she be-came a seamstress. She used that voice for the coal operators. But she never quite lost her Irish lilt. From Ireland to America when she was a small child, to Chicago, married, with a family, and on that cold evening, to East Bank, West Virginia, she had, for so long, marched from disaster to disaster.

In 1867, when she was thirty-seven years old, her world had col-lapsed. Her husband and her four children died in a yellow fever epi-demic. On October 8, 1871, Mrs. O'Leary's cow kicked over a lantern in a barn. The Chicago fire took the little shop Mother Jones had set up to make clothes, the last of her belongings, her way of making a living. With thousands of others she milled around the shore of Lake Michigan, watching the town burn, jumping from time to time in the lake to cool off. She had nothing left.

By the time she got off the train that evening in East Bank, she was a paid union organizer, the only woman to be a "walking delegate" for the United Mine Workers. She was signing on miners for the United Mine Workers District 17, which at the time covered the whole of West Virginia. She was paid three dollars a day, with her expenses, which mostly consisted of train tickets when she was unrecognized and could ride the train instead of sneaking through the woods. It was a job that was so dangerous that most men wouldn't do it. West Virginia was known to them as Russia, the worst state for miners in the country. Some organizers had been killed. Some had gotten away and sworn never to go back.

Early in the fight for the miners, few people, certainly not the faraway shareholders, cared or even knew about how they lived—scrip instead of money so that they could only buy at the company store, short ton payments, child labor, sixteen-hour days when conglomerates controlling the mines piled up the greatest fortunes in American history. The accident rate was appalling. There were closures without notice when corporate owners decided to cut work in mines that weren't earning enough profit, in order to control coal prices. Today this is known in the business community as "down-sizing." When there was work, the coal fortunes trickled down to an average yearly pay for a miner, with or without family, of about $450. These practices were only noticed by a minority of rabble-rousers, intellectuals, fire-eaters, muckrakers, and other undesirables.

At dawn the next morning, Mother Jones took the first ferry across to the north side of the Kanawha River, and went to Mr. Marshall's store in Cedar Grove and woke him up. She told him she had come to organize the Kelly's Creek mines. He let her in and gave her breakfast. They were old friends.

It was her second visit to the Kanawha Valley. By 1901 "her boys," as she called the miners, were passing her from mining camp to mining camp. They called her Mother Jones, the Miner's Angel. One old man in a sobbing crowd of men called out, "She ain't a woman. She's Jesus Christ, come down as an old woman for us." He was either drunk or hysterical. His wife took him home.

The meetings were clandestine. She was not allowed by law to trespass on private property. She went anyway. She was forbidden to walk the roads or the rail lines on company property. She walked in the creeks. When shooting started at one meeting, she was carried piggy-back across the creek to the safety of the woods. She had to get out of one mining camp at night because her boys found out that the superintendent and his men were plotting to kill her and an organizer who was with her, burn them in the coke ovens and then say she had left town.

If she was the miner's angel, she was the owner's devil. They called her Old Hag, the most dangerous woman in America. They said she was an anarchist. Since the assassination of McKinley, everybody who was dangerous was an "anarchist." It was a cover-all term of abuse, as "communist" was later, and as "liberal" is now. She was actually a socialist, but no coal operator knew or gave a damn about the difference.

She took the "walking" part of her job seriously. For weeks she trudged through the hills, up the hollows, the miners watching for her and protecting her. It took courage. Any miner caught sheltering her, or even giving her a cup of tea in a company-owned house was blackballed in the mines and thrown out of town.

The legend spread that she was afraid of nothing, from governors to mine owners to snakes. She walked right by a copperhead and never paused. She went past the foremen and walked deep into the mines with a carbide lamp on a miner's hat she borrowed to find her boys, sat with them on the gob pile, and organized while they shared their beans and fatback and cornbread with her. She refused to eat anything the miners couldn't afford to eat. She was Catholic, but if she had been told that she was behaving like the saints she would have said, "Go to hell."

She shocked the ladies by wearing hip boots, a miner's shirt, miner's pants under her skirt to keep warm when she was working. Fall moved toward winter, 1901 into 1902. Because both banks were leased to a coal company, she stood in water above her ankles in Kelly's Creek at Cedar Grove, near what the towns people called the Big House, signing on miners for the union as my mother, a little girl, watched from the parlor window. The creeks were deep. She tucked her skirts up around her waist to keep them dry, her pants showing, which shocked the miners' wives, her thick men's boots failing to keep her feet dry. She worked with the energy of a woman who had replaced her past with zeal for what she was doing, as if she had already died and had nothing left to fear. Through that winter she slept outside when everybody was too scared to let her in. She disguised herself as a peddler. She dressed as a male miner. But she put on her pretty black dress when she went to see the mine owners and the governor, used her lady voice, and shocked them into politeness. In the mine she swore, they said, like a section foreman, and when she spoke at meetings her high voice rang out so that it bounced against the hills.

Coal towns had been too quickly fitted into the narrow hollows by the companies. The companies had built the church, the assembly hall, the company store. Mother Jones called them Pluck Me stores. The largest and most comfortable building was usually the "club house" where the unmarried managers, the office clerks, and visiting business-men stayed. It and the superintendent's house had indoor plumbing. There were a few model "villages," well-built and attractive, but very few. They tended to be the ones photographed when West Virginia mine owners were criticized.

Most of the miners' houses were pathetic. They were built with one board-and-batten layer, and some inner facing between the family and the weather, on stilts with single wood floors instead of basements, with one fireplace for warmth and cooking and heating water for the miner's Saturday night bath. Behind every house a privy had been dug. These were the houses that she stayed in when a miner and his family were brave enough to have her.

In the fall of 1901, the mine owners had not yet hired the Baldwin-Felts Detective Agency to provide mine guards. They simply closed the mines until local strikes were over and they had come to agree-ments with Mother Jones. Then, early in 1902, Mr. Justus Collins who, with a Kentucky conglomerate, owned the Collins Colliery at Glen Jean in Fayette County, hired guards from the Baldwin-Felts Agency and kept his mine open with scabs. Mother Jones and Mr. Collins were the two people who ushered in the new and more dangerous phase of the mine wars.

By 1902 there were nearly forty mines on lands that had been owned Before the War by the Tompkins family on both sides of the river. At least ten of them were on the land that had been divided between Preston and John. Christopher Tompkins, my great-grandfather's first cousin from Richmond, had kept a summer home at Hawks Nest, in the wild, romantic mountains. Far from the mountain scenery of the summer home, Cousin Christopher had opened a coal mine south of the river at Paint Creek, but that had been ruined by the Civil War. After the war, he still owned thousands of acres of upcreek and mountaintop land on Paint Creek and Cabin Creek. There was so much coal on the land that farmers dug their own mines into the hills behind their houses and sent the children in with buckets to pick it out when they needed to light the stove. But there was no commercial way to get it out. The river barges couldn't get up far enough. Besides, Cousin Christopher said he was never going to come back to a part of Virginia that had turned coat in the war.

So he sold his holdings south of the river outright to the first Yankee who made an offer, Mr. Pratt of New York, for a few dollars an acre, glad to get rid of the traitorous land. He had been a Confederate officer. He needed the ready money.

By 1902, the Pratt interests had leased the mineral rights to twenty-six mines, mostly owned by out-of-state companies. The coal towns of Kayford, Pratt, Mucklow, Coalburg, and Holly Grove were a few of the many that had opened.

On the north side of the river, the subsurface of the land that my grandfather had sold to his brother John, up Kelly's Creek, had been leased to the Kanawha and Hocking Coal Company, and the tiny towns of Blakely, Mammoth, and Ward had grown up. Preston and John had leased the Cedar Grove mines to Kanawha and Hocking as well. So the decisions and the power had moved to Cleveland.

My grandfather found that if he leased out his land he wouldn't have to declare bankruptcy when he failed at running the mine as a cooperative. Bankruptcy was a disgrace no one in his family would excuse either in himself or in his brothers. Leasing was another way to get money and retain surface ownership, and local mine owners fell for it in droves. It was the beginning of what looked at first like rescue and turned all too quickly into a new kind of servitude. No longer were the owners' names local. They were men who never saw the Kanawha Valley—Rockefeller, Davis, Elkins, Mellon, Mark Hanna.

So the pattern of ownership was formed. The surface of the land stayed "in the family." Hell went to "out-of-state interests." Instead of the golden future that was forecast for West Virginia when the mines opened and the railroads came, it was a boom-and-bust, every-man-for-himself economy.

Later, in 1912, in a speech during a strike, Mother Jones said of the Kanawha Valley, "They was gentlemen back in oh two." Local patriarchy was dying. It was not yet dead. My mother remembered Christmas of 1901 when her father gathered them all together and told them that there wouldn't be Christmas for the family, because money was "short," and that what there was had to go to the town Christmas tree where he had always had presents for all the children of the miners. Nobody, she said, proudly, had any idea that there was no Christmas at Cedar Grove when the big tree was lit with candles in the parlor and all the town children filed in for their presents, which he gave them with his own hands, as his father had done before him when the slave children called "Chrismus Giff!" at dawn on Christmas morning.

The Emancipation Proclamation had emptied most of the slave cabins. In "oh two," they were rented out to Kanawha and Hocking for their miners, but Mr. Tompkins still considered that he had a duty to "his people."

Mother Jones had left the coal town of Cedar Grove until late in her conquest of Kelly's Creek. It was not completely a company town. The boat yard and the mill were working, and the railroad owned property. All through the growing town there were still areas owned by my grandfather, and he could still say that he had kept the house and the acres around it away from what were being called, by all West Virginians, the "outside interests." "Outside interests" cornered the mines, "outside agitators" were trying to organize them. West Virginians, who had sold to whoever would buy, sat in the middle, innocently claiming that "outside" was ruining their land and starving the miners.

When Mother Jones tried to find a field to have a meeting in the town of Cedar Grove, there was little land that did not belong to the companies or to the local mine owners.

Behind the facade of the Big House, little seemed to have changed. Everybody still had their place at the supper table, and there were still silver napkin rings with their names on them that enclosed damask napkins. By 1902 there were two grown half sisters, Myrtle and Bertha, old enough to court, brother Pressy, two younger brothers, Roger and Bado, two Tompkins girls, my mother Rachel and little Helen, two long-staying cousins of Addie, and a tutor and nurse for the youngest. Mr. Tompkins sat at the head of the table and served the meat. Mrs. Tompkins sat at the foot of the table and served the vegetables. After the long prayer, said by Mrs. Tompkins, there was usually a babble of voices.

At the supper table one winter night in 1902, all the family discussed the terrible Mother Jones who looked like a little old lady and had a mouth like a section foreman. Mr. Tompkins said she had sent him a message that she wanted to use his land to have a meeting but he wouldn't let her, and besides, most of the subsurface had been leased out, so he didn't have the right.

For once, nobody at the table said a word. The only sounds were the scrape of forks, passing of hot potatoes, reaching out by Mr. Tompkins for plates to serve second helpings. The whole table had retreated into a silence where everyone seemed to be someplace else or waiting for somebody else to say something. My mother, who was ten, said she had never been in the dining room when it was so quiet.

Finally Addie spoke.

"Mr. Tompkins," she said, "do I own the bull field outright?" He had turned over some of the property to her when there was one of the boom-bust fears of bankruptcy.

"Yes, my dear, you know that," he told her, and then, according to my mother, there was another silence.

Then Addie announced, "Then Mother Jones can use my bull field for her speech."

Grandfather forbade the children to go to the meeting, and Addie agreed. "I don't want a single one of you children going out there with that bunch of miners. Those men are armed and dangerous," she told them, laying down the law. "Now I mean it," she added, not trusting them.

My mother was the only one who disobeyed. A few nights later, Mother Jones spoke in the bull field and my mother, thank God, provided me with an eyewitness. She crept down the back stairs and scuttled out through the dark up the creek to the field where the miner's lamps lit the black sky like fireflies mingling with the winter stars. Beyond the dark crowd of men, the famous Mother Jones stood in dirty clothes on a feed box raising hell, so far away that my mother, hiding by the fence so nobody would see her and tell Addie, could only see the shape of her, even though she was lit up with pitchpine torches. But she heard her.

"She was a little tiny woman. She hollered just like a Holy Roller preacher, and she gave the miners hell. She told them they were cowards and didn't have backbones and didn't stand up for each other. I thought she was mean to them," she said, when I asked her years afterwards if she had ever seen Mother Jones. "My God, she used language I never would let pass my lips, and she had grown men crying. I wouldn't have missed it for a farm in Georgia." Then she smiled and said, "I was the only one brave enough to disobey my mother."

It may have been the first act that would form her political attitudes and her passions, but she let them fight within her against her father's and later, her husband's, hide-bound attitudes. There were only a few times that she let her secret out. But she remained a life-long Democrat. Sometimes her self-denigration at youthful folly dropped away, and she let out what she had been. In 1976, when she was eighty-four, we watched the Carter nomination from different cities while the old Democrat ward heelers who had been white supremacists joined hands and sang "We shall overcome." When it was over, my telephone rang.

She sounded like a young girl. I could hear the bright excitement. We talked for a long time. She said, "I'm going to tell you something I have never told a living soul."

She stopped speaking, daring me to break the silence. "I cast my first vote for Eugene V. Debs," she said, almost whispering as if someone out of the past could still hear. But when I asked her about it two months later, she laughed at me. "The things you get in your head. I never said such a thing. How do you make up things like that?"

But with all her denial of her mind and her past, she remained, at a politically pragmatic and critical level, one of the most intelligent women I have ever known.

*J*n 1906 business was booming. Go-getter was a compliment. Horatio Alger was the young boy's Bible, and Herbert Spencer was the most popular philosopher in the country—a best-seller up the hollows and around the fires, in the company store, and on the trains that ran so often moving, moving, go-getting, all up and down both sides of the river.

Social Darwinism was the future, and few questioned it. The goal and dream was "individualism." In *Social Statistics* Spencer wrote that the poor should be eliminated, "to clear the world of them and make room for better." He explained, "If they are sufficiently complete to live, they DO live, and it is well they should live. If they are not sufficiently complete to live, they die, and it is best they should die."

New words were bandied about by coal operators: vested interests, conglomerates, floating loans, bond issues, all of it the language of the bubble they called a boom. The bubble had not broken on Wall Street since "oh three," and the recovery had been swift. Underground, in the mines in Montana, Colorado, and in the states that produced anthracite and bituminous coal, something else was happening, but, like the coal itself, it was only beginning to come to the surface.

Many of the poor that Spencer wanted to get rid of were from a vast wave of immigrants who passed day after day through Ellis Island while jobbers who spoke their languages offered them jobs that all too often were as innocent scabs. Most of the immigrants had no idea what a scab was. At Ward and Mammoth, up Kelly's Creek, three or four languages were spoken in the mines. The valley hummed with work, and the money went out of the state.

All through the summer of 1907, speculation on Wall Street was going mad. Teddy Roosevelt had tried to control it by getting new anti-trust laws passed and reactivating those that had not been enforced. Big business totally ran the country, and Roosevelt foresaw trouble. But he only managed to scotch the rush for vast financial control, not kill it. He used anti-trust laws that had been condemned as "arcane" by the business world to bring suit against some of the most powerful trusts, including the J. P. Morgan interests. They saw the first anti-trust laws as corrals, and they tried hard to kick their way out.

Most of the controllers of the "big corporations" accused Roosevelt of attacking the great American demi-god, "free enterprise." The rest of the country hailed him as Teddy the Trust Buster. Whispers of trouble, like dangerous creaks in the mine ceilings, were reaching the surface by summer. Some people thought that the financiers were staging rumors of panic to defeat Roosevelt.

In a world where individuals held so much uncontrolled economic power, anything could happen, and it did. It had started in Montana in the late nineteenth century. To say that the "Rockefeller interests" were trying to corner copper in Montana is not exaggeration. "God gave me my money," Mr. Rockefeller explained, and neither he nor the people who worked for him brooked interference.

Most of the owners sold out. One did not. He was a wild speculator named Frederick Augustus Heinze, who refused to accept the leadership of the Rockefeller combine, which, in Montana, called itself the Amalgamated Copper Company. Heinze had cornered copper smelting. He stood up to the Amalgamated Copper Company until he got his price, and then, triumphant, he moved on to Wall Street.

The Rockefeller corporation did not forgive him. They spread the rumor that he was a trouble maker. But at first his anarchic style went well on Wall Street. He found a partner, Charles Morse, who was as wild as he was. Together they floated a stock venture that had more stock than copper to sell, and called it United Copper. Its stock billowed up and up and up on margin buying, loans floated, all the paraphernalia of moving money without money.

Share selling and buying became so wild that the country was literally running out of ready cash. It was Standard Oil's turn to take revenge. United Copper interests already controlled much of the stock in the Knickerbocker Trust, one of the leading New York banks. It was time to stop them. Stories were leaked to the newspapers that United was teetering. On Thursday, October 17, 1907, the bubble burst. United Copper crashed. The Knickerbocker Trust shut its doors. Lines to withdraw what money was left formed, blocks long, around the New York banks. The panic bled out to the rest of the country. Banks began to shut their doors. The ability to refloat loans to cover losses sank like the stock market shares. Brokers and borrowers ran through Wall Street like wild horses without reins and their chaos spread.

Mr. J. P. Morgan disliked Teddy Roosevelt because Roosevelt had dared to sue his corporation for trust violations. When Morgan heard that Roosevelt was going lion hunting in Africa, he is said to have voiced the hope that the lions would do their duty. At the end of the terrible weekend in October of 1907, Morgan was coming back on his private train from an Episcopal convention, surrounded by tame clergy who were enjoying a comfortable free ride back to New York, when he heard the news. He was seventy years old and he had a terrible cold, and more financial power than any man in America.

He went home. He called Wall Street's leading financiers to his house and locked them in a room until they came up with enough money to save the Trust Company of America, the largest bank in New York. The rescue would, in turn, act as the setting up of a domino so that the other banks and trust companies could follow, and the closings would stop.

Mr. Morgan went into another room to play solitaire and blow his famously huge nose. After several hours, the men in the locked room had come up with enough money to save bank credit. Mr. Morgan had guided the country through its latest financial disaster. His price for success was high. He demanded that the president leave his business interests alone.

Teddy Roosevelt gave in to his demands. The latest panic subsided. It had seemed to exist only in New York and Washington, but the crisis that had threatened to devastate Wall Street had already trickled down into the rest of the country, and it did not disappear. Local banks closed. Nobody had any money beyond the money in their wallets, their pockets, under the mattress, or in the piggy bank.

By October 11, "ready cash" had almost disappeared from the Kanawha Valley. No greenbacks in the pocket. No change to rattle. Literally, no money. Some of the banks had closed for good. Others were closed for "reorganization," promising to repay their depositors when the temporary shortage of cash was over.

At four-thirty in the afternoon of November 25, Mr. Tompkins left the company store which was part of the Cedar Grove Collieries that had been built as soon as his mother died in 1873. It was pitch dark by four-thirty, almost the shortest day of the year. He walked the ties of the railroad that split what had once been the family farm and that ran from all the way down Kelly's Creek, past the mansion, spurred out toward the river, crisscrossing the valley like a cat's cradle of iron and soot, built through the center of the new coal town, another layer of civilization that had gradually replaced the fine farm of 1844.

The only place to walk comfortably on a bleak dark November evening was on the railroad. The wooden ties had become a makeshift sidewalk to avoid the rain puddles, the horse manure, the hog wallows he could stumble over in the dark. There were no streetlights, only the gas and kerosene lamps of the houses. Their light flowed out in ponds of brightness, separated by the dark of the evening.

High on the hill above him new houses had been built for the superintendents of the Kanawha and Hocking mines. Stronger lights from their electroliers spilled down the hill from them and brushed the railroad. It was cold. He walked with his wide-brimmed hat pulled down nearly over his face to keep himself warm, or perhaps to avoid anyone passing, to keep from being recognized. Who knows? He was alone.

He passed the little house where Forest Hull lived with his widowed mother. It was one of the oldest, older than the mansion. It had been there since the boat yard had been opened before Mr. William Tompkins bought the property. Gingerbread carving had been added to the porch, so that it looked Victorian. Forest painted it white every spring. His mother made him do it. There was no light in the front parlor. Mrs. Hull was careful with money, being a widow.

He passed Mr. Calderwood's store where the gas lights were on. There were no customers in the store. Money was still too tight. The big meeting hall above the store was dark. Mr. Calderwood's and Mr.

Marshall's were the competitors to the company store for those who had real money instead of scrip.

Where the railroad spurs crossed there was nobody sitting on the discarded ties. It was too cold. Maybe a horse whinnied in the horse field across the railroad track from the mansion. He would have recognized it, because he knew the sound of every horse he had. There were fewer than there had ever been.

Did he walk as if he were still on the great farm, with the slaves and the horses and the silver in the dining room? People do that, by habit, thinking of other things when the world around them has already changed. It was, after all, too dark to see the garden that had been a formal garden when his mother was alive and had been plowed up where Mrs. Tompkins planted vegetables there in the spring. On that early evening it was a pool of darkness. When a train is half a mile away the tracks begin to sing. They hum, louder and louder. Nobody knows if he heard. Was he deep in his past? In his mind? Had he had enough?

The family swore ever after that the train came out of Ward Hollow without lights. Maybe that was part of the reconstruction of something that happened that was too harsh for the truth. Was there a second when he could have jumped free and didn't? Did he freeze? Did he see the lights ahead of him in the mansion, or was he in a darkness of his own so deep that he saw nothing?

The train dragged his body all the way back to the darkness in front of the superintendents' houses. Nobody would ever tell me what happened then. Did the men who gathered around the spread-eagled crushed corpse take him upstairs in Mr. Calderwood's store so that the family wouldn't see him until the undertaker had fixed him up?

The next morning before the late dawn somebody had spread coal ashes over the places along the track where his blood had splashed and flowed. It was the most fitting burial he could have had.

Shock and grief are blank times where people move through the days and nights depending on habits. Over the pool of blood left, a film grew, hardened, and then the habits became stories—of how the men came to the door, how Addie ushered the children into the parlor, and told them, in banal words. That is all there are at such a time. It was cold in the parlor. Someone had not gotten as far as lighting the fire, stopped in mid-chore. How many of them were glad? The older daughters hated him and did not show it. Of the five youngest, Pressy hated his father so that he changed his name from Preston to Harold. My mother, Roger and Bado, still children, and Helen, seven years old, loved him and were devastated.

He had left Addie eight children to raise, a still large poverty of land, and a November darkness that spread and stayed in a part of their hearts that they covered with lies about its being an accident, as if they could never face the fact that their father had acted, and not been the victim of carelessness on the railroad. Of course, he had been a victim—of carelessness and greed—but that was so tenuous and had begun so far away and so long ago that they could not or did not grasp it.

Mr. Tompkins was dressed by Addie, but none of the children were allowed to see him. The casket rested in the front hall on her quilting trestles so that his friends could pay their respects to his closed coffin. All the next day they came through the dark time of the year, walking the tracks, driving in carriage after carriage up the river from Charleston. Addie made her excuses when the Tompkins family carriages rolled up. She sent word by my mother that she was too ill to see anyone. She sat with her cousin Ellen Martin in the master bedroom and waited for them to leave. My mother said they stayed for fifteen minutes, which was, she said, exactly the right time to make a mourning visit. When they left, all in black with veils, and she stood at the door abandoned, she thought she would never ever see them again.

All through the rest of the day the people from the town of Cedar Grove passed slowly by the coffin while Addie stood and received them. He had been loved. They all knew the times he had gone without so they could have, when he had let them live in his houses rent-free when the mines were closed, how he passed the time of day. The town knew him better than his children. They had known him for much of his life, and they had watched with real hope after his mother died when he opened the mine and tried to make a cooperative out of it, gave them work when the railroads laid them off. The town had grown around him, and now it stayed, and mourned him, Mr. Tompkins, who they remembered as the first elected mayor of the town of Cedar Grove. Did the older people see on the face behind the closed coffin, the elegant man who had ridden high wide and handsome across a world of riches that was never going to end? He had put their sweat into horse flesh, their underground digging, even their deaths into red flowing ties and four-in-hands, and into good brandy and good looks and a devilish way with the ladies.

Did the older ones see that, or was it the real sixty-seven-year-old man, greyed and disappointed, as much a victim of boom and bust and outside corporate manipulation as they were? Maybe none of them except Captain Bannister, CSA, his best friend, remembered or cared.

A long straggling procession walked up the road from the mansion to the little brick church. The family were driven slowly in a carriage following the black horse-drawn hearse with its black plumes. Outside the long windows of the little brick church, they could see that the turf had been laid aside and the empty vault, where his parents had been interred and then moved, opened again, the stone steps that led down into the darkness, the piled grass brown with winter.

It was over at last, the turf set back as if it had never been moved, Mr. Tompkins left in the vault, the family driven slowly past the mourners back to the mansion, aware of being watched. The older girls, my mother said later, with condescending "understanding," a lilt, a look, that she saved for those memories, "acted like the world had come to an end, crying and carrying on, but you know, I didn't. I wouldn't have let myself, in public like that."

So she was left alone, and some part of her stayed alone forever. She never admitted aloud that his death was anything but an accident, but she had no respect for suicides. She judged them as weakness. Whatever it meant to her through the years of her silence about it, denial or secrecy, his death became the most important loss and mystery of my own life, long before I was born.

$\mathcal{T}$he days of my mother's first death were slow, leaden, makework. For two days Addie didn't say a word. She moved fast through the house, cleaning, cleaning, swatting the curtains, heaving buckets of water. If anyone tried to help her, she pushed them away without a word. Then suddenly she began to give orders, signaling without calling their names, as if she didn't know them very well. She put the girls to work giving away almost everything that had belonged to Mr. Tompkins. She put his best clothes in mothballs for the boys when they grew into them. She spread the clothes the boys would never use among the people in her church and in the tenant houses. She seemed to be trying to sweep, swat, scrub, polish her grief out of the cupboards, out of the closets, out of his office, out of her sight. At least it seemed that way to my mother.

She gave his chess set to Captain Bannister. She sent my mother down into Charleston on the train to deliver what she had decided should be sent there—his best gun to my mother's Uncle Will, the cruet stand to the Swann farm, the teapot to the Patton house.

From morning until night the girls trailed up and down the stairs, down into the town, up Horse Mill Hollow. One pair of trousers had a hole in the seat, and Addie gave it to the undertaker to bury a man in. When my mother went down into the town she could see parts of him, everywhere, as if the town had become him.

She was left alone. Left alone as in lonely, and also left alone in the best sense, as in "let me alone," the adolescent cry when we all have learned to listen beyond familiar speech and noise. It was new to her, and shocking, this slow replacement of stunned grief with a new kind of breathing, and she never acknowledged it. It showed only in what she did for the next four years. The clues for me to those four years of a kind of blooming on her part are not chronological or clear. She talked little about them. What I remember are shards, like broken pots found in a dig into the past, and what remains is this attempt to put them together.

Her inheritance from her father was an adhesion in her heart that closed away the child in her from the grownup she was becoming. She was never healed of that, child and bright woman, alternates, not one, ever. They had different voices. She began to construct a past out of hope; hope for something that had already happened. I can still hear her Elsie Dinsmore voice, "When I was a little girl." I hated it and was ashamed of myself. Shame came easily then, and still could if I let it.

She shared with me the books she had been given by her father. She tried to share the manners and the prejudices she had inherited as the correct things to do and think. But she would not share the accomplishments that she took most pride in. They were hers when she had been first, hers and her father's. It was all she had of him. Addie gave her nothing, not his diamond tie pin or his little silver hip flask or his cigar case, or the gold watch fob he had inherited from his father, and always wore. "It should have come to me," she said, years later.

There was not a woman in her life who was not her rival—her mother, then her sisters, then me. It was her guiding force, her deepest longing. When I wanted to ride, she said I could never learn because we didn't have horses like she had when she was a little girl. "You ride hacks," she said with some contempt, and took no more interest. "I could ride anything he put me on," she told us, ignoring or not knowing the fear that had become etched on her face.

The worst blow she suffered was that with his death she had been relegated from first to last; for her whole life she had to be first with someone. Part of it was revenge her older half sisters didn't know they were taking, even Addie, who said, quite simply, that she never had loved her, she was too much Tompkins, but she respected her and that was just going to have to do.

She was made into her mother's unofficial business partner when she was fourteen. The only time she admitted to having been afraid was when Addie sent her in the chaise, driving through the dark to put the rent money in the safe at the Company Store, when everybody in town knew she was carrying it. She did it every week, in winter, through the dark. "It was dangerous. All those drunkards and coal miners. Mother never bothered to think about that. My father never would have dreamed . . ." she said.

The older girls starched their petticoats and looked for men to marry, all except Minnie, who had already married twice, and whose doctor husband, Addie swore, had introduced her to morphine. No daughter of hers could have done it on her own. It had to be somebody else's fault, a man's fault. It was a house of women, women who, from the hints my mother left around for me to stumble on, seemed to talk about, dream about, agonize over, cry over, giggle over, entrap, seduce men.

She, from fourteen on, was contemptuous of it all. Romance was something sleazy to her. Love was a joke. Touch made her flesh crawl. It always did. I learned it early when I fell against her by accident, half asleep in the car when I was three, and she recoiled with the flesh of her body.

The girls pored over the catalogues, Montgomery Ward, Sears and Roebuck, and the popular ladies' magazines, to make their spring and fall choices. Bertha told Myrtle she didn't have big enough breasts, so she sent off in secret for a breast enlarger. When it came it was the picture of a man's hand. Teasing went on in yells and whispers, "Myrtle wears a rat. Myrtle wears a rat." It was easy to tease Myrtle.

But when Minnie disappeared again, it was Myrtle who rode the train to Charleston, heavily veiled in one of Addie's mourning veils, to try to find her. She had to go, my mother told me in one of those truths that escaped like little licks of flame from hidden fire, to the whorehouses near the K and M railroad station. But she heard her tell Addie when she came back that the madam had said she wouldn't have Minnie, she was a crazy dope fiend.

None of this showed in the pictures I have of the time. They deny my mother's stories of neglect and unhappiness by their existence, as my own adolescent pictures challenge my memory. It is a time when the skin is too alive, the nerves too alert, the world too new, exciting and fearsome, and you are told to smile for the camera.

But there is one picture of my mother at fifteen, and the picture has caught her words, her secrets, her memory when she would let it surface. She is sitting in the hammock between my uncle and his fiancée, the most beautiful of all the women who would be part of her growing up. She, too, is beautiful; she wears a ruffled waist. She is the essence of silent anger, eyes as accusing as a goddess who has just found out something she has decided to punish.

She was beginning to learn how to regain her place from last to first. It was seduction, only she would never have deigned, a word she loved to use, to call it that. In another picture, she sits in the back porch hammock with its pillow and its seraglio cover of vines and fringe, the same hammock I would love to lie in more than twenty years later. She is dressed in a Peter Thompson suit. It is too small and binds her breasts. She is too old for what she is wearing. She is practicing the come-hither smile she has learned, seeking that state of being first that she will, all her life, recognize as love, that and nothing else. The boy beside her looks either wary or scared. No. He looks as if he is seeing through her.

In another picture, taken the same day, she lies in the hammock, and if her eyes were not so wary she would look like the siren she imitates. Those are the pictures which prove one of the stories of her neglect through those years; she set her stories well. "When the catalogues came we all chose our dresses, and Mother didn't even tell me that she didn't order what I chose. When the girls' dresses came they were grown-up, just what they had ordered, but when mine came it was another Peter Thompson suit, too little for me. It bound my, you know, bosoms,"—she said "bazooms," as if making a joke pronunciation would evade the reality. Then sadly, and still a little afraid, "Nobody told me anything. When I started to bleed I thought I was dying and ran down and jumped into our swimming hole in Kelly's Creek to wash it away."

I didn't believe her—this in a house where the older girls talked about their periods, their beaus, and one, Minnie, her lovers. She had shut herself and her memory away from them. "I was too old," she said, "and they treated me like a little girl." She smiled, every time, even her gestures repetitive. "I think it was because the men were beginning to pay attention to me and I wouldn't have touched one of their beaus with a barge pole. My life then," she moved so easily into that mixture of reality and legend that gave light, shadow, and lack of focus to her time from fourteen to eighteen, "was dedicated to higher things than a lot of men hanging round." But she did admit that when the young lawyers looking for coal leases rode up from Charleston and tethered their horses by the front gate, she ran and dressed up and waited, sometimes all day, for them to come back and notice her. They did. Many years later an old man told me that she was prettiest girl in the valley.

Other photographs belie so much of her tales of neglect. There they are, the sisters, in the pictures posed down by the great tree by the creek, one in front of a rail car on the new tracks between the house and Horsemill Hollow, another rollicking on a horse fence, hugging each other to keep their balance. In them she looks gay, a real smile, all of the sisters, half sisters, friends together, laughing so that you can almost hear them.

In another they are sitting on the lawn in front of the house, each with a beau. Aunt Helen, a child, peeks from behind my mother's silk dress with the lace collar that frames her face. My mother's mass of hair that reaches to her waist is piled in a great puff around her head, with a knot at the crown. It is beautiful silken heavy hair. She sits with another unknown young man. She is sweet sixteen and completely adult, as part of her has been since she was a child. Myrtle sits smiling with a beau of her own, and Bertha's hand is in Ernest Michie's, who would be my Uncle Mick.

"Then," she has told me, "it was important, the time you put your hair up and wore a corset, and several petticoats, all starched and ironed, like sitting on a pillow." She said, not bragging, taking it for granted, "I had the prettiest hair, Tompkins hair." With the ever-present joking condescension she never lost, she added, "Once Bert put on ten petticoats to go to the fair the next day. She slept all night sitting on the stairs with her legs straight so she wouldn't muss them."

In so many ways the years between fourteen and eighteen were the most fulfilled of my mother's life. She had been set adrift, and she turned an anger that could have festered, and did in many ways for the rest of her life, into an energy beyond family that led her to break out of the citadel that had been made of Cedar Grove, and its high walls of protection against a world that they had learned to ignore. She led another life.

She knew so many people in Charleston, not half-children like herself, but the men her father had taken her to, and the aunts. Addie sent her on business errands to people she had known for years. She had already learned politics so well, eavesdropping at her father's side, that nothing surprised her for the rest of her life. In a Republican household she became a lifelong southern Democrat, dragging accepted tendrils always of her father's teachings. She thought it right to be responsible for "colored" people. She told with some pride the story of her father's meeting with Booker T. Washington on the train from Cedar Grove to Charleston. "He shook hands with Booker T. Washington, but he didn't take off his hat." This subtle balance of prejudice and tolerance would haunt her.

The very well remembered and constructed myth that was her life alone was not alone, only remembered that way. She had a companion, closer than a brother, and together they made up a majority of two in the secret advocacy of the United Mine Workers, Eugene Debs, and the socialists and above all, for her, the suffragist movement. It was Forest Hull, the only other person in the new town who had ever heard of the *American Mercury*. They made their decisions together, read together, acted together in melodramas in the hall over Mr. Calderwood's store. She was a poet. He was a painter. Their life together had to be kept away from the others. It was part of the excitement, brave silence before ignorant and prejudiced tormentors, never forgotten.

When women's right to vote was brought up at the dinner table, still filled with people (never fewer, according to her, than sixteen), there was loud laughter, and then Addie said, "I don't need the vote. My boy Jim votes for me." Jim was the black man who had replaced Uncle Obe when he died. He did the heavy work. She said it often. It amused everybody but my mother, head down, furious, and resolved.

Once, like a fool—my mother said that of herself—she left a poem she had written where somebody would find it and read it, but my coal baron Uncle Mick picked it up and said, "Sissy, where did you copy this one from?" She swore she never wrote another. But she did. She saw herself all her life as a writer who never had a chance, as if woman after woman, her own age, had not climbed barricades. She would never have been the writer she yearned to be because her mind was split, as hard minds often are, between the sentimentality with which she viewed her own childhood, and the critical view of life she had developed.

Her taste was sometimes good, often syrupy. She loved Edna St. Vincent Millay, William Butler Yeats, and what she called "bessellers." She looked with disdain on the one talent that would have made her a writer instead of a critic. It was the capacity to open oneself to the world, to be fooled, to ask the questions of a child. She knew better than that. She would have made a good academic critic. Some of the memories that formed her coldness were as stark as winter fields; some memories embellished; some taken over from other people, made into stories that had happened, not to them, but to her, time telescoped.

The most exciting thing that had ever happened to her, she said, and she was years too young to vote herself, was taking Carrie Chapman Catt all around West Virginia to make speeches for Votes for Women. It was the first attempt at state-wide suffrage for women. My mother's voice and her face changed when she talked about it later. She came out from behind the mask of childhood as a fierce, intelligent, and determined advocate. She told about the floats in the parades, really seeing them again, the white crepe paper made into flowers, the streamers, the ladies all in white not looking ugly and masculine at all the way *Judge* and *Life*, the two comic magazines, made them look. She heard again the derisive calls of the men, the cheers of women as they passed.

She said that Mrs. Oliphant led the conservative women against the vote. After the failure of women's right to vote in the state legislature, she met the editor of the *Charleston Gazette* on the train. "Well, Sissy," he said, "it looks like the elephant stepped on the cat's tail." She told it as a joke that never failed to please her.

Addie, at the same time and in the same house, lived a different and private life that grew more isolated as she grew older. She set to work clearing away the failures of Mr. Tompkins. She learned as she did it that she could do it, and the weak defenses of her ignorance fell away. She did not have time to give a damn anymore. They were Addie's years of breaking down her own barricades; she was no longer mistress or wife, was mother when she had time; she had been left the decisions as Mr. Tompkins's mother had, widowed at forty-two, near the same age. It was almost as if both men had planned it that way, chosen the kind of women who would take the reins they had left loose, hold things together, do that traditional job of Southern widows that had never been recognized, holding a place together, making decisions that they had learned to do secretly from watching their own mothers, left in the same traps of familyhood.

But Addie had had no mother to teach her acres. She learned it for herself. I have a picture of her then, too. She stands in front of the rambler roses, her first grandchild, my oldest cousin, Bertha's child, held high in her arms like a trophy. Her waist is still small. Her face has filled, but she still looks handsome, and practical, and totally in charge of whatever she was concerned with. In another picture, the one I have always had with me, although I never saw her like it, she looks lovely, imperious, at ease like a soldier is at ease. Her battles had only begun, when she had thought—she must have—that they were past.

Addie put away her lover-husband's watch, its gold fob, his fine leather wallet, his dress studs, for the boys when they were older, and she kept for herself every silk tie he had, even the worn ones. She put them away in a silk bag, and if she got them out again in the first years after his death, nobody ever knew or noticed.

"A great big girl like you settin down," was one of Addie's favorite terms of disapproval. But on fine days in summer, she released the girls from fruit picking, canning, dusting, sewing, jelly making, churning, to name a few of the ways she expected her girls to fill their days. Sometimes she went with them, and sometimes she let the girls go alone, chaperoned by their big brother, take picnics on the train and ride for thirty miles through the green valley to Kanawha Falls.

The train rolled through clean country, by long narrow waterfalls off the mountain cliffs that had carved deep clefts in the rocks near the tracks, past the half cave where everybody said the pioneers rested for the night when they came over the mountains, past farms, and tipples where the coal was dumped into coal cars to go east.

Kanawha Falls was the meeting place for the upper valley. Great Uncle Aaron Stockton's place was still there, no longer an inn. When the heavy summer heat lay over most of the valley, the rushing veil of water at Kanawha Falls cooled the air. The pool below the falls was clear and deep, and the island where they picnicked was green with flowering mast and trees and underbrush from the spring freshets that lodged between the trees and smelled of rain and spring all through the hottest days of summer.

I went to Kanawha Falls last year. The smell of the island is, to me, the smell of river-summer, a damp smell, a green smell, and mixed with it, the deviled eggs, the watermelon, the big thermos of lemonade, chocolate icing, pickles, fried chicken, and the wet serge of the bathing suits my parents and their friends wore when I was small.

Generations of people in the upper valley learned to swim there, in the calm deep silk water space bounded by the island, the shore, and in the distance, far away enough so that they were and are a deep murmur, the great falls. The island protects the water from the strong current caused by the meeting of the Gauley and the New Rivers, as they rush over the quarter-mile span of rocks, a blue river and a brown river whose colors are tossed together in the air above the falls to form the dark green river, the Kanawha.

In the brightened photographs that have helped to guide me through a time I cannot know, there are three, taken at one of those picnics in summer. They reflect and expose what I have been told of their lives then, the clues, the lies, the hints. First, someone has taken a picture of one of the flat boats kept at the falls for rent. My mother holds the boat still with the oars. Big Brother, poised at the bow, is ready to dive. My mother's head is down. I have seen her that way so often, shut off, absorbed. In the boat behind her, his sweetheart, Mary, sits, demure, and at the stern, Myrtle looks daggers at her half brother, who is showing off.

They wear large billowing blouse-like bathing costumes, and their hair is protected by bathing caps like tam-o'-shanters, tied with bows. Brother wears a wool bathing suit in two pieces; the legs come to his knees. The top is like a large tee shirt.

The second picture has been taken within minutes of the first. My mother looks up, not smiling, as he flips high over the water. In the distance beyond the boat, two men have pulled their boat to shore and are walking up the bank, and in the shade of the water willows, too deep to see anything, there may be fishermen.

The third picture was taken later in the day. It is the one that has astonished me and made me understand something I have been told, but not known with my whole self, all my life. Eight people lounge on a blanket that they have brought. They have been swimming. Some of the women are drying their long heavy hair. They wear loose, easy summer dresses. I think they have hidden behind the pile of brush and changed, teasing each other to watch for snakes and men.

My mother is wearing a loose summer dress she called an artist's smock. The picnic has been cleared away. Big Brother sits on a fallen tree branch looking over them. My mother's face is hidden behind her hair, which flows down to the ground. She is half kneeling, turned, watching through the veil of hair a young man on the other side of the group. He lies on his stomach in a striped shirt with the sleeves rolled up, propped on his elbows, smiling at her.

It is the moment of the meeting and falling in love of my parents. He is twenty-four and she is eighteen. It is the most passionate picture I have ever seen.

From that day on they lived for each other, each first with the other, as my mother had once been with her father, and my father with his mother, and whoever stood in the way of that was punished. For all of their lives together it is as if they had, as they must have longed to do that minute, to push the people who lie between them in the picture, out of the way so they can touch and be alone.

Everything that has gone before in my mother's life is buried under that summer awareness between them, he a passionate Puritan, she, one who hated such things as being crazy over men, and all the pain and viscous filth that, to her, went with sex. She had never let herself be fooled, she was too genteel for that, and she had never forgiven anybody in her life.

It was always, of course, different with them. What they felt for each other had nothing to do, ever, with that moaning and groaning, that sighing and giggling, that went on among her sisters. They were both far too high-minded for that. They never said so. They lived it. She tended to recognize higher planes than those ruttings, as she saw them, of passion and mistakes and adolescent sorrows my brother and I would later fall into, reminding her of something soiled that she had rejected with disgust and disdain in the four dedicated, free, bright years between her father's death and her husband's taking her, not physically yet, but with his watch over her, as her hair dried in the sun and shade of the picnic ground at the falls on that day in summer.

My father fitted, for her, every preconception of a fascinating man in 1912. He was of the right profession for romantic novels of the time, a mining and civil engineer. He had traveled. He had been in the last Indian war in 1910 when the Indian reservation in Oklahoma had been opened to the Sooners, who stood at the border all night long, waiting for the signal to run in and stake claims.

The rumor had spread among the waiting land grabbers that the Snake Indians were on the war path. My father had lain on the ground all night with a rifle at the ready. I was always fascinated by this story, and I would get him to tell it, always hoping that he would get beyond the inevitable last line.

"I was laying there all night long on the ground, and as far as I could see in the moonlight there were men, all along the line, waiting, and waiting. The moon went down."

Then, always, my disappointment: "I was so sore from laying on that damp ground that I got a pain that went all the way from my shoulders right down my back to my legs . . ." I never got him to go beyond that. But he had crossed the border with the Sooners, and he had given his claim to a pretty young school teacher who had naturally curly hair. In 1911, he was back in West Virginia. He was the mining engineer at Boomer, his first job. He had been back for a year on the day of the picnic.

He was, she said, the handsomest man she had ever seen. He had, then, a passionate mouth that he kept folded for all his life, except at rare times he felt joy too great to hide. He was so intelligent that he had entered West Virginia University at Morgantown when he was fifteen, so small that when he played quarterback on the football team, they were able to throw him over the line of scrimmage for touchdowns. All his life he was called Prep by men who had gone to school with him. He had that network, as strong as iron, to come back to whenever he went away to seek his fortune.

His mother had been his goad. She had seen his potential, forced him to study, forced him to play the piano, forced him to go to school at the private academy at Montgomery, where, still fourteen, he was valedictorian of his class and delivered a speech entitled "Ambition." She was the daughter of a Methodist minister who had been in the Civil War. At ninety-eight her father christened me. He had been a strict, belligerent man. I remember his white beard, all the way to his waist.

He gave each of his great-grandchildren a Bible when he christened them. In the front was his autobiography, written in his own hand. I have to remember it; the Bible is long gone. He had been born sometime in the 1830s. He had been ordained to preach the Gospel in 1855. He had joined the 33rd Virginia Infantry in 1861, but not as a preacher. He had been a prisoner of war, guarded by a Negro who prodded him with a sword. He said he would deal with him when he got to heaven.

After the war, he wrote, he was reordained to preach the Gospel, and God had called him to Farmville, Virginia, and (this I remember word for word) "with the aid of God and the Ku Klux Klan I was able to take my pulpit." He did not mention his marriage or his large family.

When my father was a small boy he was walking with his grandfather in the courthouse square in Fayetteville when the old man saw a playing card lying on the ground. He flew into a rage and stamped and stamped on it, dancing like Rumpelstiltskin, with his white beard flying. This was the rigid Methodist world my father came into, the sad, unfulfilled mother who bore him, the graduate of a Methodist college in Ohio, a woman who had little beauty and who once told me that she never had a bright dress in her life. She said bright, not what color.

Much was expected of my father, and he expected much of himself. He brought with him, then, Puritan Methodism, vaunting ambition, a handsome face, an athletic body, a good-old-boy network of iron, and a passion for my mother that lasted all his life and shut out the rest of the world. His Puritanism met her disdain and they saw the world eye to eye, as few people I have ever known. Except for politics. They went together every election and killed each other's votes.

From that time on, whatever she did was, in his eyes, perfect. She, who was contemptuous of men, he who disliked women, fearing his mother and his own passion, saw each other as exceptions to all that. Nobody else measured up to their mutual archetypes. They filled them for each other. But they both remained haunted by what they hated, and when they saw reminders of it, narrow-minded Puritan zeal, or sex, or weakness, they both reacted with contempt.

They shared something else, a blind place that they looked on as light. Things were to be this way, this way had the right future, the right colors, the right car, the right schools; the right to them was as rigid as his grandfather's Methodism, and the Presbyterian religious snobbery she had been born to, but they could not know it. They were both afraid to question. It was as if there were a human abyss of anonymity waiting to swallow anyone who did not abide by the rigid rules they lived by.

It has no name, this blindness. John Betjeman, in a poem, says, "Approval of what is approved of is as false as a well kept vow." If and when in later life they were disappointed, it was because the world and their children didn't live up to their vision. The vision itself was never questioned. I realize now, this far away, that they were emotionally stunted, cold with a fear hidden in some deep cellar that they couldn't reach and wouldn't ever have tried.

It contained, since they had seen so little of it in their growing up, no compassion from my mother and little, a thin weed of it that he sometimes let show when it matched his own wordless longing, in my father. I only know that when I dream of my father, he is young and dancing, happy the way I seldom saw him in front of his children. And when I dream of my mother I search and search but I can't find her.

$\mathcal{O}$n the 29th of March in 1912, Rachel Addie (she dropped that name at once) Tompkins married Joseph Edward Settle, aged twenty-four, with her mother's permission. They were married soon after my mother's nineteenth birthday in the little church that her grandfather's slaves had built for his religious daughter Virginia, who had never come to see Mr. Tompkins's family in all the years my mother had lived there.

I can't see them on that morning unless I name them. He is Ed Settle, always called by both names by his friends, of whom there were many. She is Rachel, no longer Sissy, her childhood name, except that her sisters and her brothers said Sissy always, calling her back. I have been afraid of her far too long. If I see her as my mother I will lose those glimpses of that young woman, lovely, nervous, a little triumphant. She was not and has not been mine, ever, and in that recognition is a freedom that pours through me, even at my age, seventy-nine, as if I were sending an urgent message to myself as a child. There is an emptiness when fear is gone. Empty.

She would have liked being Rachel. Once, when I introduced some friends to her, she took against them at once. "They treated me like your *mother*," she emphasized, annoyed.

All Rachel ever said was that it was a small wedding. Why did she tell so little? She was a woman who loved to tell stories, but they stopped at her childhood, except for incidents, a little laughter, and sharp, often witty opinions, about politics, human weakness, gossip, and disapproval of her "in-laws," who she expected not to like. But the wedding is blank, and yet they lived so totally for each other that one of the remarks, said often, in her family at "home"—Cedar Grove, a place she never really left—was that they never should have had children.

Was it morning? Did Addie sit in a front pew, relieved to get rid of one of the girls? I know that she was in the church for the second time—the first was when she buried Mr. Tompkins. Did the sun shine in the high Gothic window and find Rachel's beautiful chestnut hair? Or did she wear a wide-brimmed 1912 hat with a huge crown; did she wear georgette, a favorite, apple-green, her own color? No. I can see her making the decision. For the last of March, a suit from Miss Hostler's in Charleston, the correct place to buy the correct thing to wear.

I think it was what would later be called beige, a jacket nipped in at the waist, and falling below her hips, with covered buttons, a tailored collar, and a skirt to just above her ankles with a pleated insert with more buttons. Maybe she let herself wear a ruffled blouse she would have called a waist. Elegant. Good Taste. An unwritten law. How many petticoats was she wearing, and did she cry before the wedding? I think not. I think she was triumphant. She sounded that way about my father. She demanded and consumed all his attention.

Did my Uncle Roger give her away? He was her most beloved brother. He had, she always said, her father's dash. Aunt Helen was only nine but I think she must have chosen her for her attendant.

Who else was there? I can see only the lines of wooden pews, their curved arms, not yet painted white as they would be in my lifetime. They were polished by years of hands, when the slaves sat on one side, the family on the other, and what they thought of as the valley gentry came in their carriages to church. I think she looked frail, standing there beside the man who was much taller, handsome, whose brother was his best man. Her face softened always when she looked at him. He never, in my lifetime of knowing them, suffered that hard disapproval that was her most effective weapon. So she could have looked tender, her father replaced by her husband. Maybe the fear and fury were blotted out that day, the resentment of the four years that she had seen as cold indifference after the love of her father.

Her mother never entered into this. Rachel was ashamed of her and Addie knew it. She was going to walk out of the church new, a Tompkins, to take her place without the tendrils of old mistakes, scandals. I think that she took for granted that she could live as if she had sprung, like Athena, from her father's brow.

But Ed Settle was not her father, and he was not the elegant handsome man who was rescuing her from something she did not bother to name. He was, to her, a vehicle to everything she looked for and would expect for the rest of her life. She died disappointed in those expectations, though she had long forgotten what they were. She never knew that, like Gatsby, she had already left them behind her, in the bricks of the little church, huddled in the nearly empty pews.

She expected new things of herself if she had to be a woman, the vote that would change everything she had hated, all the four years that she wanted to write, not ever knowing that it is not something you want but something that you are, no matter how much you kick against the pricks.

Ed Settle was a handsome, intelligent, ambitious country boy. He was, all his life, in the few times they were apart, an emotional, warm, concerned person. He was, I believe, a sweet man. His daughter-in-law, who my mother could not stand, knew it. His grandchildren knew it. In my growing-up there were a few times that I caught a glimpse of it. But it had to be hidden from her and from himself, like a minor vice.

Newly wed, they moved to his job at Boomer, above Montgomery, where he was the mining engineer for a mine where not one word of English was spoken, and where he learned a peasant Italian that he never forgot. I think it may have been his favorite job. He told more stories about it than any of the other jobs he had, told directly, not remarks or news to Rachel that I so often overheard and remembered.

He told about the vineyards the Italian women planted, the good food, and the way they were organized so that there was little trouble from them. He said they feared "the black hand" more than they feared any American law. He told often about how they didn't understand that children could not go into the mine on the coal face, only at the breaker shed, where they sorted coal all day, pea coal, lump coal, nut coal. He said he had brought the bodies of ten-year-old Italian children out of the mine after one of the fairly common explosions. His pride and most of the energy of his life was in his work; he spoke of it more easily than anything else.

My mother, already pregnant after the first month of her marriage, set up housekeeping in a two-story clapboard house with a porch and a garden. They lived in a row of houses much like their own, in that strict caste system of the mines. The miners lived in Jenny Lind shacks. The miner's wives terraced the steep hills of the hollows to grow gardens. There was the next tier of two-story houses, clapboard, for the higher caste made up of the families of the superintendent, the mining engineer, the company doctor, and sometimes the family of the man who ran the company store. Even by 1912 there were few mines where the owners lived near enough to know them. Boomer mine was owned by Mark Hanna, from Cleveland, one of the movers and shakers of the Republican Party.

My mother, too, planted a garden, vegetables, as Addie had taught her, and flowers—cosmas, and marigolds and zinnias. The neighbors' chickens broke into it, over and over. One day my father came back from the mine and found that she had shot the heads off every chicken that belonged to her neighbors and flung the bodies over the fence into their yard.

She said that she had warned them over and over and that was enough, and besides, she added, "I was used to living in a big house where nobody dared come on the property without being invited. Bounce saw to that." Bounce was a white bull terrier bitch who was so mean she ate her own pups if they weren't taken away and raised by Uncle Obe with a bottle. But Bounce had died of old age when Rachel was still a child, following her father along with the dog. Cedar Grove was already becoming a weapon and a dream of the past.

Both of them had lived in the world of mining for long enough to take violence for granted as a part of life, like the awful stillness that fell over all the valley within hearing when there was the underground rumble of explosion in the mine. It was usually dynamite being set to bring down coal from the coal face, but sometimes it meant death, and until the rumble had died away and they heard no scream of the alarm whistle, they waited.

In 1912, when the Kanawha Valley mines came out on the strike led by Mother Jones, Ed Settle took his brother, Frank, up the steep hill to the mine entrance. It was his duty every day, strike or no strike, to inspect pit props, faulty ceilings, gas, any danger—a door left open, wind that was an underground warning. As they climbed up near the entry, they saw two bunches of daisies set on pit props driven into the ground on either side of it. They looked, my father said, quite pretty, like a holiday or Decoration Day. He told my uncle what they were for.

"If you stay on this side of them you can smell the daisies. If you cross into the mine, they put them on your chest. You better wait out here. They got a sniper on watch and he might be too far away to see your face."

Then he strode into the mine. He did have a stride that went with what he always wore to his work—silk socks, good leather boots, highly polished puttees, jodhpurs, and a leather jacket. He was a dandy but a little ashamed of it. He looked over his shoulder and called out, "I can go in. They don't keep the engineer out. They depend on me," he added. I think he had a brag in his voice.

My mother went to Cedar Grove to bear my brother.

Most of the six years between their marriage and my birth is shrouded, not in secrecy, but in forgetfulness. There are only shreds of memory left around, neglected, that they threw out, and left for me to find. My mother's stories hardly ever went beyond her glowing childhood, my father told only of his exploits.

At some point they lived in Fayetteville, the county seat of Fayette County, West Virginia, the town my father thought of as his home, although he had been born in Deepwater on the river. In Fayetteville they were surrounded by his mother's Carr family. Rachel spoke so often of her mother-in-law's criticism that it must have been true. My grandmother was an emotional woman who cried easily. Rachel found it disgusting.

It is a truth universally acknowledged in the South that the mother's family is "better" than the father's, even though the father's may be descended from kings and the mother's have just crawled out of the swamp. Rachel made friends, she said, with the nice people of the town, but she never admitted that most of the "nice people" were my father's relatives. It didn't fit the picture she was building for herself of her family being better than his.

Fayetteville then was one of those pretty county seats in a farm county where early-nineteenth-century farmhouses were side by side with the new big houses that had begun to be built when the Fayette County coal fields opened. Rachel remembered the houses before people lost their money, and once she spoke of a Christmas tree that their close friend helped them trim. He was, she said, a distant cousin through her great-aunt's marriage to Aaron Stockton. His name was Ebersole Gaines. He would be a friend all of his life. She said he had never had a Christmas tree before. His mother was too strait-laced for that. And then she added—always—"He was at Princeton."

For the rest I have to rely on things found then lost again, as the one poem my mother published in the *Chicago Tribune*, a few pictures, a sudden memory of Chicago. All this was later, in the more silent time of their lives. Maybe they kept it to themselves and remembered it together. I think they did. At some point they lived in Virdun, Illinois, where Ed Settle had been moved as the mining engineer. A song reminded them once of going into Chicago from Virdun and listening to the German band play waltzes. Chicago was their city all their lives, a private city in a private world. Living in Virdun was one of the few times they ever got so far away from their families that the cord that held them stretched to thread.

For two years the papers had been full of death in France, terrible losses, terrible gains. In 1916 Woodrow Wilson had run on the motto, "He kept us out of war." Barely a month after his second inaugural, on April 6, 1917, the United States declared war on Germany. Wilson announced that "the world must be made safe for democracy."

Ed Settle wrote to Cedar Grove in the fall that Rachel cried all the time when her brother, Roger, who had been one of the early volunteers, had been sent to France. Quoting the Bible, he wrote, "she would not be comforted." That letter was from Virdun, Illinois, so I must have been conceived there. I have always thought that I was conceived around Halloween. At least I hope so. I have always loved Halloween.

Ed Settle was moved again, a corporate move. He became the superintendent of a small mine up Straight Creek on the border between Harlan County and Bell County in the mountains of eastern Kentucky. The war-time boom in the coal business was making fortunes for the corporations that owned so many of them. One of the rare pictures of that time is of my mother, about six months pregnant, standing in front of the two-story clapboard house, this time on Straight Creek. But it is the same kind of house, the same fancy structure on a windy base, the kind of house that would fall quickly from neglect. The front yard had been allowed to grow up in weeds. Behind her I can see the beginning of a long flight of bare wooden steps that went all the way down to the level of the hollow.

She smiles, a little shyly, at whoever is taking the picture. Her maternity dress has a wide double sash that controls her full womb. Under the dress there would have been, at the lower end of the burden, a similar strap, like a cradle to hold me up.

When she was in her last two months of pregnancy with me—a difficult one, I was told, and I felt guilty about it for years—it was inevitable that she should come back to Cedar Grove. I only remember stories of the time, as usual some true, some false, and the false has to be weighed for its elements of truth. When you are the child of story-tellers, it is better to check one's facts.

My brother was six years old. I had heard, as children hear in passing, that my parents were afraid for me to be born in a coal camp with a company doctor. In the midst of war and moving, I was another crisis. My mother feared being pregnant. She thought she was going to die. By instinct, she went back to the only home she had ever really recognized, to bear me.

She must have hated it, the heat of July, the bigness weighing her small thin body down, the awkwardness, the ugliness. In the last month of her pregnancy she sat or lay in the back porch hammock she had been used to all her life, waiting and fuming and wanting and hoping, I'm sure, at least for a breeze from up Horsemill Hollow that when it came cooled the porch and smelled still of honeysuckle.

There had been American soldiers in battle before, but the first American soldiers as an army went to war under General Pershing, to stop the great German offensive in the second battle of the Marne that began on the 18th of July, 1918. The telegrams were already beginning to arrive. The women listened for knocks at the doors like they listened to the dynamite booms, waiting to know.

I see her lying as comfortably as she could, half sitting up in the hammock with pillows behind her, the papers strewn around her, learning a new language of salients, and place names she had never known existed, always thinking she knew, a feeling, where Roger was. There were new rivers, the Aisne, the Marne, the Ourcq, new places, Champvoisy, Oliz-et-Violaine.

On Sunday in the late afternoon of the 28th of July she began to go into labor, and Ed Settle took her to Charleston to the Macmillan hospital. He drove her in his new open Chandler touring car slowly down the river so she wouldn't be jogged, in the cool of Sunday evening. She was in labor until three o'clock on Monday, the 29th. On that day the *Charleston Gazette* printed the official news that nearly three hundred Americans had been killed in the counter-offensive.

This was not true. There were, between the 28th and the 29th, six thousand Americans killed capturing the German ammunition dump at Fère-en-Tardenois, an eighth of all the American soldiers killed in the war. The paper also announced that there was a round-up of a hundred "slackers" in Kanawha County.

It would be easy to say I remembered. It is too deep for that. God, what a thin channel to life it must have been, how taut the muscles of her fear, her pain, but I did fight through to life when I burst forth screaming in that room in the Macmillan hospital. That fight went on for years, she trying to stop me out of her fear, I fighting to be born.

But I carried a scar without knowing why. One of the nurses came in, looked at me, and said, "Did you have this baby to keep your husband out of the war?" I know now that it wasn't true, not altogether. Ed Settle was already in a reserved industry; he was "making good money." There was a cover from a magazine, framed in their bedroom, a tender sentimental painting of a woman with flowing hair, holding a new baby, and her husband, looking like Ed Settle, leaning close to her.

Totally instinctively, looking ever since for reasons that would satisfy the people who asked me, I joined up in World War II as a private in the Women's Auxiliary Air Force of the RAF. But when I dream of war it is of World War I, not the one I was in, and for years I could not hear a World War I song without sobbing. The first poem I wrote at the beginning of the next war was about Cambrai, where there had been a blood bath in 1916. It began, "In the greengrown center of my memory tree lies Cambrai, carved there by only a story; I was not born, nor you, but the earth fell under the fall of our fathers . . ." The rest is gone, the only copy lost, but that stays in my mind.

Rachel couldn't feed me. I weighed the same at six weeks as I had at birth. The new formulas for babies were tried. Nothing worked. Rachel said I never stopped crying, that I nearly drove her crazy, that she did everything she could but the baby book said not to pick me up when I cried because it would spoil me. From that time I still have a ruptured navel.

One day Addie picked me up. She said that if something wasn't done I was going to die. She held this opinion all through my childhood, which meant that she paid more attention to me than any other grown-up woman. There is another memory. Whenever I am sad, I can feel a large hand spread across the weak part of my back, and I sometimes dream of being held that way. Is it Addie who had enough of what she would have called fool ideas about letting babies cry until their navels were ruptured and their backs were arched and frozen?

Is it Addie's hand I have felt from a time when I was small, vulnerable? Or is it Serena's?

Serena worked at the house. She brought twin babies with her when she came, and they lay in their basket by the fireplace in the kitchen while she washed dishes and cooked. She was so big that the owner of the picture show made two seats into one so she could be comfortable. Her face was rosy over the blackness. When Addie picked up seven pounds of frail baby she marched with me into the kitchen and handed me to Serena. She nuzzled me to her huge breast. I stopped crying. From that time on for six or seven weeks, sometimes I was told one, sometimes the other, I joined the other two babies in the basket, and my mother and my Aunt Helen and Addie went back to the main problem that summer, worrying about whether Roger would be killed in the second battle of the Marne. I learned Château Thierry, the Argonne forest, Beaulieu wood, with my first words.

Rachel took a healthy baby who could, after Serena's hot milky comfort, take a formula, back to Straight Creek in the fall. I remember lying in a white wicker baby carriage on a platform at the top of a long flight of wooden steps, in the sun, alone, peaceful, listening.

They ordered a Kiddy Koop from the company store, and Rachel put me in it when the sun was out. The mountain people who had come down from their farms to work in the mines came by on the way to the company store to see the wild baby who had to be kept in a cage. Addie called long distance from the wall phone in the back hall at Cedar Grove to see if I was still alive. I caught influenza, along with millions of other people, in the worst pandemic since the Middle Ages, where far more people died than were killed in the war.

In the summer when I was three Rachel took me on the train to visit at Cedar Grove. She brought a carry cot with her so I wouldn't try to sleep in her lap.

She dressed me beautifully, from the time I could stand. I wore a grey taffeta coat with a grey taffeta bonnet. There were tiny pink roses around the ruffle of the bonnet, and roses and smocking on the coat, which had been made by the nuns. Until I was twelve I had a silk dress every year, "made by the nuns." Where the nuns were I was never told.

Now at last it is my own recall, and real, and vivid—the first true sight of Cedar Grove as we walked up the walk. She gripped my hand so I wouldn't run. The rambler roses were out. They covered the front of the wide front porch. Behind their deep shadow was the door, its fanlight above it and its fine side windows. The red-brick house was the biggest house I had ever seen. It rose up and up against the sky. In front of it two cedar trees were surrounded by mounds. But the right side, from the brick walk to Kelly's Creek, was a huge pond, and some boys were playing at going to sea in a washtub. They paddled the washtub between trees that stuck out of the water. They were cousins. I found out later that it was the worst flood since 1860.

Three of my cousins were in a bedroom that Rachel said was called the cyclone when she was a little girl because the boys, her brothers, made such a mess of it. It was dark in there. My cousins were coughing and they couldn't have light because they had whooping cough. My Aunt Myrtle's son, Elsworth, was in there, and Bill Grant and June Bug. Aunt Myrtle took me into the room so I would be exposed and "get over it early." All I remember was the dim dark of a daylight room behind sucking green blinds.

Great-grandfather William Tompkins (born 1793), a gunsmith who fought in the War of 1812

Great-grandmother Rachel Grant Tompkins, who ruled the roost as a widow from 1857 to her death in 1878

Cedar Grove, 1995, the house that William Tompkins built with salt money in 1844

Henry Preston Tompkins, my grandfather, born 1847, family "bachelor" and rake

Addie

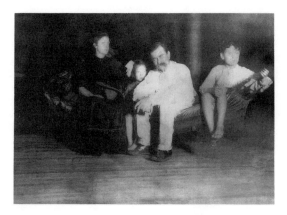

Addie; my mother, Rachel; my grandfather Henry Preston Tompkins; and my eldest uncle, Henry Preston, Jr., in the hammock on the new porch

"Pressy's children": My uncles Preston, Roger, and Bado; my mother seated with her doll; and Aunt Helen, the baby. The playhouse, later Aunt Myrtle's chicken house, was built for my mother's seventh birthday by her father.

"Grandfather's girls," from left to right: Aunt Helen, three years old; Aunt Myrtle, seventeen; Aunt Bertha, nineteen; Addie, thirty-seven; my furious mother, eight. The portrait over the piano is of Aunt Minnie, and the one over the fireplace is of my grandparents.

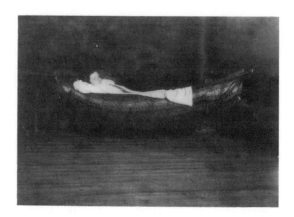

My mother, at age fifteen, in the front porch hammock

The girls in summer, with their beaus. In front of Addie's porch: my mother, Aunt Helen peeping from behind her, Aunt Myrtle, and Aunt Bertha

The first meeting of my parents, at a picnic at Kanawha Falls

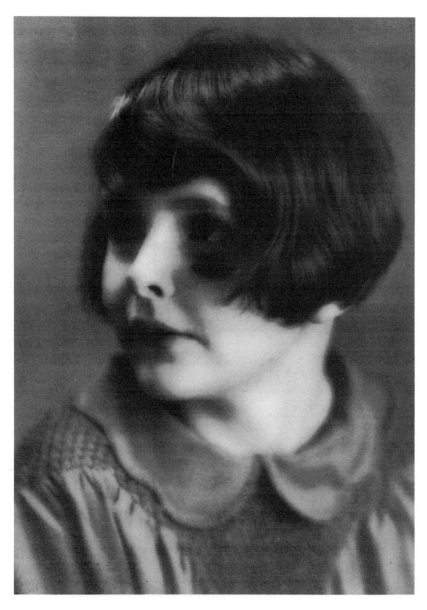

Mary Lee Settle, four years old, Pineville, Kentucky

Dignified Chinese amah, twelve years old

The Dunce Boy, Barter Theater, summer 1938

Photograph for Scarlett, Barter Theater, summer 1938

Roger Tompkins's last ceremony of innocence before Uncle Bado's death, Cedar Grove, Thanksgiving 1974. Roger, third from left, holds his glass up; I am in the back, third from right; Uncle Bado and Aunt Violet hug each other, front right.

The Little Brick Church. The historic marker shows its many changes, including its various names.

*E*arliest memories are half-dreamed, half-recalled flashes of still being. Linear memories, when events had beginnings and endings and the days are recalled in time and movement, began for me when I was two, and we moved from Straight Creek down to a pretty little cottage with a garden beside it and a big back yard with a two-story barn in Pineville, Kentucky. It was the happiest time of my parents' lives—and so my brother's and mine, too. The years run together, whether I was three or four or five, but the memories are as real as if I were still there.

Pineville, the county seat of Bell County, Kentucky, lay in a cup below Pine Mountain on the bank of the Cumberland River. It had grown up around the courthouse, a brick building with columns set above high steps in the center of the town, surrounded by grass and trees, a park-like square where people strolled and met and passed the time of day. Later it would be the meeting place for strikers, for Baldwin-Felts detectives, but not while we were there. In 1921 the wartime coal boom was going to go on forever.

There were two doctors, two or three county-seat lawyers, one druggist, one ice-cream parlor, one grocery store, one cloth and notions store run by Miss Mabel Osburn, and on a corner of the courthouse square, one bank that belonged to Mr. Reese, who drove the only Packard in town. There was a little hospital behind the bank.

Towns are benign or cold. Hobos know this. They mark them by hex signs. But in the midst of violence, coal mining, mountain trouble, unions, and owners, Pineville was, and still is, benign. The village it took to raise this child.

It was as far away from the dirt and sadness of the mines as Rachel and Ed Settle could get within driving distance of "Daddy's" mine. He drove his Chandler to the mine and came home late. Daddy's mine. That was all I knew. I have found out that it wasn't "Daddy's" mine, that he was still at the mercy of faraway owners. He went earlier and earlier to the mine, and he came home later and later. My mother said not to bother him because he was too tired.

In the early Twenties, Pineville was a haven of bankers and mine owners and operators, where people went east to finishing school and prep school and college on coal money—attractive, ebullient young people who smelled nice and went for rides in open cars and on picnics at a swimming hole up Clear Creek. Afterwards we all sat in the dark around an open fire and watched the animals' eyes all around us light up like little stars, and they sang "Little Corey," "The Sweetheart of Sigma Chi," "It was Sad When That Great Ship Went Down," "If I Had the Wings of an Angel," while I drifted to sleep in Bobby Low's lap. Bobby Low and Genevieve were my parents' best friends. I was closer to him than to anybody else in my life.

At the corner of our street, opposite the courthouse square, was the post office, in the same building as the picture show. I went to pick up mail for my mother because I didn't have to cross a street. One day, when I was five, I stood and watched the courthouse steps. A man with high-buttoned shoes was being carried on a stretcher down the steps. He was one of the Tollivers (the Kentucky spelling of the southern family name Taliaferro) who had been shot through the courtroom window with a sawed-off shotgun by one of the Falins while he was on trial for shooting a Falin in the Tolliver-Falin feud. It was the first time I ever saw a dead man, but I only remember his high-buttoned shoes.

On the corner in front of the courthouse was the center of life, the Flocoe. It had marble-topped tables on wrought-iron flared legs, a marble counter, and tessellated marble tiles on the floor. Until I was at least four years old I thought that all the places you went to for ice cream were called Flocoes.

Addie belongs in Pineville, too, by the weight of her absence. She never visited our house for the whole of our lives there. Rachel's freedom from her was like a light turned on in her eyes, an easy gaiety, laughter free and unpinched.

My father was playful so seldom that I remember almost every time. It was as if he had let joy into the house for a minute and then shut the door on it again. His duty, as he saw it, was to worry, and we were a part of it. Our duty seemed to be to honor this. It was a way of life. I remember the relief from it, the almost unconscious little jig he used to do, clicking his fingers. It was his gesture of pleasure. I remember him smiling, with his hat pushed to the back of his head. As he recited A there's your arch in Archibald, I remember his gleaming leather puttees, his britches, his handsome coat, and in winter his silk underwear and long silk socks that hung on the clothes line to dry. I remember that he made a Puritan excuse for wearing them. He said silk kept him warmer in the mine.

They were part of a "crowd" of young people, some of them with families, all in their late twenties or early thirties. The women played bridge. The men played golf at a little club. I have a picture of the ladies, the way they looked, riding on a float in a Fourth of July Parade, representing, I imagine, the Women's Club. The float has a yard-wide crepe-paper band—red, white, and blue with stars—wrapped around what must have been a truck bed. Over the roof, which acts as a shade for the ladies, there is more red, white, and blue with stars, and fringe hangs down to make a little gazebo.

My mother is driving. She wears a wide-brimmed hat that I remember trying on, brown and green and white stripes. Her summer dress is more tailored than the others' summer hats with ribbons and voile dresses with ruffles. I can smell these dresses and these ladies—the scent of sun-dried cloth, lemon Florida water, and talcum powder—as I look at the picture. I can tell by their clothes that it is 1922. All of the women own copies of Emily Post, and take the *Ladies' Home Journal, The Woman's Home Companion*, but not *The Delineator*.

There are two tables set for bridge, set for me forever, the way the ladies of my mother's crowd look. In the parade they represent how American ladies live. They are being served tea at the tables. Behind them stands a young black maid in a white uniform. She is in profile and I am sure I recognize her—it is Ruth, my young nurse, playing at being a maid.

For me, most of the time, it was a town of women, the way women should dress, the way women should behave, smell, move. Mary Brank Moss, Margaret Bell, Fannie Lehmann—they all wore dresses nearly to the floor with tucks and sleeves and with collars of lace, organdy and filmy cotton and handkerchief linen in the summer, crepe de chine and taffeta when they dressed up in the winter. Their hair was long still. I saw it down when they dried it at the swimming hole, in their knit bathing suits that fitted their bodies. The New Year of 1923 came in in our living room around the Christmas tree they had all put up together. It went all the way to the ceiling, and Bobby Low put up the top star.

Genevieve is my lifelong idea of a beautiful lady. She had long blond hair and soft curved arms. She smiled a lot and held me on her lap without being afraid I would crease her dress. White voile curtains that breathe in the slight breeze, eggshell-colored bedroom furniture with little carved borders, Coty's powder in an orange box with white powder puffs printed on it, a pale orange embroidered silk Japanese kimono, feather-light, waving blond hair flowing down her back—all of this brings Genevieve close to me again. She must have spent a lot of time in her bedroom. I remember her there. Nobody told me that she was frail. People were, in those days, cared for and watched for years, the frail ones, their graceful light gestures.

The white cottage we lived in had a porch wrapped around the front and a garden beside it where the flowers had names I liked to say - cosmos, delphinium, marigold, calendula, zinnia, corn flower, rose. I can still walk into every room. My parents' big bedroom was in the front, surrounded by the porch on three sides. I slept there, too, first in my Kiddy Koop.

I remember standing up in it and screaming for someone to come in and get me out of the dark. I could hear grown-ups laughing in the living room. I remember thinking, "I can cry longer than they can stand it. Then they will have to come and get me." But they must have won that stand-off. I don't, of course, remember wearing myself out and going to sleep in the dark. But I do still remember my quite cool will to defeat them. Later I had a "thimble" bed that was supposed to have belonged to Jefferson Davis. My mother had already started collecting antique furniture and making stories up about it.

I don't see both my parents in that room, but I do see my mother, her face dead white, her hair flung around her pillow, blood coming from her mouth that she spat into a chamber pot. I thought she was dying. I was terrified of her. She looked like the evil witch in my fairy tale book. She only told me to go someplace and play. She had had a wisdom tooth pulled.

The living room had wicker furniture that was to follow us on too many journeys. There was a wonderful soft sofa, and a big upholstered chair where I read with my head on one arm and my legs across the other. I learned to read, first by memorizing when I was read to, which was often, then on my own, before I was six, from *The Thousand and One Nights Entertainment* which I found in the *Harvard Classics* that made up our library.

It was in the dining room that my great-grandfather christened me. Then he knelt and prayed for a long time; he was a Methodist. So I poured the water from the River Jordan back on his head. He was ninety-eight years old that year.

Loada ruled the kitchen and we learned from her to say, "For the love of the lamb," instead of swearing. We teased Loada by chanting, "For the love of the goat, for the love of the sheep, the cat, the dog, the donkey."

Ruth was my nurse. She was a dignified young lady of sixteen, and I recognized that. She used to take me home with her, to a small house with a narrow hall. She showed me her clothes, white voile, flower-trimmed hats. She made them herself. Once she took me to the Cumberland Hotel where the movie actress Pearl White stayed while she made several episodes of one of her famous cliff-hanger serials. Her wigs were on stands the shape of heads. I thought they were real heads and screamed and had to be taken out of the room.

Ruth and I went everyplace together—to her house, which I knew like our own, to the picture show where I saw Charlie Chaplin. I didn't like him. He made me cry while everybody else laughed. We didn't have to sit in the colored section because Ruth was my nurse. I loved Ruth. She hugged me when I was hurt, and held me if I cried, teased by the other children because I was called "four eyes" and "red head red head five cents a cabbage head."

When my mother took me back to Kentucky in the fall of 1921, after our visit to Cedar Grove where I had caught whooping cough, I was over the illness, but the strain of coughing had caused my left eye to cross so far up into my head that it could hardly be seen. There is a picture of me, standing by the front steps of the white clapboard cottage that we lived in. I look goofy, smiling when I was told to, one eye cocked upwards, my head tilted, trying to see.

My father wanted a beautiful daughter. Instead he had been handed a child with big Carr feet—he hated big feet—and a crossed eye. I know now that my father was horrified at the prospect of having a daughter whose "looks" were ruined when she was three years old. I was a crisis again, an expensive one this time. Rachel and Ed Settle had a cross-eyed child, and they had to do something about it. They made the decision to have my eye straightened. I remember being taken to Cincinnati on the train at night, wrapped in a blanket. Genevieve went with us. We stayed at the Gibson Hotel.

I already loved to walk alone. I was taught that if I wanted to walk ahead of them, I had to say my name: "Mary Lee Settle, three years old, Pineville, Kentucky." What I added on my own when I walked in the street in Cincinnati, was, "Bobby Low is my daddy."

After the operation, I was supposed to wear a patch over my "good" eye and do exercises, following a finger left to right, right to left, up and down, so that my "bad" eye would strengthen, but everybody forgot, and I was too small to know how important it was to do it on my own, so I was nearly blind in my left eye. I was "four eyes" because I had to wear little gold glasses which I learned to flush down the toilet, but they only got the plumber to get them out, and told me they cost a lot.

Genevieve was married to Bobby Low, but he lived at his house with his mother, and Genevieve lived with her parents. They had run away to marry. Mr. and Mrs. Reese, Genevieve's parents, lived in a large house with a porch on three sides and a beaten biscuit machine you could hear thumping. One night when they came to visit I saw a great gold cross in the sky and called them to see. I can still see it. They looked and looked, but could only see the moon. Mrs. Reese wore grey georgette that night and had a pince-nez pinned to her single big bosom. Mr. Reese ran over my brother in his Packard and fractured his skull.

Bobby Low was a tall, lithe, ruddy man. He smelled of good tobacco and sometimes whisky, and he had gentle hands. He lived up a road on Pine Mountain at the edge of the town, in a brown house with the town on one side downhill, and a whole mountain where he worked his bird dogs on the other. About once a month I ran away. I put all my belongings in a red wagon, and I pulled it up the hill to Bobby Low's, and sat in the swing on his porch until he found me. He taught me how to wait, how to scratch a dog on its belly, not to be afraid of the woods, to listen to classical music on the wind-up Victrola and not to wiggle, to love silence, because gabble put the birds up. I learned to carry a little BB gun broken over my elbow with the barrel toward the ground, and the different sounds of animals, the scream of the panther, the whirr of the grouse, all of this before I was six years old. He was my Jesuit, my father.

What I look back on as an interrupted lifetime lasted only five years. By 1925 the coal boom was over. Mines were already shutting down. How could I know that our lives were ruled by a boom-and-bust industry? Life for children is forever. All I knew then was that when I was six I was untimely ripped from an Eden. It was an Eden for my parents, too. Rachel and Ed Settle would keep the friends they found there all of their lives.

I sat on a suitcase in the back of the Chandler sedan. I remember being very still. Bobby Low was there and Genevieve. All of our furniture had disappeared. The house sounded hollow. Nobody explained anything. I don't think that it was a mistaken decision to spare me and my brother. I think they were so shocked by what had happened that they forgot us as people, packed us in the back seat to take my mother and me to the train, and left. Left Pineville. Never went back.

My father and my brother Joe Ed were going to drive straight to Florida, where there was a boom, in the same Chandler sedan that I had mashed my fingers in over and over because my mother was too impatient to give me time to get in the back seat. My mother and I went first back to West Virginia, where we stayed at Cedar Grove, and then on the train to Florida in a Pullman car with a berth and green curtains that swung with the train rhythm. Marcellus and Mary Brank Moss had already moved to Orlando. I think that was why my parents chose it. Nobody told me anything.

A few years ago I went back to Pineville.

I drove through Cumberland Gap. I passed the sign that read Pineville, Kentucky, population 2600. It looked somehow as if it had been stamped down, as if time itself were a strip-mining machine. The grass was deep on the courthouse lawn. The town had been severed by a state road to bring the coal trucks down the Cumberland River. The road, so arrogant, so high over the roof tops, was also a dam. Pineville, like much of eastern Kentucky, had been a victim of strip mining. With the trees and topsoil gone upriver, a flash flood had inundated the town. It had not shrunk. It was the same size, but the late twentieth century had diminished it, and had battened on the country around it.

I must have known without knowing that it had happened. Long before I went back I had sat at night in the stern of a boat in the Aegean, while a tape of bluegrass music was being played. "My son, I can't take you back to Muhlenburg County. Mr. Peabody's coal train has hauled it away." I tried to keep my sobbing quiet.

But there was the courthouse still, there the buildings around the square, as they are in so many county seats. The post office had been moved. The Pineville Hotel across the street from us where we went for Sunday dinner sometimes, and ate corn-on-the-cob with little handles stuck in the ends of the ears, was gone. Some of the buildings were boarded up. I drove around the square and looked for the Cumberland Hotel, where Theodore Dreiser and John Dos Passos had stayed for a few days during the coal strike in 1931, and where the town blades (I'm sure Bobby Low was one of them) had crept in late one night and stood toothpicks in front of Dreiser's door when they saw the woman he had brought with him go in. At six-thirty in the morning the toothpicks were still there, and Dreiser was accused of adultery, or "unlawful cohabitation," a felony then in the state of Kentucky.

The Cumberland Hotel, too, had been torn down. I was disoriented, and ready to leave. Then I saw the sign, on the corner where it should be, across from the court house—The Flocoe Drug Store.

The door was still catty-cornered, the fine tessellated marble floor was still there, still, to the six-year-old eyes within me, the finest I ever saw. The marble counter had not been moved. There were two men sitting having coffee at a small round marble table with wrought-iron legs, the way they always had, in the same place, in the same room, in a small county seat on an easy sunny morning. I said aloud, and to myself, "Thank God, they haven't changed the floor."

One of the men got up and introduced himself. "I'm the druggist," he said, "Mason Combs." He was not only the druggist, but the town's leading artist, and the recorder of its history.

"You're not Buster's little brother?" I asked.

"Why, yes. Who are you?" he asked me.

"I'm Mary Lee Settle. I used to live here."

"Why, you're Joe Ed's little sister," the other man called. He came over to welcome me.

It had been sixty-five years.

I asked about Bobby Low, and I had not been wrong about him. He had died twenty-five years before, a judge, one of the most beloved men in the little county town.

I drove my car to where our house had been. It was a concrete parking lot and service station. Then I drove, six years old within, slowly down the street, seeing and remembering the house where I got in a fight at a birthday party and got a front tooth knocked out, the Reeses' house where they made beaten biscuits on a machine on the back porch, Mr. Marting's where I played chess, and then the turn uphill to Bobby Low's house with the unchanged corduroy concrete street paving.

It had been a quarter of a mile, a long way for a little girl to pull her worldly goods uphill to find her father. I sat there in the car for a long time. The porch swing was still there, or another. It didn't matter. Something was healing inside of me. People can't know, when they are victims of far-away decisions, that in the back seat is a six-year-old child, hurt and afraid. Nobody asked, or imagined it, or noticed but Bobby Low, and his last words to me were, "Don't worry, little onion, you'll be back in no time."

He had been right. There was no time between leaving and sitting there in my car in front of his house sixty-five years later.

I went to say goodbye, to the cemetery that was on the next foothill below Pine Mountain. A horseshoe road, paved so long ago that it was too narrow for any modern car, ran uphill past marble tombs on the left and down again on the right, back to the main road. The coffins had to be carried by hand, as they always had been so long ago.

I walked slowly up the left-hand side, past marble tomb after marble tomb. I passed Mr. and Mrs. Reese, and Mary Brank and Marcellus Moss, who had been sent back from Florida to be buried there; I passed Mrs. Lehmann and the Martings and all the others, playmates and enemies and their parents and their grandparents, and they all came back to me, the way they had looked, the way they had spoken. I walked within a memory too strong to be called memory—a reliving.

But Bobby Low was not with them. I searched the little graveyard for nearly an hour, but I could not find him. At the top of the horseshoe road, so far uphill that I could see the whole curve of the Cumberland River, I turned to the right to go back downhill. Behind me, near the stone wall that separated the cemetery from the house, two little dogs were playing, a feist dog and a country beagle. I spoke aloud again, as I had in the Flocoe, hardly knowing it, "Please God, help me find Bobby Low." It was the prayer that had echoed through all my years.

Within two seconds the little beagle had jumped up on my leg, wagging his tail. I petted him and walked on along the road. He followed me and jumped up again, then ran back to the left. I followed him. He kept checking back, every ten feet or so, like a bird dog, to see that I was still following.

At the end of a small footpath, I could see Bobby Low's house on the next foothill through the trees across the ravine. The dog turned to eleven o'clock from the path, froze on point in the field where we had run the dogs sixty-five years ago, me so small that the tall grass was up to my shoulders.

There, directly between his ears, the gravestone read, *Robert Gibson Low*—on his own mountain, in sight of his own house. Some kind of search I had hardly known I was following through the years, through love affairs and half-forgotten faces, through parts of my books and the recall of voices of animals, of guides, of the woods at night, through clues that saddened me without my knowing why, had been ended. I had been allowed to say goodbye.

I said a prayer for both of us. Then I went back down the hill. The last I saw of the beagle, he was standing against the sky with a plastic wreath in his mouth. His other job at the graveyard seemed to be to move plastic wreaths from one grave to another.

*M*y father followed the booms of the Twenties and they burst in his face. There must have been almost no money. It was never mentioned, so how can a child know? We were simply packed up and moved.

In *Going Away,* Clancy Sigal wrote: "Let me tell you, a cross-country trip in your own car, at your own speed, is the cheapest psychoanalysis I know." I think my father must have faced a lot of facts on that slow road to Florida in 1925. He resolved never to go into the mines again. He had been trained as a civil engineer, and if he had to start over it would be as his first love. Even before Rachel, he dreamed of building bridges. He told me so. For years I dreamed of bridges that stopped halfway across rivers. And the dark, swift water.

After we had said goodbye to my aunts in West Virginia, my mother and I arrived on the train to Orlando before Christmas. My parents drove my brother and me straight down through a vast flatness of the Everglades and of scrub. Huge birds flew over the car. We saw an alligator. The road was unpaved in places, but the Florida sun had baked it hard and the car bumped. There were canals that my father said were to irrigate the land and draw off water from the Everglades. He surprised me by talking easily as if there hadn't been the disaster my mother had told my aunts about. He told jokes, and he seemed almost happy on that drive. We had long since learned to watch for signs of that happiness as you watch the weather.

We went to Moore Haven, near Lake Okeechobee where my Settle grandparents had a dairy farm. The house was built of cypress and it perched on great cypress poles seven feet high to withstand hurricanes.

I had never been out of the mountains, and I sat with my silent grandfather on the high porch of their hundred-year-old house and looked all the way to no-place through vines of red and yellow bougainvillea where the humming birds whirred like tiny brilliantly colored nerves, with wings so fast they were only a blur. He sat there every day in the same wooden rocking chair at the same time and read *The Saturday Evening Post*, passeling it out so it would last exactly a week.

It was a Christmas like nothing I had ever seen. The poinsettias grew six feet high. The banana trees held upside-down bananas that were green and pointed up to the sky instead of hanging down. We picked oranges and lemons and brought them into the house when my grandmother asked for them.

Grandfather Settle owned thirty Jersey cows with big sad eyes. He got up to do the milking every morning just at dawn, which he said was the best time of day. He took the milk in huge cans into Moore Haven and ladled it out to his customers. We went together in his milk wagon, slowly, the horse at a walk along the canal so we wouldn't joggle the milk. I don't remember him ever saying a word. I was finding out where my father had learned his long silences—a silent family, except at those rare times when my father opened his mind to us about his visions and his concerns.

My Settle grandmother was the first grandmother I could love. I didn't know Addie well enough yet, and I heard little about her, but my Settle grandmother had been to Pineville and had brought me a present, a big shell from Florida. When you put it to your ear you could hear the sea.

She was ugly-handsome. She had, as my mother pointed out, big Carr feet. She scrubbed the kitchen floor and put newspapers on the ugly, worn, yellow-and-brown linoleum until it was dry. She made me citron cake, and she let me cry when I needed to. This was a new experience for me. Emotion. Shown emotion. My parents had been told by Dr. Sattler in Cincinnati not to let me cry until my eye had healed. My mother remembered it as a time when I was spoiled rotten to keep me from crying until when I threatened to cry, she finally got fed up and said, "All right, dammit. Go ahead and cry." I don't remember it like that. I was afraid to cry.

There was a depth of emotion and intelligence in my Settle grandmother, who had been a Carr from Virginia. That a part of me was at peace with for the first time. She had graduated from a small Methodist college in Ohio in the early 1880s, a very rare accomplishment for a woman—except for a Methodist. There was still, she explained to me, the Methodist passion for education of both men and women, which had come down all the way from when Methodism was the intellectual's church in the late eighteenth century. I learned a lot about the Methodist church from her. She talked about holy poverty, but sometimes she seemed to envy people with money. Most of the books in the little living room were about the Holy Land, and I read them all, and the Children's Bible.

At the small, white Moore Haven Methodist church where she lived, she said, in the depths of her belief, she sang in the choir. A Christmas pageant was being planned when we got there, and she took me in and asked if I could be the littlest angel. It consisted of kneeling behind a sheet with a big light shining on me and two other angels. I wore a single cardboard wing, almost as big as I was, pinned to my back so that I was a shadow of an angel. All I could think of was that I had to keep very still or the people in the church would know it was just me and not the shadow of a real angel.

On Christmas morning the sun shone on us. We drove in the wagon to church and my grandmother and her friends cried and hugged each other. There were presents on a tree that was the wrong kind of tree for Christmas, but the little stage with the Holy Mother and the Holy Father and the Holy Jesus and the animals was right because He had been born in the beauty of the lilies in a place that was a lot more like Florida than West Virginia or Kentucky. My grandmother told me that.

She knitted me a bright green scarf to go with my red hair, and she told me that she loved the color. She said that when she was a little girl, a preacher's daughter, people gave them sensible things because they had no money. She said she was always given brown clothes.

My brother and I were taken back to Orlando so we could go to school. First we lived in a one-room apartment where the beds went into the wall in the daytime. We moved three times in Orlando, the second time to a ground-floor apartment with grey furniture, the last time to a house where we had kumquat fights from a tree in the back yard.

We had already missed a semester. I know because it was the first time I heard the word semester. I would walk out into the back of the apartment house and say new words to the poinsettias that were so high that I could hide behind them when my mother called me until I was ready to answer. I had begun to be aware of words, how they sounded, what they meant. A friend and I walked home from ballet class and she said her feet were "agony." I thought it was the ugliest word I had ever heard. Agony.

Something was beginning between my mother and me; I was disagreeing but not saying so. She was contemptuous of my Settle grandmother and she seemed to want me to laugh at her, as she would later want me to like the "nice" people in Charleston and tell funny stories about Addie. It broke the confidence I had in her; she had a sense of humor and she told me I didn't, so she could see the funny side of my grandmother's being an "Amen Corner Methodist" and people in Florida being "city tacky," and I couldn't. She couldn't "stand" my grandmother Settle. She always said, if I cried or if I laughed too loudly for her to approve of, that it was the Carr coming out of me. I could imagine the Carr flowing out to offend her, even the color, a yellow-grey like my grandmother's hair. But my grandmother didn't like her any better, although she never said so. She just told me a secret my mother didn't know, that the Virginia Carrs were better than the Tompkins any day.

The Mosses must have already gotten rich. They had a Colonial house with a wide central hall and stairs that went up like the house at Cedar Grove. They had been "abroad." They had the first cabin trunks I ever saw, with labels on them—Paris, London, Rome. Their maid taught me the Charleston in the kitchen. Their daughter, Frances, who I had fought with in Pineville, and knocked out one of her baby teeth, lorded it over me.

I was entering a new path, alone, reading from the library where I walked nearly every day through quiet streets under huge trees with the Knights of the Round Table, Hans Brinker, Mowgli, the Phantom Rickshaw. What was coming alive has never aged and never changed. I had begun to see.

It was a constant worry and embarrassment to my mother. She tried. I don't think she ever knew that she was failing, only that I was disappointing. She wanted me to "have the best," which was the right things to do and the right clothes to wear at all times and an appreciation of art and good taste. Above all, she wanted me to be graceful, which was not easy, since I was half blind and stumbled around and fell down when I tried to skate. My knees were always bloody and the scabs were exciting to pick at.

Once, she planned a special treat for me, to go to a class that the Denishawn dancers, who she said were the best modern dancers in America, were giving at the high school. She said it was because they were wintering in Orlando and were doing something for the city.

She held my hand as we walked into a beautiful room. It was sky high; the floor was polished so I could see myself. The walls were hung with wonderful ropes and swings and signs. It smelled of polish and disinfectant, and sweat. It was the first gymnasium I had ever seen. I loved everything about it; I realize now it was the clean lines, the functional looks, the true colors.

In a corner of the big room a row of mothers sat. There was a man in black tights down to his ankles. You could see his bulge. He lined about twenty awkward, scared little girls in rows, and then he said, "When I start the music"—his voice went whispery—"I want you to tiptoe down the beach and feel the sand under your feet, and lean over and pick up a lovely shell, and listen, listen, listen . . ."

He showed us how to do it. He tripped across the gymnasium floor, swooped and picked up nothing and held it to his ear with a moony expression on his face. His arms were curved. "Be graceful," he said over his shoulder, and he turned around and started *Humoresque* on a little wind-up Victrola.

So I plodded along the gym floor on my big Carr feet, and I didn't feel any sand and I stooped down with my behind in the air and picked up an imaginary shell. . . . That was as far as I got. I saw my face in the shining floor. I saw my hands swoop down. In that beautiful room he was trying to tell me we were someplace else. Unfortunately my brother had taught me the words to *Humoresque*. "Passengers will please refrain from flushing toilet while the train is standing in the station I love you."

I got the giggles. I rolled on the floor. The other little girls caught them from me. We rolled and laughed and had a wonderful time. That was the end of the class. My mother grabbed my hand and squeezed it so it hurt and told me she was never going to let me go to dancing class again as long as she lived. I was to find out later that as long as she lived was a favorite time frame for her punishments. She died at ninety-two.

Now I realize how unfair I might have been; it was self-protection to withdraw from her. Her hugs were harsh. She was too preoccupied. It was not a time of ease for her. She seemed to hold in her body a fragile, brittle courage you could feel if you touched her. I had become a little afraid of that dangerous poise.

What was happening to my parents only impinged on a life that for me was becoming withdrawn, safe, and private by necessity. Only now can I see that that year and a half we stayed in Florida must have been a terrible change for them; from a house they took pride in to a one-room apartment, from friends they valued to strangers, from the security of being at ease and well-liked in a small, safe town to the constant worry about money. I do remember that they made friends in Orlando, probably through the Mosses. My mother exchanged "good" books with a woman friend, and played a new kind of bridge called contract; my father played golf with men. They never dreamed of sharing these pleasures. I never learned to play bridge until I was grown, and my father, who was on a golf team, was always too busy to teach me or my brother. We were both already leading separate lives.

But my mother looked too thin and had sick headaches, and I brought her ice wrapped in a washrag. My father started coming home late and worried as he had in the last year at Pineville. Once in a while, he told my mother, letting us listen, he had to keep a watch on the concrete mixers because rival contractors poured sea water in the sand. Subdivisions were springing up everywhere. Another new word, subdivision, long division, subdivision. New cities were planned. My father was designing and overseeing foundations of new towns, the water and sewage disposal, for the Mizener brothers, who were leading Florida boom developers.

I remember being taken for walks outside of Orlando where a few houses were just skeletons with men swarming over them and there was an incessant din of hammering and empty acres of scrub with sidewalks and paved streets and no people. Mr. Moss and Daddy discussed investments as we walked.

New words that came from civil engineering were part of life—venue, bond issue, blueprint, stress (not people but metal). I had to be careful not to sit on the pointed brass plumb-bob that my great-grandfather and my grandfather had used when they were engineers. It was always in the back seat of the car.

Once I stood at a window and watched the trees through air so still I could feel a great holding of breath. Then the line of royal palms across the street slowly leaned almost to the ground through the stillness and the yellow air. Orlando was on the edge of the 1927 hurricane.

My father went on the rescue team to Moore Haven, which had been flooded when the levee at Lake Okeechobee broke and flooded the lowlands. Only my grandparents' house was left of all the farm houses, because of the cypress piling. My father said a hundred years had petrified the wood. Friends I had played with were drowned. I was told they wouldn't be there when I went back. But I never went back, not until a few years ago when I drove through central Florida. The farm and all the small farms, with the old houses and the bougainvillea, the small banana groves, the barns and the humming birds, had been swallowed by mile after mile of agro-industry.

One morning the doorbell rang. My mother was still in her dark-green tailored taffeta dressing gown with the wide skirt. It swished when she walked, which was a protection in case I was doing anything I wanted to stop before she saw me. She came back into the bedroom, which was behind the living room, and she opened a yellow telegram. I was sitting on the bed, watching her. She stepped back as if she had been hit. Then her face went paper white.

She said, "Genevieve is dead." She looked at me. "She wasn't supposed to have children. She died because Bobby Low wanted a little girl like you."

Addie came to Florida by herself every winter, but she didn't come to see us there, either. Until I found a picture last year of two old women, as I remember them both, I didn't know that my grandmothers had known each other, and that Addie had visited in Moore Haven. But there they were, standing in front of a head-high, itchy bush that I remembered in front of the house. They were close together as if they liked each other, a woman whose son no longer loved her because she had criticized his wife, and a woman who knew her daughter was ashamed of her. They were in their mid-sixties then; they had grown to look like sisters, one still handsome, the other solemn, dressed alike in those loose dresses of summer cotton, both dresses with little lace collars and embroidery. Their long hair was bunched up in buns behind their necks and escaping down their faces. Both of them wore shoes that showed they no longer cared for looks over comfort. Both of their bodies had sagged and widened with age as if they had breathed huge sighs of relief and were no longer trying to hold anything up, not even their stomachs. These were the two I was supposed to dislike or find funny, and I couldn't. They taught me and touched me, and above all, they listened when I told them things.

The Florida boom ended between hammer and nail. Everything was too quiet and my parents talked in other rooms. I remember that grass had begun to grow through the cracks in the asphalt in the subdivision where we went for walks. Maybe my father had invested there. Most of the skeletons never became houses. There were cracks and stains in the stucco of ones that had walls. I saw a long tear down the side of one of them. There was a sadness and loss about those new, unused ruins that is not in ruins that have aged and been lived in.

That was when we came back from Florida in the Model T Ford, with orange crates tied to the running boards. I don't remember much of the drive back. But I do remember getting to Fayetteville, West Virginia, where we were going to spend the night.

It was a lovely little town like Pineville, in the mountains, with a courthouse in the middle of a grassy square. There were old trees, and solid-looking houses. We drove through the town to where the houses were on lawns, wide apart. My mother said that we were going to Uncle Ed Hawkins. She had already discussed with my father while we listened that Uncle Ed had lost all his money and that they had all had to move out of the big house to the cottage. By the time we got to the house I knew who we would see, who they were, how they were kin, and who were connections.

The car turned up into the long driveway. I expected a tiny cottage like those broken houses in Florida. It wasn't. It was a pretty white clapboard one-story house with wide wings and a portico. A group of people were standing on the little porch, waving—Uncle Ed and Aunt Em Hawkins, and their daughter Jensie, who was Ann Lee's twin, Aunt Em's sister Aunt Lizzie, who was the widow of Grandmother Settle's brother, Uncle Doctor, who had dropped dead at the breakfast table when he was only thirty-one, their daughter, Emma, who I would call Emmy Boo all through my childhood and her brother Madden, who had been in the World War. Emmy Boo looked like Bessy Love in the movies, and Madden looked like a handsome version of Stan Laurel.

I had never seen them before, but they were not strangers. I realized that whatever journey had started a year and a half before was over. I called out and waved from the car and my mother slapped my hands down and said, "Stop acting like your grandmother Settle."

My father's two lady aunts were dressed in black bombazine to their ankles with twin lace jabots. They told me they had always looked very alike but they weren't twins. They had both simply "handed over the keys" at some point in their lives to their two daughters to run the house, as they would have done when there had been servants, and retired into doing nothing except what my mother called "sewing a fine seam." There was truth in that. Aunt Lizzie made most of my clothes until she was nearly blind years later. My mother said she ought to do something for what my father "gave" her.

They had waited dinner for us. It smelled wonderful. The linen was snow-white, and the napkins had been so neatly patched at their borders that I had to squint to see the tiny stitches under the faint light of the electrolier. Over the dining-room sideboard was a painting of leaves and branches with two real stuffed grouse on a little platform in front of them. Uncle Ed saw me staring at them and said he had shot them.

After dinner everybody sat decorously in the living room. Flowers of needlepoint covered all of the chairs and the sofa and pillows. We took turns listening through earphones to the Crosley Radio Corporation in Cincinnati, to far-away thin music from the Netherland Plaza Hotel.

*I*t had taken nearly all day to drive the Model T from Fayetteville down the snake curves of Cotton Hill Mountain. It rained. My father and my brother changed another tire, the fourth since we had left Florida. My mother sat stone still, most of the way, her mind someplace else. It was dark when we finally pulled up in front of the stone gateposts of Cedar Grove. My parents sat there for a minute without moving.

I could see shadows of trees, and the huge, vague shape of the house. In the distance there was a light in the hall so dim that it only brushed the shapes of the fanlight and the glass side panels of the door. We sat there forever. I knew better than to spring out of the car and act like Grandma Settle.

It seemed a long way up the walk, up the steps, onto the porch that loomed on both sides, its rocking chairs faint in the dark. The air smelled of pine trees, not the heat of Florida, but a dampness that wanted to get into my bones.

Addie opened the door. She was a shadow that flowed from the one gas wall sconce in the front hall where the stairway disappeared up into blackness. I wanted to put my hands on my head to protect me from the space.

My cousin Elsworth, Aunt Myrtle's son, informed me at once, under the gaggle of grown-up voices above us, that he made straight As, and that he had had to give up his room and move all his airplanes because of us. He took me by the arm and made me go with him into the dark living room.

"How long are you going to stay?" he asked me. "We don't want you here." I was seven and he was eight. I never told what he had said. Our childhood was a private world, a world with its own absolutely inviolable rules. You did not tell on anybody.

Auden describes home as a place to go out from and come back to, and Frost calls it the place that when you have to go there they have to let you in. Cedar Grove was that for all the children of Addie, as if she were a great oak tree that they could shelter under, even though they were all afraid of her.

By 1927 most of the family were beginning to gather at Cedar Grove. Minnie, Addie's oldest daughter, had come home to die in the spring, raddled and broken, forty-eight years old. She had been the one who at eleven was made to stand up in court, a shy country child, and be a witness in her mother's divorce case—Minnie, who my mother let me hear was a shame and a disgrace to the family. I never knew otherwise until Miss Addie told me about her, the real woman, and then, when years later, I heard of her again.

My Aunt Myrtle and the light of her life, her son, Elsworth, came back to live and they never left until Miss Addie died years later. Aunt Myrtle left Mr. Palmer, who worked for the Pullman Company, and came home to mother. Mr. Palmer, the husband, was never seen. He had simply existed someplace else. He had taken Aunt Myrtle to El Paso, and to Cincinnati sometime in the past, and then he had faded away. I never heard his first name.

She ran the house and made remarks behind her mother's back to get the children on her side of all arguments. It never bothered Miss Addie. "Poor Myrtle," she would say, "she ain't right bright. She needs a gardeen appointed." She said "poor Myrtle" as if it were her name. Except to walk down into the town once a week to get her blond hair dipped and marcelled in hard disciplined waves, and to carry a bucket every evening up the hill field at the foot of Horse Mill Hollow to milk her cow, I never saw Aunt Myrtle leave the house.

Miss Addie said she came back because she never had felt safe anyplace but Cedar Grove, but my mother quoted her father, who had said that Aunt Myrtle wouldn't be happy cooking for angels, so no wonder she left Mr. Palmer.

Once again, as it had been at the beginning of the finding of the valley, and as it had become again when Addie was brought there, and again when Mr. Tompkins walked in front of the train, Cedar Grove, the Virginia farm house, became a fortress, this time against a growing country-wide depression when nobody had a nickel.

Uncle Roger had volunteered for World War I when he was only seventeen. He lived in the back downstairs bedroom that had once been the ladies' withdrawing room. It had been turned into a bedroom when Addie came, and it was given to Uncle Roger when he came home shell-shocked, still only nineteen. Once in a while when they were dynamiting up at the mines, he would run out into the yard before he was fully awake, and try and dig a hole to hide in. He would cover his ears and whimper. They were afraid that if he slept upstairs he would jump out of the window and kill himself.

That had been in 1919 when he came back from the Army of Occupation. How wonderful that the words are in my mind still, meaning what they meant to me at the time. Occupation meant work, or your talent that was a gift. Your occupation. A whole army occupied.

The room had not changed in the spring of 1927—the heavy carved bed and the dresser had been brought from Charleston when they came back to Cedar Grove in 1892. Uncle Roger kept his condoms in the drawer beside the mirror and my cousins explained to me what they were and where they went. They would blow them up and then let them go so they made farty noises as they flew around the room trying to escape, like panicked birds.

Uncle Roger had the wit and charm of his father and his grandfather, a slight lisp that the women said was "dead attractive" and, until he was over forty, like his father, he didn't marry. He said it was more fun to court. He was a rake and devil with the ladies and he drove a Stutz Bearcat with the cutout out so it would vroom.

It had been fitting that Minnie, the first of the daughters, the child of the Morrises who had settled the land, had come back there to die, that her sister, Myrtle, the Morris child who could not stay away, and that the children of Mr. Tompkins would not consider any course during the Depression but to come "home." In their mother's house were many mansions—little mansions within what they thought of as "the mansion" because years before it had been called that in old deeds. Home, to each of them, was a room under their mother's roof tree.

My parents had the front left bedroom with the wooden imitation of what had been the marble fireplaces down stairs before Addie and Mr. Cabot changed them. The room was the color of my mother's safety—green and white. Ivy wallpaper trailed down the walls. She took some of the Pineville furniture out of the shed where it had been stored while we were in Florida and made a frail nest of ownership. The twin beds were covered with tailored green-and-white striped bed spreads that she said were right. Things with her were always right or wrong—colors, manners, clothes, morals. There were still screws in the ceiling where Elsworth had hung his airplanes.

Aunt Myrtle's room looked over the spread of back lawn, to the far foothill where her Jersey cow grazed. It was her world, her color, and a view of what she considered her domain. She had brought back cream and pink French carved furniture from her marriage, she said, as if it were a place. She covered her dresser with an embroidered runner of little frail leaves and flowers, her bed with pink and white quilts she made herself. She had been given a long-legged French doll for Christmas and its arms and legs flopped across the ruffled pillows.

Aunt Myrtle made quilts every winter. The smell of rolls of cotton batting, gingham, scraps, the oil from the sewing machine, and the rhythm of the treadle, filled the second floor, while she thought of other things, and stared out of the window up Horse Mill Hollow. I went to sleep in the fall and winter to those smells of oil and gingham and cotton.

The next winter Aunt Helen and her husband, Uncle Mac, who had been in Mexico "with General Pershing," then in the World War, came back from downriver where they had lived beside a ravine and Uncle Mac had run a greasy spoon until the men lost their jobs at the local plant. The downstairs library where there weren't any books left was made into their bedroom. My cousin Nancy told me that she remembered lying in her cot set against the door to the dining-room and listening to them quarreling in whispers so nobody would hear them outside the room. She pretended to be asleep. It was almost always about money. She was not yet three years old.

My brother and Elsworth slept in the porch sewing room for a little while and then Elsworth moved in with his mother, making their own barricade within the greater barricade of the house. My bed was in the corner of the big bedroom that had always been called the cyclone. I could look into the sewing room through the window that had once been open to the upstairs veranda. It was where my cousins had been put to have whooping cough, and where I caught it from them when Aunt Myrtle decided it was time.

Addie's room was the most secret, the room for the woman my grandfather had called the finest lady in the valley to staunch her younger tears. The other rooms seemed gathered around it, as their owners were in life, with their little idlenesses and habits and their paler flowered wallpaper that would have been called then "the very thing."

Addie loved color and she wasn't about to have her daughters tell her what was "right." Right was what you had to look at all the time and what you liked. So without giving it a thought she had achieved, unknown to herself, and she wouldn't have cared if she had known, a deep elegance and magic in the master bedroom, scorned behind her back by her daughters, whose pastel "good taste" came from the *Ladies' Home Journal.* The Persian rug Mr. Tompkins had bought her was red, with blue and fawn designs that could have been flowers and leaves if you looked at them long enough. There was no green. She told me that the people who made it way yonder over there thought God didn't like green. They were heathens.

The "solid mahogany" high Victorian dresser had belonged to my great-grandmother. I had to stand on tiptoe when I was seven to see myself in the mirror. The surface was a wonder, level with my eyes. There was a silver-backed brush and mirror and nail buffer with initials carved in them that you couldn't read that my grandfather had given her for a wedding present, she told me. They lay on glass, easy to dust. To go under the glass so the mahogany wouldn't be scratched, she had made a long lace runner with lace flowers tumbling across it, a delicacy that made the rest even more rich and solid. There was a handkerchief box covered with little pearly shells she had brought back from Florida.

On the surface later, and as long as she lived, was the powder box that played a little tune that I had bought when I was nine and given to her for Christmas. I remember telling her that I had gotten it with my own earned money at Woolworths. All that fall I had knocked on doors and sold orders for Christmas cards out of a big book. My mother said you weren't supposed to tell things like what they cost about presents, but Addie was pleased. She like to see people stand, as she said, on their own two feet God gave them. The music box was right there in the middle of all the silver and lace and pearly shells. It was made of some painted metal that changed color when you turned it. I have forgotten what it played. I can only hear a small tinkle in the depths of my mind, too far away to call back.

When all of the others were in their rooms and she was in hers, sometimes she let me in, too. When she invited me in, I sat in a little nursing rocker and she sat above my head in the twin of the mahogany rocker with the needlepoint back in the parlor, and she talked about Mr. Tompkins.

"His manners were perfect. He never raised his voice to me," she said as she rocked. "But he did drink. God knows he did. Once I sent away for a Keilley Cure. You were supposed to put it in morning coffee and they wouldn't know, then after a while the licker would taste bad and they wouldn't drink no more. The ad said you could stop your husband drinking in six weeks. Well, all I got to say is they didn't know Mr. Tompkins. I even threw good money after bad and sent for two cures, and gave them to him one right after the other.

"About the tenth week," she said, "Mr. Tompkins said to me, 'Mrs. Tompkins, I hate to complain about the housekeepin, but don't you think we ought to change our brand of coffee? I can hardly get my morning brandy down any more.'"

Sometimes she would let fall, not a story, but a remark, out of the blue. "Oh, he married me all right, but he never was faithful to me, not for one day," she said once, and then not another word.

I remember wondering, when I should have been far too young to think such things, I suppose, which of the old ladies in the mean downriver town had unlaced her corsets for him. I could see Miss Nellie who drove an electric car, lying panting on the ground, or Miss Eliza who wore several chiffon scarves winter and summer, or Miss Rose, who dressed for dinner every night like the new people she refused even to meet, but who wore her comfortable Oxfords with it. She wore real pearls she said came down through the family when everybody knew they were bought with new coal money.

"One woman wasn't enough for him. He was triple-secked," she told me another day, opening up wonderful vistas of depravity as she rocked. Then a sigh, "He did try, though. God knows he tried . . ."

She said he never showed his licker, but she could not say the same for the younger generation who couldn't smell a bung hole without passing out on the floor. She supposed that was the boot leg licker those fool women had forced them to drink. Addie was wonderful at mixing politics, civil rights, morals, and Jesus, and coming out with an answer that contained them all. It took me a while to realize that she meant the Fourteenth Amendment which had been passed after the women got the vote, and which she said was all a piece of foolishness.

She had, long ago, sewn a patchwork jacket out of my grandfather's bright neckties, a cubist design of pink and green and red and purple and pale yellow silk long before anyone in that house ever heard of cubism. She called it her Joseph coat because it was made of many colors, quilted together with a delicate rickrack of black stitching that looked like chickens had left tracks across it. She would put it on when we talked. I had told her how much I loved it. But she never wore it outside of her room. Her daughters made fun of it.

All that summer, fall and winter, my mother sought her childhood by reading to me. She read me Sir Walter Scott who I didn't like but didn't dare say so, and then I read Robert Louis Stevenson, *Treasure Island* and *The Master of Ballentrae* and *Dr. Jekyll and Mr. Hyde.* I loved Robert Louis Stevenson. I took *A Child's Garden of Verses* to bed with me, and before I went to sleep I would say over and over, "Robert Louis Stevenson, Robert Louis Stevenson." That, which my mother chose, and *At The Back of the North Wind* by George MacDonald, which she gave me for Christmas, were my favorite books.

But the revelations of what life was really like were piled halfway up the wall paper with blood red roses, big ones, behind the bed in Addie's room. Sometimes, when I could get away with it, I took advantage of the neglect that is a gift to children when everybody is either taking a nap, or gone someplace else. I would watch out of the upstairs

French doors of the hall for Miss Addie to start down the back walk nobody used but her.

She had planted it with Rose of Sharon bushes so long ago that they were higher than her head. She would go into town in the afternoon for errands, and, I suspect, somebody to talk to, and then, like clockwork on Wednesday evening, to her church. It was her church, too. She had built it and kept the key.

Although she never knew it, and would not have admitted it, Miss Addie was the first person—not to teach me, but to leave around for me to find—the raw material of the kind of myth and poetry that first makes your hackles rise, not from fear, but from secret recognition. When she disappeared behind the Rose of Sharon, I slipped into the magic room and hid in the corner by her bed with my back against the wall so nobody or thing could creep up behind me.

Robert Louis Stevenson would have loved that corner. Piled higher than my head against the blood red roses were magazines. It was true poetry, not the awful stuff of James Whitcomb Riley, Edgar Guest, ridiculous Hiawatha, Ivanhoe who was sick all the time and nasty Elsie Dinsmore. It always made my hands hurt whenever I thought of her playing the piano for her mean papa.

Addie's magazines smelled of old newspapers. Their pages were not slick and white like *Colliers* or *The Ladies' Home Journal.* They were rough and tan. I could run my hand over them and some of the print would come off. They had wonderful names like "Ghost Stories," "True Pisic Phenomena" (at least that was the way I pronounced it in my mind), "World Beyond," "Spirit." Those were not their names, but their names were like that. They had wonderful drawings of manifestations and auras, misty figures and crawling things that looked like they were made of smoke or mud.

It was there in the corner of her room with my back against the wall that I first knew about the *House of Usher,* rewritten by some cynic for the pulps, long before I found Poe. The chimera, the hunchback, the ooze, the sphinx, the thing that climbed the stairs, the arm that reached all the way from the attic to the first floor in the hall to grab at your hair, the blob that couldn't die, and the ghosts of queens and their murdered lovers were in those books. It is not where they were first but where I saw them first that made me see Miss Addie's room when I read *The Inferno.*

Addie talked about ghosts and people returning from the beyond. She had experienced all these things and she would tell me about them— the Confederate soldier who had died in the attic who she could hear sometimes, walking around over her head, the hand that came up from the river that was all that was left of a drownded man who had been mostly eaten by catfish. She said he was coming back to beg to be saved because he had been a sinner and had fallen in the river drunk; sometimes in the night I could hear the wetness squish as he tried to get up the stairs. I learned to sleep with my head under the pillow. Addie understood the fear and that was why she came into the room often and slept in the other bed, the big bed, especially when the moon made too much light in the window and crawled along the pale painted chifforobe and reflected in its mirror.

One night the ceiling of the cyclone, made of heavy slate that had been there for nearly a hundred years, fell on my bed. It was my fear of oozie dead things, the fact that I slept with my head under the pillow that saved my life. Addie had slept in the big bed that night. She pulled the slate away and held me in her arms until I stopped shivering. She said she had a premonition. It was the first time I had heard that word. I said it over and over to myself, wondering what it meant, not wanting to ask.

Her tenderness was kept secret. Beside the gate on Miss Addie's walk that went down through the garden, and that nobody else seemed to use, partly hidden by the Rose of Sharon bushes, there was a shelf so the mail man could leave parcels without going all the way up to the house. I picked the blossoms off the Rose of Sharon, fixed them for fairy skirts and left them on the shelf, and every day when I went back they were gone and a nickel was there to pay me for them. Then I went to Jess Simmon's store, and I bought penny candy, everything but "lickrish." I bought caramels, and jaw breakers, and jelly beans and wax babies. When you bit their heads off they had sweet colored water inside.

Then Aunt Helen laughed when they were all in the kitchen talking, "She's conning a nickel out of her grandmother, acting like she believes in fairies. She doesn't fool *me*." I never did it again. I think that up to that time I had at least half believed in fairies, although I knew that a nickel was damned big for a little tiny fairy to carry, one that could wear a Rose of Sharon blossom for a skirt.

*I*t was spring when we arrived, just after school. Elsworth told me I would be put back a grade because my parents had dragged me around the country so much. I always knew what Aunt Myrtle was saying about my mother because Elsworth repeated it as something he had thought of himself.

Spring moved toward summer and we went to the creek to swim and try to catch crawdads that hid under the stones of the creek bottom; some of the stones glittered like jewels under water, but when I picked them up they were dull, just stones. A high rock, like a miniature cliff, had whirled the water for so long that it formed a pool that was about two feet deep at its deepest point. A big tree had wrapped its roots around the rock so that they looked like petrified snakes. It was our swimming hole. Elsworth told me that it was the place where Mr. Kelly had been found with his head scalped. His hair off. Elsworth said he read that that was the way they said it—hair off.

Elsworth dared me to walk the ties of the railroad bridge, high over the creek. He told me that if I was caught on the bridge by a train I would be killed and that if I jumped into the creek it was so shallow it would crack my head open and my brains would flow downstream all the way to the Ohio river, just like Mr. Kelly's. I didn't dare not take the dare, but I learned quickly to put my ear to the track and see if it hummed, which was the sound of a train coming, faintly, far away.

Summer turned to fall. Elsworth, my brother and I rode the school bus to Montgomery, ten miles upriver. I wasn't put back, which made Elsworth mad. We were both in the Fourth Grade. The rides back and forth were my favorite times of the day. I wasn't anyplace. I was in between.

In winter we came down to breakfast at six-thirty in the morning to a kitchen already warm. Aunt Myrtle had been up for an hour, had done the morning milking, and fed the chickens. If the weather was cold the kitchen was full of animals. She brought baby chicks in when it was too cold in the chicken house for them. She said she liked to come down in the morning and hear them cheeping all the way from the dining room. She had set the kitchen table with hot oatmeal and honey that Addie brought back from the woods, and milk still warm from the Jersey cow. Breakfast in winter was under the hanging ceiling light. The windows were still black outside.

Flo, Aunt Myrtle's Belgian Shepherd, lay in front of the fireplace and nursed her pups. Flo was really a German Police dog, but after the World War, the name of the breed was changed for a while. They adored each other, woman and dog. Whatever extra money Aunt Myrtle had, and it couldn't have been much, went for examinations every six months at the vets in Charleston. She said she had to breed Flo at every heat or her womb would drop, just like a woman. I see now that it was because Aunt Myrtle needed a litter of pups far more than Flo did, so the poor dog went around the whole time I lived there, dragging her pregnant body or her worn sagging tits, and falling in front of the kitchen fireplace with a long sigh.

When I got up in winter to dress, I chanted, "In winter I get up at night, and dress by yellow candle-light . . ." until my mother said it was driving her crazy. She put lamb's wool in the toes of my shoes so my feet wouldn't be cold on the bus and said, almost every time, that her daddy had put lamb's wool in her shoes every morning in winter when she went across the river on the ferry to school. She gave me loathsome codliver oil. She said the recurrent flu I had that winter had gone far enough, that I never should have been brought back from Florida for a winter because my blood was too thin. Addie reminded her that I had been caught in the flu epidemic of 1918 and that it was probably still in me. I could feel it running around in my blood.

When we rode the school bus we could see the few miners who had a day's work walking to the mines with their carbide headlamps lit against the darkness. From November to February we rode back and forth in the dark. In the evening, we passed miners, walking home from their shifts, their headlamps bobbing along the roads like lightning bugs.

Spring came again with broody hens, then more chicks. They were like Easter chicks until they shed their baby fluff. Then they looked as naked, and as gangly and awkward as I felt much of the time. The inevitable litter of pups grew up in the kitchen. Aunt Myrtle hated giving any of them away. They got bigger and bigger, like a gang of teenagers, following the lead dog, who pushed open the screen door with his nose.

It was through that year that I learned that there was only one place in the world that was "home." We had lived in other rooms, a lot of other rooms, seeking those vague chimeras, better chances. Before my father was married, it had been Oklahoma; then it was Kentucky; then Florida. But then, and still, there was only one tap root, one building, one door through which we all walked, led by my mother, who would release her body from its genteel tightness, literally spread her knees, and be more at ease than I ever saw her anyplace else.

But from the spring of 1927 through the summer of 1928, her pride outweighed her pleasure, and she seemed all that year to be distilled in shame and fury. Sometimes I tried to cheer her, even to make her look at me. Once, to make her smile and approve, I drank all my milk, which I detested, without being nagged. I touched her arm and turned over the glass to show that it was empty. A drop fell on the tablecloth. She slapped my hand and said, "Watch what you are doing!" She was trying not to cry. I never saw my mother cry in my life, but I heard her, then and later, stretched across her bed, crying over telephone calls from the grocery store, the milk man, the besiegers through the Depression years, asking for bills to be paid.

All the year we lived at Cedar Grove, the women moved past each other, preoccupied. It was Addie who paid attention, Addie who listened, and sometimes Addie who had to do her duty. When we didn't suit her, or did something she had expressly told us not to, she would walk slowly to her tree. It had supple branches. She would break one off and swing it against her skirt to get the heft of it. Then she would say sadly, every time, "If you won't listen, you'll have to feel," and land the branch on a bare leg with a singing swish.

Addie was worried about my mother, and I didn't know why. So she gave her fifty dollars she had saved from what the rest of the family called "The Tompkins Estate" and she called "a piece of property," which consisted by then of a couple of bigger houses in the town, the brick house on the hill above Horse Mill hollow, some town lots, a few fields, empty, abandoned slave cabins that had been built way up the hollow, slowly falling under the weight of wild vines, or turned into miner's houses that in the Depression were rural slums; and, of course, the Tompkins's hopes called coal, oil, gas, gold, silver, under the ground. I saw it all guarded by the same kind of trolls who threatened the Billy Goats Gruff.

Fifty dollars was all the money in the world that year. Addie told my mother that she had saved it "for a purpose," another of her favorite phrases that had the impetus of a command. She told her to go and buy herself "something decent" to wear. She said it always cheered her up.

My father drove my mother to Charleston and she came back with a brown silk dress that had a brown circular cape with burnt orange and fawn stripes. Everybody gathered around and felt it with their fingers. The smell of silk was different from the smell of cotton and gingham. It was edgy, like the *Evening in Paris* perfume I stole from Aunt Helen's room.

I have found a picture of my mother in the "outfit." She stands against the roses, one hip flexed, like a model, but she looks emaciated, trying to smile and not succeeding. Her eyes are again as angry as when she was fourteen after her father's death. If my father had not gone every day to Charleston to find jobs as quickly as he could through his network of school friends, and moved her away in a year, she would have died. That picture is the picture of a dying woman, fear and disappointment so deep that it lined her delicate skin. She was only thirty-two. Elsworth told me everybody said she had lost her looks.

Especially in summer, Cedar Grove was a haven for my cousins, a dumping ground for parents who had not yet moved back, and who were relieved to get rid of them for a while. The boys were a little like Flo's adolescent pups. They moved and played in packs. There were usually only three or four of them, but sometimes it seemed to me like an alien army.

Out of sight, out of mind must have been said first about the young who find, in large houses, that they have a secret freedom—the freedom of neglect. The grownups couldn't see us. They were too deep in their own concerns, and the talk raging among them.

So to amuse themselves and pass the time, my cousins taught me about sex in Uncle Roger's bedroom, which included taking their pants down to show me where he put the condoms. My older cousins also taught me fear. I was an apt and perfect pupil. After all, Addie had told me that lots of things that ordinary people couldn't see were manifest to those with the second sight, and I didn't even have the first sight. Anybody, meaning my cousins, could come up on my blind side and scare me out of my wits.

The attic at Cedar Grove was the most terrifying place I have ever known. There were spaces behind closed doors under the eaves that not even my brave cousins would crawl into. My cousins would lure me up there to play with them. I fell for it every time. Flattery, for a little while, was stronger than fear. I was entertainment for them because I became hysterical almost at once.

We sat in a circle on the linoleum floor. All along the walls were hump-backed trunks. Some of them went all the way back to 1820, and hadn't been opened since the family moved into the house in 1844. In the mornings I could see Addie in the vegetable garden far below, moving slowly through the grape arbor, or bent over, her ample gingham rear to the sun, forking up potatoes. If it was late afternoon when they caught me, I would watch for a kind of psychic reassurance, as she walked down through the Rose of Sharon path, dressed up to go into the town.

But neither flattery nor teasing would get me to climb those dreaded stairs at night—not then, and not today. I knew, because my cousins had told me, what was up there. There was the decomposed body of Aunt Minnie, hidden in a trunk. Her auburn hair and her fingernails had grown so much after she was dead that they filled the trunk so full that if you opened it you couldn't see a thing but hair and long, long fingernails, hiding her shriveled body. Her old skeleton arm would reach out and grab me. I never considered that Aunt Minnie had been dead less than a year.

There was the arm, too, that was three stories long, that had belonged to the wounded Confederate soldier hidden from the Yankees in the attic, that would reach all the way down and pull my hair when I walked through the front hall. For years I went down the stairs there near the wall, avoiding the open stairwell.

There was the hand in the darkness of the corner behind one of the trunks, still looking for my great-grandmother's table silver and pearls that she hid during the War and that had never been found. The fact that she lived for over fifteen years after the Civil War, and that she was so aware of what she owned that she sued an uncle for an apple-butter kettle didn't enter into this story. I could hear the hand scurrying across the linoleum. It sounded like a rat. They said it was trying to find the pearls in my hair. It was there, right behind me, crawling closer and closer to my blind side. I would, quite satisfactorily, bat myself on the head and dissolve into hysterical screams, scream after scream. I would half run, half fall, down the steep attic stairs to find my mother. She would grab me and say, "Don't let them see you afraid." She would put me to bed in her bed, which was a treat for me, hold my hand and stroke my forehead. "Don't let them know," she would whisper, as if she were saying it to herself.

I have wondered since if the face and touch of fear we conjured in the attic wasn't a substitute for the real fear we could do nothing about, not only because we were children, but because we were living through a brutal time. The true fear of those years had no name, no picture, nothing to see in the night, or touch, or drown in. It was a miasma worse than any child's thrill at ghost stories. It had no name. But it had a sound. Waiting. Heavy and wordless.

It permeated the rooms, whispered when the back hall telephone rang. On the hottest days of summer, grown people sat looking cold, waiting for "things to improve."

Few people born or growing up during those years of the Great Depression are free of it. In the coal fields it had started long before the recognized year of 1929. Like the Florida real estate boom, it, too, had burst in the mid-twenties. By 1927, the mines were working only a few days a week. I have been to war, and I carry both scars, but to me, the scar of what the Depression did to people, the guilt for existing when my parents couldn't "afford" me, has been more painful if less recognized.

Addie, my aunts, and my mother had seen their lives change so slowly they took it for granted: from green fields, riding horses, servants, farms, to coal towns on the same surface of the land. The "estate" was carved, smaller and smaller; more Jenny Lind houses were put up, more tenant shacks. It never stopped. I walked several miles up Horse Mill Hollow in the fifties. The last house, if it could be called that, had cardboard in the windows marked Crosley Radio Corporation.

I had made my liberal pilgrimages through slums in England, which are, or were, some of the worst in the world, monuments to class indifference, but I have never seen and smelled anything like that place. Rural poverty and despair has its own smell—rotted vegetation, neglected shallow privies, summer cholera. When I went back to the kitchen at Cedar Grove where my mother and aunts were sitting, almost in the same positions they had sat in when I was a child, I said, "Who has let people live like that?"

My mother laughed. "We own it. They are squatters. We don't get any money."

My aunt Helen said, "Give it to her. It's no good to us."

They laughed together and went on talking about things that were, to them, more important.

What seems brutality happens slowly, hardens, inures. In the midst of more coal dust, more railroads, and more fear, Addie, my aunts, and my mother wore their habits like armor. Every afternoon they cleaned up, brushed their hair, put on their good summer dresses. It was a ritual. About four o'clock in the afternoon they drank iced tea, and gossiped, and I listened. They spoke of sex and who ran off with whom, and sometimes even better, who had just walked off and left everything. They had, like the social protection they inherited from their parents, a siege mentality.

In World War II in London I saw this; women sitting, urgently casual, having tea. Their faces reminded me of home. When people speak of violence in the streets, I, and others like me, withdraw a little, not wanting to admit survival, not wanting to say, "Get used to it. This is the world you have made." There has been a fashion for writing about waste and empty lots by writers who have seen no trouble beyond what is personal, luxurious sadness producing lovely, drooping musical prose. In the face of that innocence I have been silent. It is, to me, the crying of children who have not been invited to a party that never was.

The aunts in their summer dresses that smelled of drying in the sun, were, as they say, "quite well aware." Coal country. The stories were taken for granted. The grownups had lived for so long in that harsh world they overlaid with doilies and good taste, that, to them, it was normal. The women talked easily about violence and disasters as they sat on the porch, rocking and reminiscing in the afternoon. I listened, hardly listening. The years before I lived there became real, repetitive, unheard, unforgotten. Terrible grownup stories are so often complacent voices droning over children's heads.

Years before, during the mine wars of 1923, the miners had announced a march on Charleston, the state capital. On the night of the march they gathered from all over the valley, the crowds of men growing as they poured out of the hollows and swelled the main stream of the march. The strike leaders, including Mother Jones, had warned everybody to stay in their houses or be shot.

That night the women were alone in the house. My quiet and lovely Aunt Violet was Uncle Bado's new bride, the daughter of Mr. Holland, the mine superintendent at a mine near Winona in Fayette County. My Aunt Helen was then twenty years old.

Addie watched from the parlor window as the marchers appeared in the distance up the night-dark hollow road from Ward, and began to pass the house. They carried pitch-pine torches that swayed and lit the sky. The march was noisy. Men shot into the air. They yelled and sang all at once. Aunt Helen kept saying, "Mother, please please get away from the window." Addie didn't move. She said she wasn't about to miss anything.

When the miners had almost gone, they heard the last of the gunfire down at the Kelly's Creek corner of the lawn. The noise of the march had passed and it was dark again, when Addie heard the weak voice of a man calling, "Miss Addie, help, I'm shot."

She didn't wait. She told Aunt Violet to come with her. They lifted a shutter off one of the long windows of the parlor and carried it down toward the creek.

A young boy lay at the side of the Ward road, bleeding. The two women put him on the shutter, carried him in, and laid him down on the floor of the front hall. Miss Addie told Aunt Helen to get towels to staunch the blood while she called a doctor. Back at the wall phone she called the two white doctors in the town. Both were afraid to come out. She hung up on each of them in turn while they were still explaining.

Finally she called Dr. Davis, the black doctor. She said, "Doctor Davis, are you a doctor or are you just a plain nigger?"

He said, "Mrs. Tompkins, you don't have to talk to me that way. What do you want?"

She said, "There's a man been shot. He's layin in my front hall, and if you don't get over here quick, he's gonna to bleed to death."

"Why didn't you tell me that right away? It's a good thing I'm black, isn't it?" Doctor Davis told her. "I can sneak around the back way and nobody will see me."

Dr. Davis must have run all the way. He was there to stop the bleeding in five minutes. He told Miss Addie to call the ambulance at the miner's hospital, the Sheltering Arms, across the river.

When they were waiting for the ambulance to come, the boy whispered to Aunt Helen, who was still kneeling beside him. "I've got a gun. If they find it they'll put me in jail. Will you hide it for me until I come and get it?"

Nobody ever knew whether the young miner lived or died. He never came back to get the gun. It stayed for years, unloaded and rusty, in the chifforobe drawer in the cyclone behind Addie's bedroom.

As long as I was growing up at Cedar Grove, either in the first years when I lived there, or later in the early Thirties when I was parked there with my cousins in the summer, I never really took in surroundings and events beyond the fence—and I never forgot.

The mine at Cedar Grove had had so many names. Then, in the twenties, it was called the Tompkins Fuel Company. Uncle Preston and Aunt Mary lived in Charleston. He went every day to an office in a bank building on Capitol Street where a McDonald's is now. I was afraid of the little, mean elevator. The company name was printed on the door of their office in gold letters.

Uncle Roger ran the mine. It limped along through the Depression. Addie said he came home dirty as a breaker boy. He said that if you wouldn't go into the mine with the men you had no business having a mine. I realize now that he was voicing the last, sad sense of responsibility of the patriarchal mine owners.

Most of the other mines had been bought for peanuts during the Depression by impersonal, solvent corporations whose offices were someplace else. When the grownups talked at the dinner table they talked a lot about "outside interests." Uncle Roger was the only one, Miss Addie said, who was worth a hill of beans although she didn't necessarily like him best, she would add. She said she couldn't help her likes and dislikes. They came from Jesus anyway.

Uncle Roger was courting a twenty-two-year-old school teacher in the tradition of his father. At nearly forty, he had decided to marry so he could have a son. One Saturday he let my cousin, Jean Michie, and me ride in the rumble seat of his Stutz Bearcat when he went to visit her at Ward, up Kelly's Creek. Her mother ran the clubhouse where the unmarried mine officers and visitors stayed.

We sped in his Bearcat past nearly a mile of makeshift shelters beside the road, where miners and their families had used whatever they could find to make places to live when they had been thrown out of the company shacks because they were on strike. Some had tents, but most of them had put together shelter for their families from anything they could find; big boxes that pianos were shipped in to the company stores, frames of raw wood hung with rain-stained and sun-faded quilts; blanket-covered sticks that made three-sided caves where small children sat in rows and stared at us as we passed, as quiet and watchful as litters of wild animals. We paid little attention. We were busy singing, "Put that cut-out in," to my Uncle Roger, teasing him.

When we got to the entrance of the town of Ward, there was a huge chain stretched across the road with armed guards at both ends. One of the guards saw who it was and lowered the chain to the road surface. I still remember the bump as we drove slowly over links of the chain at least six inches in diameter.

Ward was a ghost town. Only the clubhouse was occupied. We had tea, decorously, on the upstairs porch, watching while Uncle Roger impressed Polly Woodrum's mother.

There were terrible arguments that scared me at the dinner table. They called them conversations. That night the edged words that sometimes turned into shouts while Addie paid no attention were about the miners and their families who lined the road. One of the men said they were a public menace, and ought to be, "forcibly removed."

My mother stiffened. She asked, in that awful quiet voice she could use, "And where are they supposed to go?"

"Oh, of course, you're for them. You're just a Democrat," he said.

"How can you be a Democrat when your whole family are Republicans?"

She looked all the way around the table at her family. "Because I HATE Republicans," she said.

One of the "in-laws" who later became a member of "The Knights of the White Camellia," an anti-union, anti-black, anti-Catholic, anti-foreign, anti-Semitic group, interrupted. "It's all the fault of the goddamn Quakers. If they weren't up here feeding the bastards they would go back to work tomorrow."

"Don't use the Lord's name in vain," said Addie.

That was how I found out that the miners had been thrown out of their houses when they struck. I remember my Uncle Preston explaining it to me in that patient voice for stupid little girls who couldn't understand grown-up decisions, "You see, honey, the mine *owns* the houses; the miners *don't*. Of course when they won't work they have to leave so somebody can live there who will work."

Gradually I picked up new words for what he was telling me—yellow dog contract, and scab.

When the men sat on the porch in 1927, waiting for supper, there was a barrier of silence around them that we learned not to try to scale. The word my mother used for it was "worry." "Your father is worried. Don't worry your father." A mantra to protect him. The left side of his handsome face twitched. He had developed terrible headaches called *tic dolorosa*. When I learned the words *Via Dolorosa* I thought of my father on the porch, with his face twitching because, as Elsworth informed me, he "couldn't provide for his family."

He was suffering from the Depression, as surely as if he had caught a disease. He stared out over the front lawn where we were playing, but he saw nothing, only his worry. Worry is catching. The word ruled our lives. All my cousins who lived there or were dumped there in that front yard and around the creek or on the river, or whispering in the attic or daring each other, caught it and avoided our fathers. As the evening came on, lowered through the rambler roses and turned them dark before any of the other colors faded, and the lightning bugs began to show their lights, riding the air, they sat like frozen towers, saying little.

If I went too close I heard words that I did not know but always remembered: float a loan, foreclosure, condemnation rights. It was where I learned words for what they said, not what they meant to them. Condemnation, like damnation, was the right to be condemned. Was it a right? Or a punishment? There was nobody to ask. To them, these were words and phrases they had been taught to respect and fear. They were icons from the manic depressive economy they never questioned. They seemed to be sitting and waiting, day or night. We learned not to make any noise when they were there.

They were all loyal Republicans. They had made a choice that would govern the rest of their lives—either to believe in a hope that must have seemed so frail, because hope was the only road out the past that had brought them to the rocking chairs on the porch, or to believe only in a past that had it "gone right," their hopes would not have been so brutally crushed by forces so far beyond their reach.

They seemed perpetually to be listening. They expected themselves to be go-getters. There were no go-getters from 1927 to the early thirties on the porch at Cedar Grove. There were only the worriers, as if that itself were something they could do to change things.

At night they gathered in the kitchen as if it were the safest place in the house. All the aunts and the uncles could barely wait for Aunt Betty to clear the table from the dishes of the silent supper, clean the kitchen, and trudge off up Horse Mill hollow, so they could gather around the kitchen table, scrubbed white through the years, and play Setback.

"High Low Jick Jack and Game!" We could hear the shouts from the kitchen when we were in bed. They were the sounds of pleased grownups when the children were not around to, what was the term the women used? Cramp their style.

My Aunt Helen would call out, "Be there!" as she drew a card. Uncle Preston told stories about his prowess on the football field. I heard him say, "I broke my neck and still kept going," and they all laughed in a distance as close as the touch of my hand, as if it were a family joke the children had no part of.

One night they sat until late and forgot to send any of us to bed. I sat outside the screen door watching the lightning bugs and eavesdropping, wishing I were someplace else, unnamed. How did I already know that night that they were waiting there, playing Setback and clinging to a past glory that had already, so long ago, let them down? But I did know. They were waiting for the wall telephone in the back hall to ring and save them.

Finally the telephone rang the two rings for the house. My uncle Preston went to the phone and listened for a long time. Then he dropped the earpiece in its cradle and rushed, which I had never seen him do before, back into the kitchen.

"Gas!" he said, and they all made a single sound, talking at once. Happy. Relieved. Somebody made a joke and they all laughed. The whole atmosphere of the kitchen had changed. The overhead light seemed brighter. Load can be lifted from whole houses. Or whole rooms. The load, for a little while, was lifted from the kitchen.

They went on playing Setback, joking, calling out, "High Low Jick Jack Game." The telephone rang again.

My uncle walked into the back hall and picked up the receiver. He listened. This time he left the receiver dangling on its wire. I thought he had forgotten and went to reach high up and put it back in its cradle when I heard him say as he stood at the door of the kitchen, "Salt."

Salt was the nemesis of drilling for gas. Salt and gas too often lay at the same depth of drilling. It had been salt that had made the fairly short-term fortune in the 1830s, and that had given the family its pride and expectations, when William Tompkins had discovered a way to use the gas that came with the salt to burn in the salt furnaces.

Salt proved, over and over, their tormentor in the Depression—salt in the gas wells that the fathers drilled over and over, borrowed money for, speculated on, sat in the rockers on the porch at Cedar Grove and waited for. Once in a while, when they got tired of waiting, Uncle Roger and Uncle Preston would disappear into Uncle Roger's downstairs bedroom, rootle in the closet, and share a drink of clear moonshine out of a mason jar. It was supposed to be a secret.

Nothing was a secret from any of the grandchildren, we who lived hated loved and had our being on a different level, just as Addie told me the ghosts of the past lived in the same house, on the same ground.

*I*n the midst of ghosts, family, the Depression, too many people, daughters who didn't like each other very much, and secret sorrow for the death of her eldest daughter whom nobody ever mentioned, Addie lived alone.

For over twenty years as a widow, she had been welded by events into the chthonic woman I remember, used by her family as people use legends, to prove their lies, to react to, to fear. She had long since earned in the town the title of Miss Addie, the title that then was given to the Southern ladies she hated when they had inherited, held power, and reverted at last to the virgins they once had been.

Addie ran the property without either help or notice. She would pass the men on the porch as if they were in a different country, and most of the time she wouldn't say a word. The men were too involved with schemes and disappointment to recognize that the houses she collected rent from, rent that often then furnished the only ready cash, needed fixing.

She liked to have a grandchild with her, as she carried a board, a folding ladder, a sheet of tar paper for a roof. I went with her whenever she would let me, and carried a hammer and some nails. She said that if you wanted things done right you had to do them your ownself. What she was really doing was saving money, nickel by nickel. She climbed up and fixed the hole, the tear, the sagging of age, while I handed tools up to her.

I never heard her say a word against any of her sons or sons-in-law, but she did advise me as we walked. She had no problem with editing the Bible. One morning as we were walking toward Horsemill Hollow, she spoke out of something she had been thinking about, "No wonder," she said to nobody, but let me hear, "the weak will inherit the earth. They will have worn all the strong out." When, later, I found out that the word was "meek" it didn't seem to make as much sense.

We went out of the back gate and closed it with its heavy iron weight so the dogs and the chickens wouldn't get out. We walked across the back railroad tracks, laid before the turn of the century to bring coal down from Ward and Mammoth. In the bad times the grass grew between the ties.

In front of us was the main part of Addie's kingdom, Horse Mill Hollow. She said she owned the surface and the houses and the bees and the trees free and clear; but the "estate" owned the mineral rights where their mine disappeared under her hills for several miles. The rest of the family, who remembered, or thought they remembered, when the dirt on the window sills at Cedar Grove was pale chaff from the mill instead of black coal dust from the gob pile, never called it anything but Horsemill.

The wide mouth of Horsemill was dominated by two houses. One was the brick house up on the right hand hill where Colonel Bannister, who had fought for the South, had lived. The other was the overseer's house, right in the middle of the hollow entry in the widest field. Addie's cousin, Aunt Ellen, had lived there when my mother was a child. When I was there her relatives, Senate Martin and his brood of children tumbled out and around the once pretty little house, and the yard was a tangle of broken toys, old tractor parts, tires, and even a barber's chair that Senate had bought cheap. But behind the house, as neat as Addie demanded, a vegetable garden was foursquare upon the rich ground.

Addie told me that Aunt Ellen had had a pretty garden and curtains at the windows and nice furniture. She reminded me of the mahogany work basket with the curled legs where she kept her swatches of wool. She said Aunt Ellen had left her that in her will. Every time we passed she said Aunt Ellen was crazy for hanging plants and that her front porch was like a jungle. But she had long since left the perils of this wicked world and had found a home in heaven. Then she laughed.

"I used to set there on the porch with Ant Ellen. We used to talk on and on. One day we was settin there and a young girl come up the hollow and Ant Ellen she commenced to tearin that poor girl's reputation to shreds. How she done this and that and was no better than she ought to be."

"So I said, 'Ellen, you never have been a purty woman. You don't know how a purty woman gits tempted.'"

She was quiet for a long time, a little round grandmother who seemed tall to me, walking beside her. She wore the poke bonnet her daughters disliked. She had grown fat but she had been pretty, you could tell that, and I wondered at the time, not of course, knowing anything of the family scandal that we were surrounded by as by the vines that grew around some of the deserted, fallen houses up Horsemill, if she had been purty and tempted.

The houses near the foot of the hollow had been built for the household servants. They were still the best and strongest houses in the hollow. I could see that Horsemill had once been a little community, like an open jail with pretty gardens, where the overseer commanded the entrance.

In 1927 the "estate" that Addie ruled, fixed, cajoled, commanded, was a rural slum. Jenny Lind houses, as frail as prosperity in that deep cleft in the hills, had been built between the cabins, filling the space for miners and their families when times were good. They were all occupied. Whatever whitewash had been on them to protect the board and batten had long since been drenched off by rain and winter.

There were few men on those mornings. They were usually someplace else looking for work, or down by the tipple where Addie couldn't find them, or in the mine the few days a week Uncle Roger could keep it open.

Addie visited with the women. She was more at home with them, their easy conversations, their country pauses, than anyplace else except in her own room, the head of the dinner table, and in her garden. They seemed to take each other for granted. Addie told me some of the women were a lot younger than they looked. To me they seemed the lost color of the houses, and their clothes sagged like the vines. But in front of every house Addie owned, a garden was squared and kept up.

She never would have dreamed of putting anybody out of their house when the mines shut down and the men couldn't pay their rent, but she made them plant gardens. That was her rule. She would go along inspecting the gardens of tenants who hadn't paid a red cent of rent for as much as a year, she said, and who would have gone hungry if she hadn't watched them.

"If you don't lay down the law," she told me, "they would just lay there like a hog in a waller."

I followed her, imitating Addie, the owner of property in her own right, walking literally in her footsteps to keep up, agreeing with everything she said. And she said a lot, there in the summer mornings as we walked farther and deeper into Horsemill. "I don't bother them and they don't bother me," she told me.

The path got narrower, until at the end of the hollow, where it turned up between the wild trees toward the top of one of the little mountains, there was nobody, only the silence of the woods, the faint run of the creek on days when it had rained, and the hum of wild bees. Addie knew where the hives were. She wouldn't let anybody go with her to gather honey. She said the bees knew her. She wore a wide-brimmed hat with a big heavy veil like she was going to church in the woods.

The only Jenny Lind shack she didn't go to except when she had to was the bootlegger's who lived on the foothill behind the field where Aunt Myrtle kept her cow. They had a wild dog on a heavy chain, and they had put their pig pen across the front path. They kept a sow in it who was so mean she ate her own piglets, Addie told me, so that those revenuers who came up the hollow wouldn't go near the house.

We could smell it from the road—pig shit, summer cholera, rotting vegetation under the hot sun. They had protected themselves with a wall of country poverty. Addie walked through it when she thought she had to and told the women to bring their children for a glass of milk every day or they would hear from her.

Addie not only made her tenants keep their gardens. She worked her own garden, hoed along the rows of snap beans and peas that had crawled up dead branches balanced like teepees that she set for them where once, she told me, there had been real Indian teepees and where she turned up arrowheads with her hoe. She told me branches were better than anything else for peas and beans. They had more room to grow.

By June the garden was lush. She raised enough vegetables to feed the brood that worried on the porch and "lay down for a while" in the afternoon, sometimes in the hammock, sometimes flinging themselves across their beds with sick headaches.

Addie taught me to garden that first summer by giving me two seed packets, one of marigolds and the other of zinnias. She handed me a long pole with a sharp blade at the end. I didn't know what it was. She didn't tell me. "If you want the flowers to grow, feed and water them and keep the weeds out. God put plenty of food for them in the ground so long as them damn fools let it alone." She took for granted that I, at eight, knew who the damn fools were. "Now make yourself a long row, dig pretty deep so the roots can breathe."

We turned the new potatoes, and picked the corn she had shown me how to plant with pig manure at the bottom of the hole. Sometimes she said the three seeds she let me drop into the stinking holes were one for the birds, one for the Lord, and one for us. Other times she said they were for the Father, the Son, and the Holy Ghost. We carried water from the well in buckets, across the backyard and along the rows. When the Catawba grapes were ripe I carried the basket and she reached up and freed them from the vines on the arbor over our heads that made such a romantic walk, and sometimes we sat down on the ground together and ate grapes, staining our fingers with the purple juice.

The other cousins played together. They were older, and male, and I realize now she took me with her because I didn't have anybody to play with. I never did learn to play, as in "play like." It was all real, and you could eat it and smell it and drink it.

So I learned and still learn from Addie, as in so many things. I learned to wait, to watch every day for the dead seeds to show a hint of green, my own seeds, then green shoots. She showed me how to thin them out.

She said "The Lord sure is profligate," surprising me with a big word I had only read and never heard, and throwing the seedlings away muttering, "Some fell among rocks. Oh Lord, how long?" I recognized then her inner voice which so often erupted and crept out of her mouth in a whisper as if it needed more space. She lived by the Bible which she read every night when she went to bed.

I have planted gardens ever since—a garden in Essex in England, an allotment in Oxford, a garden in Turkey which, when the water dried up in the town, I tried to keep alive with Coca-Cola. It didn't work. To watch a garden die from lack of water is to know dying, how slow it is, how life struggles for a last gasp of here and now.

*A*ddie had her own religion just as she had her own poke bonnet and her own way of talking and her own opinions. She was a Church of God Holy Roller, and she rubbed the family's noses in it whenever she could, so maybe my mother was right when she said Addie did it for revenge. But through the years it had grown beyond revenge into a way of living in the world. For her it contained passion and mystery instead of the straight-backed, cold-hearted Presbyterianism she had suffered from her enemies.

Every Wednesday night she put on her hat and her black coat, winter and summer. The coat was what she called store-bought, but she made all her dresses herself. She wore a grey voile dress in summer, and in winter a black bombazine, with a lace jabot like the one I saw later in pictures of Mother Jones. She walked down the side garden path in the late summer light, or in the winter dark, never missing a Wednesday. Nobody from the house ever went with her.

Every summer Holy Rollers wandered from valley to valley for Revival meetings. Preachers would turn up at the front gate with their bedraggled families, thin, shy wives and children, dressed in sun-faded hand-me-down gingham that made us whisper and giggle when we were out of Addie's hearing. At those times Addie took over the attic.

She pushed the trunks that held the family's past back in the corners. She made her grandsons help her, catching them before they left for the river. She didn't care that the trunks held not only the dead and festering bodies my cousins swore were there, but my mother's legends, too, some real, some hoped. My mother said that Miss Puss and Miss

Boonie's ball gowns they wore to White Sulpher Before the War were there, and their kid gloves, still in tissue paper, and their fans and their dance cards. Addie shoved them all back as if they were rocks in her way, and put up old First World War army cots that were never used any other time. She spread sheets on the cots, and opened the dangerous floor-level windows at both ends of the attic to air out the musty frightening smell. She put back the iron trellises that were always over them that my mother said had once held roses from Woods in Richmond. The windows were never opened any other time.

Sometimes there were as many as four families up there. I could hear them, shuffling and whispering, like the pigeons that lived in the eaves and that my cousins said were ghosts moaning. At night I could hear Addie talking with them, their voices going on and on and on all the way into sleep.

When the preachers and their families left Addie told them to wash the cot sheets, and they hung them on the back clotheslines with all their clothes for the next revival. For a day the wash would look like something, according to my Aunt Helen, that the cat dragged in.

I always tried to catch one of her preachers in the bathroom but I never could. I think they must have been embarrassed in the big house, and so the scrawny men, their slat-bodied wives and their towheaded children crept around so nobody could see them.

My mother wouldn't let me play with the children. She said I might catch cooties or something worse, but she didn't say so in front of Miss Addie. The children dragged up and down the steep attic steps behind their parents, making little noise, almost trying to hide behind them like little ghosts themselves.

Aunt Betty cleared the table after the preachers had eaten and gone to the evening session of the Revival, and made it again for the family. She said they ate like a pack of wolves. These were the children of Depression and empty roads and day coaches and street corners that, for a week or so, the length of the Revival, had found enough food, and a roof over their heads.

I never considered what they must have thought of us until years later. They must have seen the worried men, the frightened women who were my parents, my aunts and my uncles, as rich people. They had enough food. They lived in a big house, they dressed like people in another world, so that the overalls and galluses of the men who slipped past them on the porch were a living sign, like a banner, that they were different.

Addie's easy familiarity with Jesus seemed to be there always; she filtered her stories through that awesome approval. It provided her with a background that I remember better than I attended then, and the authority, straight from Jesus's mouth, to tell her family what to do.

She always sat at the head of the table and served the meat and Uncle Roger sat at the foot and served the vegetables. Each of us had our places, and our napkins in their silver rings. Children sat by parents. It was the same for all the years we had dinner at that table.

Addie said a blessing that went on for about ten minutes, while Aunt Myrtle fumed about the food getting cold, and the smell of meat and pickles and fresh homemade bread haunted us. She began the same way every time. "We will now bow our heads in prayer." Then she went around the table to every grownup who was there with her harsh messages from Jesus. She prayed for all of them, even the ones who then lived in Charleston.

"Oh Lord, spare Berthy's children from suffering from her terrible habit and make her seek Thy strength to quit it." Poor Aunt Bertha was a bender drinker. When she retired to her bedroom in a rose-sprigged dimity nightgown with a bottle of gin, the aunts said she had the flu.

"And dear Lord keep Ernest Michie from spending all his time in a poker game at the Ruffner Hotel, leaving that poor woman home where she ain't got nuthin else to do but drink." Uncle Mick was my Aunt Bert's husband. When he finally realized that she was lonely, he bought her a parrot.

I could feel my mother stiffen when Miss Addie got closer to her. "Oh Jesus, we talked so many times about Rachel's overweening pride. Oh Lord spare us her lordin' it over everybody when she ain't got nuthin to lord it over lesser mortals about." She passed over my father. In-laws tended to be spared. Whether she liked them better or felt that they weren't any of her business, I never knew.

Having passed over him she let fly at her favorite, my oldest uncle Preston, the child born at the dawn of my grandparents' passion. Her voice began to sway and sing, "Oh Jesus, keep Pressie from the awful despair that overtakes him because he wants to be again like them useless Tompkins's used to be and get rich quick and he hates to toil and moil like the rest of the world. And Jesus help him get over that Tompkins mean streak." Usually Uncle Preston and Aunt Mary were in Charleston so he only got her instructions to him through Jesus on Sundays when the whole family gathered for Sunday dinner.

Then she got to Aunt Myrtle and the prayer was always the same, "Oh, Jesus, make poor Myrtle understand it's no use."

These crushing admonitions, or others like them, depending on what her grapevine had brought back to her about her children, happened every evening, and when she was finished with them, all around the table, she ended with, "and when we are through with the perils of this wicked world, give us a home in heaven. Amen." There were no private vices or hidden sins in her family. She saw to that.

Out of sheer relief, and to break through the pall of silence above us, the grandchildren began to accuse each other of peeking, and the prayer was forgotten in the noise of dinner until the next hard wisdom was ladled out before the food.

Sometimes she turned her religion full force on one or the other of the children. The first I heard about what she intended for me was in an argument with my mother. Addie said that anybody who didn't believe in miracles was a damned fool. Damned fool and city tacky were her two terms of abuse. City tacky had to do with people who "had to take out a mortgage," wore clothes that all matched, and didn't look after their piece of property.

She said she was bound and determined to take me to a healer who would make me see out of a left eye that had been nearly blind since I was three. My mother absolutely forbade it. She said to Miss Addie over my head, "This child is too susceptible. I have enough trouble with her, high-strung as she is."

As soon as I was left at Cedar Grove with my mother out of the way, Addie, one Sunday morning early, told me to get dressed because she was taking me to church. I put on my church clothes, strapped patent leather shoes, white knee socks, the clean white underwear in case I got in a wreck, a little beaded bag, a voile dress with embroidered flowers around the neck. Addie had told one of the tenants to drive us. We sat in the back seat of her black Buick that she never drove, and instead of going down into the town to her church, we drove about fifteen miles downriver, nearly to Charleston.

It wasn't a church at all, and nobody but Miss Addie and me had their Sunday clothes on. It was a huge tent like a circus tent that smelled of heat and the sawdust on the earth floor. The color of the canvas was tan, so that the sun on it made a holy light inside. The sawdust smelled sweet. The tent was packed with people, sitting on plank seats. I sat there listening and not listening to a preacher who said it was in the power of Jesus to heal anybody who was worthy. When the sermon was over, people started getting up and talking about themselves. Somebody was barking like a dog. Somebody else was singing all alone. People were beginning to sway and call, "Oh Jesus!" over and over. Some people were yelling but not saying words, just noises. I was scared. Addie whispered that they were bearing witness to miracles and speaking in tongues. One woman swayed back and forth like she was keeping time to some music only she could hear and she called out, "I had fourteen stomick operations and then I come to Jesus," over and over.

A couple of rows of plank board seats in front of us, a quiet man had fallen to his knees, and I knew he was completely alone there with all those people, and all that noise. He was almost whispering, but I could hear him, "God forgive me, please God forgive me."

Addie got up, and she must have been a commanding presence even there with all those strangers, because everybody stopped bearing witness. She said, "I have brought this poor afflicted child for you to pray for so she can gain back her sight that sin has taken away." I wanted to tell her that it wasn't sin, it was whooping cough and an operation to make me pretty instead of cross-eyed, but she went on, "Will you all bend your knees to Jesus and pray for this disabled child that He will vouchsafe to give her back the sight of her left eye?"

The full tent of people shuffled and groped and fell to their knees; it sounded like huge birds landing. I was left there alone, sitting up in the tent. They began to pray, first one and then another, including Addie who was kneeling beside me in the sawdust, her elbows on the bench and her eyes tight closed as if she could see and talk to Jesus inside her head. She had pink patches of sweat on her forehead under her Sunday hat.

I had no doubt at all that the miracle would happen. I was interested in when. So while they prayed I kept closing first one eye and then the other, light, dark, light, dark, to see just when Jesus would vouchsafe me sight in my left eye.

When the meeting was all over, Miss Addie brushed the sawdust from her black dress and we got into the car. As we were driven back up the river, I kept telling her that I could see a lot better. I didn't want to hurt her feelings, and I didn't want to admit I had been too sinful and unbelieving for anything to happen. So, sinful in the sight of Jesus, I went on wearing my glasses.

We were not the only ones to share in her massive and all encompassing familiarity with Jesus. Every January Addie went to Florida alone. She said she didn't want anybody to go with her. So she would get into the Buick with her suitcase to be driven to the train, and she would be dressed exactly as old ladies dressed then—the black coat, a black dress, the black hat with flowers on it that she wore to church, the kind of shoes she sent off for that didn't hurt her feet. She would settle herself slowly into the back seat and never look around to wave goodbye.

After Lindbergh flew the Atlantic in June of 1927, he seemed to stroll into everybody's life. I think that there has not been a hero since with that pure quality of presence to people who would never see him, imagine being with him, all free in the air and brave. He walked in mist, that tall, thin figure, through our imaginations, replacing knights and fathers, and older brothers, and movie stars. All that summer we sang, "Lucky Lindy up in the sky, lucky Lindy, flying so high . . ." I can still hear the tune. I played it so many times on the wind-up Victrola, that one of my aunts said, "I wish to hell I'd never heard of the damned Atlantic ocean."

Miss Addie had her own way of recognizing this gigantic feat. In January, 1928, she went to Key West to the Pan American building and bought a ticket on the first overseas commercial flight. It took an hour to fly ninety miles over nothing but water from Key West to Cuba.

The building is still there, one of the prettiest in Key West, casual and white, with the sun and shade making patterns on the wide board floors, a spacious twenties bungalow where Addie would have sat in one of the white wood deck chairs in her grey voile dress because it was hot, with the breeze touching her grey hair, waiting with four other passengers to be driven to the air field. There were eight wicker chairs on the plane for the passengers, but only four people had had the courage to sign on. Addie, at sixty-three, in her black hat and her grey dress and her sensible shoes, was one of them.

The plane was a trimotor Fokker F7. The crew hoisted her up the little ladder into the plane, and I can see her settling herself down the same way she snuggled her bottom and made herself comfortable in the back seat of the Buick.

Down below, two mechanics swung the propellers until the engines fired, and the plane began to shiver, then lift, and they were airborne.

A young man was huddled in front of Addie; she said later the poor thing was grey with fear. So she leaned forward and tapped him on the shoulder.

"Son," she said, "I talked to Jesus last night, and He told me He was going to look after me. Now he can't look after me without looking after you, so set back and enjoy yourself."

It took years to realize what Addie's religion stood for besides Jesus. One day I went to a huge revival in a convention hall on a Sunday afternoon. I wanted to hear the singing. There were two thousand people there. I went up into the balcony and found a seat in the crowded place. When I had been sitting for a little while, I began to be conscious of a withdrawal around me, an isolation from the people sitting so close to me. The singing of the hymns couldn't break through it. I finally made myself look around at the man next to me. He looked at me with a hatred so pure, so final, that I found a pause in the preaching and the singing and left. I was shivering.

I had been dressed differently, fed differently, had been given the luxury of courage because of the way I looked. What poverty and harshness I had endured, I had chosen, not had thrust upon me. I was encased in the armor of class that had been my parents' dedication to what I considered a set of useless mores. They had provided a barricade against the abyss of the anonymous struggle to survive. I had, for a little while, felt the hatred it engendered.

Nobody can say that religion is not economic, political, and social. The fundamentalists in this country, the fundamentalists in the Middle East, the Hasidim, the Shiites, have all in the past been brutally dispossessed, and their descendants have in them the genes of revenge.

Addie had it, too; it was personal with her. She had thought, sometime in her youth, out of the vast naivete that is young hope, that she could cross some imaginary line and rest in peace, but she had learned that it was not to be, not in the perils of this wicked world, only in what she called "a home of heaven."

There is a terrible Southern saying, "Some people can steal a horse, other people can't look over the fence." In spite of Addie, I was being trained to steal horses.

I never heard a kind word said about my Aunt Myrtle by her half sisters. It was otherwise with her nieces and nephews. We loved her. A child herself who still loved dolls, she was a fount of plain, daily, touching, affectionate love in the house.

She had been the only blonde. By the time we were back at Cedar Grove in the twenties, her hair, like all the others except my mother's, was short. She wore a washboard "marcelle" in a hay-like permanent that made the waves stand like a halo within a few days. She renewed the permanent until her death when the blond had turned, without anyone noticing, into grey—not grey—she wasn't allowed even that, but a faint yellow like old egg shells.

My mother and my aunt said she never turned her hand to do a thing, that her favorite ploy when the men were there, the men being gentlemen callers from the mines, those who were "nice," i.e. management, was to run out on the porch and announce "Dinner's ready! I've warmed the plates and everything." That was so far from the truth about the Aunt Myrtle I knew and loved that they could have been joking about another person.

While Addie took charge of the garden, Aunt Myrtle took charge of every living thing, children, broody Leghorn hens, baby chicks, white turkeys, the shoats, Flo's pups, the Jersey cow that she milked every evening, and sometimes in the morning, too, when the milk was heavy.

She let me go with her to milk the cow. She called, "Soo cow," only once. The cow, like all the animals, came at once to her call and butted against Aunt Myrtle's arm while she laughed and petted the hard boney head, and said, every time I went with her, "Look at those big beautiful eyes."

Then she sat down on the stool I had carried—it was my payment for being allowed to go with her—and thrust her head against the cow's flank. She didn't move for a minute; she seemed to be feeling some kind of peace through the cow's breathing hide. Whatever it was it made me catch her silence, so that when she wrapped her hands around the cow's udders, the fine stream of milk hitting the bottom of the tin pail sounded almost loud. She tried to show me how to milk, but I couldn't. I shrank from the touch of the cow's udders, and the cow caught the message and tossed her head, but Aunt Myrtle quieted her and said not to worry, that my hands weren't yet big enough. She carried the milk back to the milk house and poured it into one of the waist-high milk cans. After that she lost interest in what was done with it.

Addie inspected the milk, poured some of it into a separate can and when enough cream had formed and soured she got out the churn, poured the creamy milk into it and sat like a woman playing a cello on the back porch while the sound of the churn went on and on until the butter floated in globs on the top. She formed the butter into big pats with her hands and stamped the top of the pat with an old iron shape with the indent of a cow on it. So, to the rhythm of the churn, a-thunk-a-think-a-thunk as if Miss Addie were willing it to form butter, I wandered around the back yard and the back porch with the sound following me.

Aunt Myrtle had, without anybody but my mother being very aware of it, changed a lot of things around the house to make it nearer to her heart's desire. She had made my mother's playhouse into a second chicken house. She kept the old chicken house next to it for the broody hens. She whitewashed everything so that the neat line of pigsty, corncrib, the two chicken houses, looked like a little village street.

The corncrib had been there since the house was built. It was a latticed shed on stilts with a high-pitched roof to give the corn plenty of air, like a small tobacco barn, only much prettier. I loved the shape of the steep roof and the sides that were narrower at the bottom than at the top. I thought it looked like the witch's house in Hansel and Gretel.

It was Aunt Myrtle who pushed the sow aside to take her piglets away so they could grow into shoats in Senate Martin's pig pen, rented for the price of one of the shoats. She didn't turn a hair when it was time to kill and the pigs' screams, like a woman in terror, rang through the hollow. She had given them all names. They sounded faintly English: Reggy and Ronald and I remember William the Conqueror. She kept a big hand-colored picture of the Prince of Wales in an Argyll sweater in her room. Maybe Mr. Palmer had been English. Nobody ever said.

In the summer when my cousin, Jean, and I were sent to stay at Cedar Grove she took us down to Mr. Calderwood's store. It was cool inside, no matter how hot the walk along the dirt road beside the railroad track had been. Mr. Calderwood left the dark green blinds drawn over the big windows to keep the store cool, which made it dim and mysterious. Sun dust danced in the shafts of light that escaped the blinds.

Hoes, rakes, and scythes hung shadowed along the ceiling. When there was a breeze they moved a little and sighed on their hooks. Mr. Calderwood had a long pole with a snagger at the end like a frog gig to loosen them from the hooks and lift them down. The long room was scented with great cylinders of cheese, slabs of corned beef, a barrel of dill pickles, apples in sawdust, greens and corn and runner beans and penny candy. Mingled with it all was the smell of bolt after bolt of cloth.

Mr. Calderwood, who was an old man, and who had been there since my mother was a child and played Little Eva in Uncle Tom's Cabin in the room over the store that the whole town used for meetings, would move slowly around behind the counter that ran along both sides of the store, from the meat counter at the back where he usually sat when there weren't any customers.

We would follow him on the outside of the counter, just as slowly, toward the scent of new gingham and silk and serge and denim and canvas, bolts of it, piled all the way to the ceiling, colors of jelly beans, sky, grass, and mud.

We always chose the jellybean-colored cotton, and Mr. Calderwood just as slowly as if the whole thing were very important, which it was, lifted the bolts down, measured the cloth, and said, every time, that we had grown a lot. I remember picking yellow and a wonderful lavender, and once, pink, since I wasn't allowed to wear it any other time because it didn't go with my auburn hair.

Aunt Myrtle bought what we chose and paid for it out of her own money. She said it was a present. She let us watch her make the dresses. Another sound that comes back when an insect, or a lawn mower far away in the distance reminds me, is the treadle as she pumped the fancy wrought-iron floor of the sewing machine and the cloth ran under her fingers as she shaped a sleeve made of a ruffle, the long whirr and flying feet as she turned the tape around the top of the hem. She measured us, saying every time how much bigger our waists were, how much taller, oh how we had grown. The dresses were always the same. She made the bodice and the flared skirt down to our knees. The sleeves stuck up like little wings. She told us stories as she finished the hems by hand, most of them about what was happening around us, how many chickens, how she was planning for the next brood.

Every time, when I took my dress back to our house in Charleston, my mother put it away. She said it was all right to wear it at Cedar Grove, but not in Charleston.

Aunt Myrtle seemed to have no past, not like the others. She lived, in those days, entirely in the present, concentrating on the dresses, which she made in an hour or so, and then letting us trail down the back steps behind her for her next duty, with Flo drooping along behind us. She said once that you never had to exercise a dog in the country if you just let it follow you around as you did what you had to do on a farm.

It wasn't a farm anymore; it was four acres around the house, a hillside for the cow, a few lots in the town, a corn field, and tenant houses, but she treated it, and so did Addie, as if it were the old thousand-acre cup of a valley before anybody else got there, or there was coal dust and trains shunting, and poor families with unemployed fathers who straggled down to the back porch and asked politely for drinking water, hoping for something more, which they always got. Addie would stand at the milk house door with a ladle and see that every child had a full glass of milk.

In the late afternoon, when everybody had quieted down, and the whole place buzzed with a silence made up of slight breeze, insects, a dog snoring, and no talk from the sisters who were in their rooms having their rests, Aunt Myrtle would cook.

Cakes, chutneys, jellies, pies—one, the chiffon pie, was the subject of my first published poem. Only somebody edited it and used the word "punkin" because it scanned, and sounded cute. I hated pumpkin pies. And "cute." Hogs ate pumpkins. I didn't like the taste, and I didn't like the word, to say it, the sound of it.

Aunt Myrtle she makes CHIFFON pies, us kids we look with hungry eyes. . . .

That's all I remember. I was deeply influenced at the time by James Whitcomb Riley. I had written some poetry and everybody crowed about it; my mother said, "I always knew she would be a writer, like I would have been if I hadn't married."

It wasn't mine any more, but it was published under my name, my first publication in the *West Virginia Review* when I was ten years old. Or nine. I don't remember. It had been made into lies. I had said chiffon pie. Then and there, standing on the stairs at Cedar Grove, aware of being the only person in the history of the world to stand just in that place at that moment, I swore on the altar of God, a phrase of Mr. Jefferson's who we were studying and who my father said we were kin to through the Carrs, that I would never write another word in my whole life.

Aunt Myrtle saw Elsworth and me out of the back door and down through the town to the river on summer mornings to take the john boat and raise the trot line he kept across the river. Often it had been cut by passing barges, but during those summers there was so little coal shipped that the trot line stayed just under water, waiting all night for the catfish, and once in a while a bass, to take the bait.

She never considered our safety. It was our pleasure and our joy that concerned her. Like a child herself she sent us to do what she had done when she was little, but she never put it that way. It was just what you did. I don't think my mother ever knew that in summer I was down on the river long before I could swim, holding the john boat steady with the oars while Elsworth unhooked the fish. There never were many, but being on the water before the morning river mist had lifted, when you could hear the frogs from the bank, and the whole world seemed to be yawning and waking up is to tie you to the river forever.

I once wrote, *Where there is a cut, there will be a freshet; beyond the freshet, a spring branch; beyond the branch, a creek; beyond the creek, a river, flowing and interflowing like the capillaries, the arteries, the veins of a man. But where it flows from, only the underbrush, the high trees, the silence, and in the midst of the silence the mountains, the Endless Mountains.*

I wrote it years ago, in the beginning of *O Beulah Land,* when I lived in England, and was calling forth my own memories of the American rivers that were the maps of our wanderlust, the route we took to settle the country. It is still true, the gathering of waters, the silence, the trees. Now the Endless Mountains are called the Alleghenies.

When your childhood has been spent on the river, the river will, wherever you are, flow through your dreams forever. It is the first measure of direction you learn, upriver and downriver, long before east or west or north or south. We learned to trace the way to the ocean from the creek where we caught crawdads under the rocks. Childhood on the river was the place of secrecy and silence.

At the raising of the trot line in the dawn the water was so still under its veil of dawn mist that only the hollow thrum of the oars in the oarlocks moving a fan of water on the surface, could be heard, that and the sound of shore birds and the plosh of water rats or snakes or beavers from the shore as they slid into the river to find their food, as we did when we raised the trot-line across the river, always hoping to find fish.

We stayed until the sun melted off the mist, the river was like shining glass, and the dragonflies flirted with the surface of the water. We were waiting for the first paddle wheel down river, so we could do what was forbidden, ride the stern waves, daring each other to row so close we were showered with the spray.

The river was my test of bravery, my entry into growing up. I learned to swim there all alone. It was at Glen Ferris. The town had been called Stockton after Aaron Stockton's house, but it had been renamed when the metallurgical plant came to squat below the house at the edge of the falls to suck in its energy. When I decided that it was time, I slipped down one early evening and sat by the river where a swimming place had been built above the falls with an L-shaped concrete wall to slow the current and make a large pool ten feet deep. Nobody was there. I had it to myself. I sat for a long time, getting my nerve up, and then I let myself fall in, and struggle across the open side of the triangle of concrete, dog paddling until I reached the far point of the wall where steps had been made. Nobody ever knew I had done it. I just couldn't swim and then I could swim. My parents thought I learned at the children's swimming class in the pool that my father built for their country club.

I still huddle there, eight years old, on the stone quay, and make myself small until I finally get the nerve to jump in and swim across the long side of the right angle triangle, clutch the far rocks of the pier at last. It taught me that whatever it was, I *could do it*. Every year I still go on the river for the day in a bateau. Now the river is the James, flowing east. I still love the silence and the timelessness, the quiet hidden dangers, the flowing water.

Sometimes in the morning when we came back from the river, Aunt Myrtle would have packed a lunch for Elsworth and me so we could hike up to the cliff that looked over the town. We walked a mile up Horsemill past the shacks and the pigpens and the little gardens. Beyond the last house where the road shrank into a narrow woodland path; we turned up the steep hill through the woods to the cliff, grabbing for little branches to pull ourselves up.

All the way I prepared myself for the jump across what must have been only a foot but which seemed a huge chasm. It was a deep cleft in the rock. Elsworth told me that if I fell into it they would never be able to get me out. He said it was a hundred feet deep. It couldn't have been because the cliff was only twenty feet high at the front, and level with the hill at the back. But I couldn't see the bottom so I took his word for it. We had to jump across it to get from the back of the cliff to the front where we could sit and eat our sandwiches and watch the family far far below, toy figures moving their habits back and forth, Addie going out of back door and across into the garden, Aunt Myrtle counting her chickens *after* they hatched, Elsworth said. My mother and my Aunt Helen were tiny figures sitting on the upstairs back veranda. Elsworth said they never turned their hand. We ate on top of the world, far above the Big House and the little town that seemed, from so high, to be gathered in its shadow.

Elsworth always took an air rifle, in case. What it was in case of he wouldn't tell me outright. Once we saw a wildcat streak up through the woods, and once, the faint hint of a disappearing fox.

One day we were walking back from the cliff down the hollow road. A huge black snake lay all the way across it, at least ten feet long, and fat, like a python. He told me to stand "perfectly still" if I didn't want to get hurt. He rested the rifle on my shoulder. He told me to hold my breath. He shot twice. Both times he hit the snake's head. It struggled off into the woods and we went past. "It will stay alive until sunset. They always die at sunset," he told me, as if he killed snakes every day, resting his rifle on my shoulder. We never told about the snake for fear we wouldn't be allowed to go back up Horsemill.

When Aunt Myrtle sent us to the cliff, she said we had to get out before Miss Addie found us and put us to work. That was the dark side of Aunt Myrtle, and it took years to realize it. She didn't like grownups, and she wanted the children to herself. So she gently told us, whenever she could, where Addie or our parents had gone wrong. It didn't take as far as I was concerned, with Miss Addie. It did with my poor mother, who was trying her best, when she remembered, to bend the twig another way.

The first winter, when there was no money, she managed to send me to dancing lessons with the two daughters of the Ward superintendent, who were "nice." They were being schooled at home by their Yankee mother by the Calvert Method. I guess she forgot that she was never going to let me learn to dance again as long as she lived.

Every week, a small, aging woman wearing a purple velvet beret, which she never took off, rode the bus upriver from Charleston to teach us ballet. She put a Viennese waltz on the windup Victrola and we waddled around and around on our toes to the music. She called the chair backs she lined up for us to cling to, the *barre*. The only French I learned before I was in high school was, *Barre. Position un, deux, trois, quatre, cinq . . . plié, plié, plié*, while we stuck out our little behinds.

My mother also taught me to recite, because I had to do it at school. She chose Little Orphan Annie as my "piece." She had better taste in poetry than James Whitcomb Riley, God knows, she told me as she put a brown hair ribbon in my hair, and tied my sash in back of her favorite dress, a brown and white gingham. But she didn't tell me what it was, though. She said I was still too young. Too young for something.

On Sundays Aunt Myrtle got up at five o'clock in the morning to get ready for Sunday dinner. My cousin told me that she once helped her and that her feet hurt for a week. All my aunts and uncles, my parents, and whatever children they could corral, went "home" on Sundays from wherever they lived in Charleston until there was nobody left at Cedar Grove.

After we went to live in Charleston, we would pick up Jean when Aunt Bert had "flu" and take her with us. We sat in the back seat, hoping to get there in time to help string and snap beans, but even more, to watch Aunt Myrtle catch the white Leghorn frying size chickens. She would take a Leghorn by the neck in each hand and swing them in a circle until their heads came off. Then their bodies would reel around the ground like they were drunk until they keeled over, and she would pluck them, not letting us help. She said nobody else could find all the pin feathers.

The dinner table was covered with a huge linen cloth that Aunt Myrtle wouldn't let anybody else iron; it was a snow-white sea. There were four cut-glass boats: one for pickles, one for olives, one for sticks of raw celery, and one for pickalilly or chutney Aunt Myrtle had made. At one end of the table a round dish held Addie's butter under a cut glass dome. My mother never failed to say the cut glass had always been in the family. She said it was Waterford.

In summer there were silver serving dishes piled high with new potatoes, green beans, squash, corn-on-the-cob. A china platter held sliced tomatoes that were as big as small plates, with sliced onions on them, and bits of parsley. Fried chicken was piled high on the huge silver platter in front of Addie, and on a smaller one, a large piece of fried country ham from Ron or Reginald or William the Conqueror was covered with red-eye gravy. Miss Addie liked both so we had both.

Then came the pies, apple and the beautiful lemon chiffon, with egg-white fluffed high and gently tanned. I don't think that until now I have realized that almost everything but the flour, salt, pepper, and sugar was either grown or made on the place by those two women.

After the grownups had paid the price of dinner by listening to Addie's prayer, the gabble of voices rose and we ate under them, glancing at each other and taking in what was said when nobody knew we were paying attention. As the grownup voices teased, remembered, argued, debated, we might as well have been deaf and dumb children sitting between them.

They took it all for granted and when they went home they filled the car with chickens, butter, buttermilk, and vegetables, never ever questioning the fact that they should. Their home. Their food. Their mother. Their sister.

We drove back downriver in the dark, my father listening to Guy Lombardo on the car radio, my mother silent, going from day to night, and Jean and I, half asleep in the back seat. I was hoping we would never get there but just keep on driving, in between and silent.

I knew then that much my mother told me about her childhood was the night's haunting, not the day's reality. Like the smiling girl with her sisters in the old photographs, she seemed, when they were all together on Sundays or holidays, to be more relaxed, happier, more humorous than I ever saw her anyplace else. Her body softened, and her face became young.

And yet, when she was not there, the dream of the place and the past seemed to overtake her. She carried her father's gentility like a banner, and somewhere in her sisters' behavior or her parents' secret was a dark dream that possessed her when she was reminded of it by any slip of behavior that wasn't straight and narrow.

One night when I was sixteen, I realized at a party that the boys had "spiked" the punch, and it was making me sick and drunk. I called a taxi and came home. I had just made it to the bathroom to vomit when my mother appeared at the door. Her face was chalk white, and her hair hung down like a witch. I thought for a second that she was there to help me, and then she said, "Die. Damn you. Die." She was not seeing me nor I her. She was seeing terrible sisters from the past, and I, too, was seeing that dreadful dead white face when she was bleeding from a wisdom tooth when I was very small.

We went "home" for every holiday. On Decoration Day, my mother and my aunts took white wicker baskets that were never used any other time, filled with rambler roses as red as blood, and put them on the graves at the Little Brick Church. My mother was the only one who called it Aunt Virginia's chapel. There was a basket for Aunt Minnie's grave, two put within the iron railings of the vault where my grandfather lay. Addie stood for a while and nobody went near her until she had finished her prayer.

For Thanksgiving Aunt Myrtle raised and cooked the turkey, a great, white, strutting, arrogant bird that seemed to know it had been singled out. I was afraid of it. She killed it with an axe while Elsworth held its neck down like Mary Queen of Scots on a block of wood. On Thanksgiving afternoon all of the children were sent to the picture show while the grownups played the inevitable Setback.

The picture show at Cedar Grove showed silent movies until the early thirties. I remember seeing *Ben-Hur* with Ramon Novarro there. And I remember Aunt Serena sitting in the double seat the owner made for her out of two seats because she was too fat to fit into one. There never seemed to be any separation of black and white there. After all, everybody who worked down the mine was black even if they turned white after they washed off the coal dust.

Christmas of 1930 stays with me as a special memory. Eighteen people sat down to Christmas dinner. Everybody seemed happy because it was Christmas, and none of the grownups got on each other's nerves.

Aunt Myrtle had been working for days. She told me so when I followed her into the milk house. Everybody brought something. It was always the same. Every aunt had her specialty. Aunt Myrtle baked the second turkey of the year; Addie, who almost never cooked, baked the ham she had smoked in the smoke house. Aunt Mary made the fruit-cake, laced with bootleg busthead whiskey she had stolen from my uncles. My mother brought candied grapefruit and orange peel that had scented our house with citrus fruit for days ahead, a wonderful ancient promise of summer and sun at the winter solstice.

Aunt Myrtle had strung a chain of bright red and green holly around the white linen table cloth. There were red candles that were never lit in tall silver candlesticks. The cut-glass boats held cranberry sauces, red and green watermelon pickle, and striped candy in broken ribbons. My mother had piled the candied orange and grapefruit peel in high glass compotes at both ends of the table. That year my grandmother said in her blessing that prosperity was just around the corner. Hoover had said so, so she put it in her prayer.

It was time for dessert, after everybody had gotten up and moved around and talked about how full they were. Aunt Mary went into the kitchen to get the fruit cake she had made in September. Addie sat ready to serve it with hard sauce. In front of her were the dessert plates, only used at holidays. As if there were an unwritten law about the candlesticks and the high compotes and the dessert plates, I never saw them any other time.

Aunt Mary came back in tears. My uncles had put the fruit cake in a jelly bag and were squeezing their bootleg whiskey back into a bowl.

Every Fourth of July, the whole huge family went in four cars up to Kanawha Falls. It was a family tradition and woe betide anybody, my mother said, who missed the picnic. When we got there, we went in boats across the backwater out to the island below the falls, and my mother told me almost every time that it was there that she met my father. She looked happy, even with the ever-present worry that seemed a pall over grownups all during the Depression. That is what still astonishes me about the holidays. For a day, they all became young again and forgot.

In the afternoon we went swimming and my father kept watch over the children from the bank, appointing himself to be the worrier in his bathing suit. Addie sat enthroned on a folding chair that was always brought for her. The water in the air above the falls was white and frail as lace. Its mist caught the sun and threw back rainbows, and then crashed into racing, white waves, and we played and waded against a background of river roar.

My uncles sneaked among the trees to take little snorts of bootleg licker, and my aunts sat on pillows and blankets in the shade to protect their complexions, waiting to put the picnic out on a red, white and blue oilcloth they brought every year. It was a wonderful picnic, always the same, ham, fried chickens, hot dogs in a bucket over a fire Uncle Bado made. Everybody said, every year, that my mother's potato salad was the best they ever tasted in their whole lives. Aunt Mary made her special chocolate cake, with melted dark chocolate dripped over white icing. Aunt Helen brought a vegetable salad and was the one appointed to remember the mustard and pickles and olives and peanuts. There was a lot of corn bread that reminded me that the hog had been fattened on that and peanuts to make its ham taste good. There were Coca-Colas we called Dopes, grape Nehis, and iced tea in two two-gallon thermos bottles with little spigots. You could smell it all in the summer, in the shade of the trees, the smell of picnic.

One year Addie decided to go swimming. She made Aunt Violet hold a blanket in front of her while she changed. Then she marched across the little sandy beach in her black bathing suit that came down to her knees, and her black bathing cap that was like a frilled night cap. She insisted that everybody else get out of the river. We stood on the bank, watching her. She went slowly into the water, and she kept walking out beyond where any of the children had been allowed to go. Suddenly she disappeared. She had walked over an underwater shelf in the river.

Nobody moved. She came up. My father started into the water. She saw us all, standing on the bank, and with what could have been her last words on earth, she called out, "You fools, you fools," and she went under twice more before my father got to her. Every time she came up and saw her large family, she called out, "You fools!"

"Whipped into shape" whether dough, clay, or children, is part of the language. But "neglected into shape" had been a greater and more saving force in forming me and my cousins in the Cedar Grove years of the long Depression. Even when we moved to Charleston I spent so much time there at first that I, like my mother, saw it as home.

My father had been in Charleston most of the days of the time we lived at Cedar Grove. He had made contact with the people who had known him as a bright, popular young man at the University of West Virginia, and in the valley. In fourteen months he was able to move my mother out of Cedar Grove where she had felt such a failure for having had, as she said, to come home with her tail between her legs.

We went to a small house in Charleston, vaguely "English" in design, as so many houses were that were built in the early twenties. There were six of them in a little court between Virginia Street and Kanawha Street. For my mother it was between Cabell and Ruffner, bearers of the names she knew, who became her best friends and stayed that way until one died and the other quarreled with her at the age of eighty. Since my mother never forgave anybody, she refused to go to the funeral when her friend died at ninety.

She paid no attention to what she called the new people, some of whom had come to the valley in the early days of the coal boom and stayed to form the crust of social ways her aunts had warned her against when she was a child. She recognized only those who came from what had once been called poor house Tories—Ruffner and Cabell and Gaines and Chilton and Caperton. She had gone back to the city she had been used to when her father brought her down on the train. She ignored its changes. She had known the fathers and the grandfathers and she thought little of any of their offspring who had succumbed to the new ways and new people.

Sometimes, when I dream of going back "home" it is not Cedar Grove, but that small house. I knock at the door. Nobody answers. It has been changed. It has not been changed. We lived there for ten years, from the time I was eight all through my growing up until I was eighteen and went away to college. I had two friends—Jimmy James who I played chess with, and Mr. Mendelsohn, who talked to me about politics and what was happening in Europe. I went there often, but I never remember any of the Mendelsohn family being in our house.

The finances of this time still astonish me. There was little money, and yet they joined the right country club at once. My mother was never without a maid, a half child named Thelma who was the smartest girl in her class at the black junior high school. She came in the afternoons and stayed to wash up. My mother put her into a black uniform with a white apron. She helped my brother pass Latin.

My mother did the cooking. She said nobody else could do it the right way. When I asked her to teach me she said my hands were too big. My brother, who was six years older, went to the high school and had a "crowd" which I envied with my whole little soul. I, who had never been to the same school for more than one year, went to the fifth grade. I walked there and back every day alone.

New life was growing in me like a revelation of noticing a world around me, beyond me, separate from me. Out there. Not to be forgotten or consciously remembered. Stored. Unknowingly. It was in the fifth grade that I first saw Miss Brown, the sewing teacher. Miss Brown stayed lodged with me until she became the physical model for Melinda Kregg, of my novel *Choices*, sixty-five years later.

We saw Aunt Bert in her house that was always half dark, where my cousin, Jean, and I tried to lose weight on Aunt Bert's machine that had a strap that went around your behind and jiggled it. There was a grand piano that she no longer touched, and a Spanish shawl draped across it with a Spanish galleon sitting on it. The atmosphere in that house was one I have recognized ever since—the house of an alcoholic—suspended, dark, a neglect of breath.

My beautiful Aunt Mary wore the coat with the fur collar that Melinda would wear to the church union meeting in *Choices* and then give to Eulaly for Christmas. When we went there in Charleston, I was allowed into my cousins' room. It was, I was informed, a great privilege. The rules were strict. I could have broken one of Aunt Mary's vases and she wouldn't have cared, but I was not allowed to touch the *SPADS*, the *Messerschmidts*, the *DeHavilands*, the *Fokker* triplane of Baron von Richthofen. They were all made of balsa wood and paper and they hung from the sun porch ceiling so that their kingdom was a dog fight when the planes moved in the breeze. There were wonderful magazines, not the boring *Ladies' Home Journal* that told you how to behave and gain weight, but *Aces*, *Air War*, and *Combat* with bright covers where the machine guns in the front of biplanes shot bullets in red streaks. They were as interesting as the *Blue Book* that my father hid under the cushion of the chair by the fireplace. The chair was his and nobody else's when he came home in the evening. I sneaked it when he wasn't there—Edgar Rice Burroughs, wonderful Mars and future stories, the forerunner of science fiction. The best—Robert Louis Stevenson, Thornton Wilder, Willa Cather—were my deepest joys; the most popular, the most pulp, were, for me, my other reading. I turned away from the mild, the pleasing, the "well written" sentimental lie, and I still do.

The first car my father bought after the Model T was a secondhand fire engine red Stutz that was so long I got sick in the back seat. When that car, or, later, the series of Buicks stopped in the driveway, my mother said so often that she hardly seemed to know she said it, "Don't worry your father."

The Depression dragged on; the banks were closing; only the privilege of state jobs thrown my father's way kept us at that strange standard of living I took for granted. After the telephone calls asking for her to pay "something on account," I could hear my mother sobbing on the tester bed that was a reproduction of George Washington's that they had bought when they moved to the house in Charleston.

I wasn't allowed to go to the river, only a backyard full of violets and a garden away, where it flowed through the city, because my father said the water was polluted. Even so I slipped away with the boys and fished from the sewer where we could always get bites from the catfish. We never took them home and we played tag to get ourselves dry so our parents wouldn't know where we had been.

In the summer when I was ten I was sent to Scout Camp. I was Will Scarlet, part of a troop called Robin Hood and his Merry Men. I hated it. All that stumbling around in the third growth timber of the mountain knowing we were pretending bored me. I only loved that camp when it rained, and I could sit in the window of the "lodge" and read. There was a story about a place where time stopped at three o'clock in the afternoon when the giant "grownupness" came and stole away children. It was a theft I much looked forward to. Later I went to summer camp on the Greenbriar River. I was being guided into the world made up of those who my parents decided were my peers. When my mother gave me the only birthday party I had in that house, she chose four of my friends for lunch. None of them were neighbors I had always played with.

1932 was a political year. We took sides in the early fall, as if it were a game. It was, to us. We tried to outshout each other. Political awareness consisted of chanting, "Roosevelt, Roosevelt, he's my man, throw old Hoover in the garbage can," or "Hoover, Hoover, he's my man, throw Roosevelt in the garbage can."

I was for Roosevelt because my mother was. She explained it all to me. She said "big business" had ruined the country and caused the Depression. She said she remembered them "coming in" when she was a child. I think it was the first serious conversation I ever had with her. She was so thoroughly a political animal that she needed somebody to talk to. But my father was a black Republican like the rest of the family. I didn't say anything when they argued at the dinner table.

Miss Simmonds was our home-room teacher and she decided that we should know about the election. She told us we had to choose a candidate and make a three-minute speech so we would learn about the electoral process. She mounted pictures of all the candidates on the wall at both ends of the blackboard. First were Hoover and Roosevelt. Next came Mr. Upshaw. He was a Dry, and we thought that was funny, especially when one of the boys who everybody knew kept redeye in his locker chose him for his speech. Miss Simmonds didn't know why we all had hysterics, catching it from each other long after he had finished. Miss Simmonds said we ought to take the election seriously. It was our privilege as citizens that people had died for and there were places where people couldn't vote. Unfortunately, in the middle of this passionate speech, somebody started everybody giggling again.

Beside Mr. Upshaw was Mr. Coxie, the candidate for the Farmers' party. The only Coxie I knew about was Coxie's Army and that was only a phrase that my Aunt Myrtle muttered when too many people turned up on Sundays without warning her.

Beside all of the candidates, Miss Simmonds had written what they stood for. Although she was a black Republican, the party of Lincoln, she tried to be fair. Beside Mr. Roosevelt she wrote that he promised to balance the budget and then explained how the government spent the money to keep us safe and keep the stop lights going, and how during the Depression there wasn't enough money coming in from taxes to pay the bills. We all knew about that. It was the carrier wave of our lives then.

Beside Mr. Hoover she put a much longer biography, how he had saved the lives of little starving children after the World War, and how he had fed the bonus marchers. I knew she had gotten that wrong because I listened to the news on the radio. It was sung, not spoken. I can still sing, "Up there in the Senate they passed the bonus bill, and sent Hoover's veto arollin' down the hill." In a newsreel we saw the camp of the bonus marchers, and how the American Army came through and destroyed the camptown with guns and tanks and bulldozers. Uncle Roger said it was a national crime.

I studied all the pictures and all the notes beside them until I came to the one I liked best. He was a Presbyterian minister and that was where I went to Sunday school. He was much handsomer than the others. He sat in a swing with his family. He believed in the public ownership of public utilities and so did my father even though he was a Republican and thought Mr. Hoover the greatest man in the country because he was a famous engineer. So I chose Norman Thomas for my speech.

In October, on a cloudy day with rain threatening, my father took me to the K and M station to see Mr. Hoover get on the train to leave Charleston. He had been at Laidley Field and the whole Republican party had turned out to hear him, but we went to the station instead to wave goodbye. Hoover stood on the back platform of the train. Why are people always smaller than we expect? There were only a few people there to say goodbye. My father said I ought to see the President of the United States.

When Mr. Roosevelt won by a landslide and there was a Democratic governor in the state for the first time in a long time, my father said the country was going to hell in a handcart. All my mother's sisters, brothers, brothers-in-law, and sisters-in-law practically went into mourning, and my mother kept smiling to herself. To me, a change of "ministration," which was how I heard the word when they talked about it, meant simply that lots of people in her family were going to lose their jobs.

My Uncle Preston had been the Republican road commissioner. That was over with the election. They moved to one of the family houses at Cedar Grove. Uncle Preston didn't give up on politics, though. He tried in 1936 to run for the state legislature. After all, it was his heritage to be in the state government. Addie had told him he was going to be governor from the time he was a child. He made speeches at the dinner table on Sunday, laying down the law of the future. The Damned Democrats and the Unions were making a mess of everything. People weren't going to stand for it. But when he announced his candidacy, he wasn't even slated. For years I didn't know what that meant. An insult. A heartbreak. Not even slated.

After the 1932 election things went back to normalcy (Mr. Hoover's word) for a while until March when Mr. Roosevelt became president, and we listened to his speech on the radio. Everybody imitated his accent, "The only thing we have to feah is feah itself." My mother taught Aunt Bert's parrot to say "My friends."

Miss Addie didn't like Roosevelt. She considered that she looked after her own people and she didn't need somebody from outside to tell her what to do. One day in summer she walked into the town and met a woman who was one of her tenants. The woman was wearing a new dress called a Hoover apron. Miss Addie said, "Where did you get that dress?"

"Why Miss Addie, Mr Roosevelt give it to me," the woman told her.

"He done nothing of the kind. I give it to you," Miss Addie told her.

The woman thought Miss Addie had made a mistake. "No you didn't, Miss Addie. That there was another dress. This here one come from the government."

"I give it to you. I paid the taxes that bought it. You people are just like hogs that lay down under a chestnut tree and eat chestnuts and never look up to see where they come from."

If she disliked Roosevelt, she loathed Henry Wallace. She called him the little pig killer. She said he went and destroyed food to keep prices up or down; she never quite made up her mind which way he was trying to control farm prices. But she did know her own people were hungry and that he had destroyed food.

Next to him, her disgust fell on John L. Lewis. When he came to Cedar Grove to make a speech to bring the miners out on strike, she burst into the United Mine Workers meeting and walked up onto the stage. The miners hadn't seen a small round woman in a black dress since Mother Jones in 1923. Nobody dared tell her to get off the stage. She thrust her stomach out and waddled across the stage as if she were laden down. Then she called out to the miners. "Who am I?"

"Miss Addie, " somebody called back and some of the miners laughed.

"Oh no. I'm John L. Lewis whose pockets are so full of miner's hard earned money he can't stand up straight. If you people go out on strike you're nothing but a bunch of damned fools." She walked out of the dead silence of the meeting.

The strike went on for months. Except for Miss Addie's houses, the miners' families were once again strung out for several miles down the public roads in makeshift tents and shelters. She said she thought the whole thing was a piece of foolishness, but she opened the bull field once again, this time to let miners put up shelters away from the road. She stood there to see they did right. She made them dig privies, and ditches for water runoff. She said she couldn't sit by and see little children be hurt because their daddies were nothing but damned fools. Obviously she hadn't read that part of the Bible which said you would burn in hell fire if you called your brother *Raca*, a fool. It was her favorite pronouncement on the weakness of man.

The day after he became president, Roosevelt declared a four-day bank moratorium to keep more banks from closing. That was the day Miss Simmonds opened my eyes to what politics meant to the heart. I went to school as usual through the backyards of houses and vacant lots, a secret path I had made for myself. I had a belt and Tangee lipstick hidden behind a rock in one of the vacant lots.

My mother always dressed me for school in a brown skirt and a brown sweater and brown hair ribbon to bring out the auburn in my hair. I had two of each and she wouldn't allow me to wear anything else to school. She said wearing dress-up dresses to school was tacky, the worst thing she could say about anything, and that I couldn't wear a belt because I hadn't developed enough yet. I longed to be like a girl everybody called Kewpie who wore silk dresses that swished. I thought she was the height of sophistication, a phrase that was becoming fashionable. So I pulled the secret belt tight to look developed, put on the colorless lipstick and went to school.

I marched up to Miss Simmonds and said, "Miss Simmonds, you can't get any money out of the bank."

She was patient, the way you are with children who don't know what they are talking about. "Of course I can get money out of the bank. If you put money *In* the bank, you can get the money *Out* of the bank," she explained slowly.

"Not today you can't. Mr. Roosevelt says you can't." I went on to my seat near the back of the room. At lunch time Miss Simmonds went to her bank. She came back furious, as Republican as a rock.

The time in a school room from two o'clock to three o'clock when the last bell rings is the longest hour in the world. I passed the time by taking a strand of my long hair and winding it around and around my nose so that the end of my nose turned white when I looked at it cross-eyed. Then I would unwind the hair and watch my nose tip turn pink and do it all again, over and over.

Suddenly I was aware that Miss Simmonds was marching down the aisle toward me. She leaned down into my face and yelled as if I were across the room, "Stop twisting your hair, you little—*SOCIALIST!*"

I have heard of a belief among the Sephardim that twelve teachers will appear, sometime in a person's life. They will be disguised. My teachers began to appear early, when they were most needed and least recognized, and at the time neither I nor they knew what they were.

I think that our parents are seldom our teachers. I grew up with a father too rigid with worry and past moral training, and a mother too frightened and frozen in an image she had made for herself to protect her like a carapace. They saw my brother and me as unfinished parts of themselves, their own hopes and their own dreams in which we, as separate beings, could not have a choice. My mother "gave up" fairly early, and retired into disapproval. She quoted the Bible, too, when she granted my wishes. She called herself the "unjust judge" who was wearied by continual demands. My father never did give up. "To the day of his death" he was "broken-hearted" in me, according to my mother. He had said, when I was an editor at *Harper's Bazaar,* that if I had finished Sweet Briar, I would have "made something of myself." When he died, I had published two books, and a third, *O Beulah Land,* was finished. Bobby Low, Addie, and Aunt Myrtle had never tried to form me, educate me, or influence me, but they had done all of these things. This many years later I can still hear their voices and watch them move at their own paces.

How could I know that something would happen that would open my eyes, my ears, my brain like a secret plant, when I was only nine years old, simply by climbing the stairs? Somewhere in me I climb those stairs again, up and up to a fourth floor attic, past the stained glass windows on the landings, sun and prism caught, with the smell of wood in an ugly house and tendrils of tunes and scales from pianos and once in a while a scratchy violin escaping from under closed doors out into the hall.

It was a time of "taking" things. Nice girls, growing up, "took" dancing and music and tennis and swimming lessons. I couldn't learn the piano, which I longed to do. There was no room in the house for a piano, and, besides, my father hated noise, especially piano because his mother had driven him to practice, among the other things she drove him to, including a long dislike of her.

My mother had to find some way to get me out of the house in the afternoons after school, since most of the things you "took" really acted as primitive forms of baby-sitting for parents who wanted to be left alone. I had what was called an impediment in my speech. My brother said I couldn't talk straight. I couldn't say "L" or "R," and I still can't, which makes me sound a little like they say Swinburne did, who started the camp language of England because he couldn't talk straight either. There was no such thing as speech therapy; but there was elocution. So I took elocution.

The Mason School of Music was in a house built foursquare upon a corner lot at the turn of the century. It was pale organic-colored brick, like a big square mushroom. There were four floors. In the two rooms where the recitals were held with their sliding doors thrown open, there were fireplaces of marble that looked like potted meat. The house was said to have been lived in by a German during the World War, who was a spy and had mysterious equipment on the top floor, which was the attic and the servants' quarters. It was a real attic, too. Even if it was empty you could tell that by the raw floors, the bare walls, the woodwork of unpainted pine. What the equipment was was not explained. But the rumor made the top floor slightly ominous, except to me.

That was because Mr. Maurice Drew waited for me up there, a seventy-five-year-old man with ears that stuck up like a faun, and wisps of white hair carefully brushed that escaped a little when he was excited and gave him a halo that glowed in the sun of the window. Mr. Drew was of the famous Drew family. He had been a Shakespearean actor, an Act Tor.

194

How he had come to be stranded in the attic of the Mason School of Music I never knew. It was as mysterious as the spying equipment, and, to me, as exotic. Had he been left behind by a showboat? Had he been fired from a road company? At the turn of the century they all came through town and the stars stayed at the Ruffner Hotel. People used to go and wait for them to walk through the lobby. Mojesca, Ellen Terry, Mrs. Patrick Campbell, Maude Adams, Nazimova.

Mr. Drew didn't have any money, and he scrounged for pupils in a way that the dancing teachers didn't have to because dancing was O.K. but you wouldn't be caught dead taking something like elocution.

Mr. Drew's two star pupils were myself and Phillip Caplan, who had a lisp, and whose father said that he didn't think he was wasting his money because if Phillip couldn't be an actor he could always be a lawyer. We were Mr. Drew's advertisements. He trained us in a cute little skit—that's the way he sold it to the Kiwanis and the Masons and the Elks when the women were invited, "a cute little skit."

I wore a Dutch costume, with wooden shoes, a wig with long flaxen braids, a cap with pointed wings, and a large blue skirt with a white apron. Philip wore wooden shoes, a black jacket with big silver buttons, wide blue pants, and a black cap with a bill. The skit was called *The Census Taker*. We spoke with what we thought were Dutch accents combined with Phillip's lisp, and my impediment.

Mr. Drew always asked permission for us to perform. My mother said, "The silly old man. I don't give a damn." For some reason she didn't like Mr. Drew much. "He certainly must not have been much good as an actor," she would sniff, "after all I've seen Maude Adams and Mrs. Patrick Campbell and Nazimova."

I, who had already picked up the secret gossip from God knows where that Nazimova was a lesbian, and a lot of other secret facts, like who the chemistry teacher was in love with and they drank, and why the librarian had a black eye, said nothing. I loved Mr. Drew and I didn't love her as much as I longed to.

So up the stairs, in a brown hair ribbon, a big one like a bat stuck with a brass pin in my auburn hair, my crowning glory, and horn-rimmed glasses, and one leg slightly shorter than the other which was a constant shame at dancing classes, climbing and climbing and still climbing, almost forever, and at the top was Mr. Drew with his faun's ears, and the biggest secret of all.

There were no Dutch girls then. I would walk in the door, and Mr. Drew would look at me, and speak.

"Stop! Still! You are *not* Mary Lee Settle. You are Brutus!"

And I was.

"Romans, countrymen and lovers."

Mr. Drew's voice would come from further and further away as the toga of Brutus fell across my body. "Remember, this is the noblest Roman of them all."

I would draw myself up to under four feet tall, and put into words at last, what had been an isolated, dim sound within me since I could remember. The rhythm, the passion, the life under life, all the sounds I hadn't known would ever be words were there. I was no longer lonely, listening and not knowing.

"Be silent that you may hear," Mr. Drew's voice, from far across the attic, "Aristocratic, tall, you are the proudest man in Rome. *ROLLL* it out over the dirty throng."

"Believe me for mine honor,"

"Honor, show honor," honor and pride stretched a little girl's body; I could feel it.

"As Caesar loved me, I weep for him,"

"Weep, weep, but not really, let your voice tremble. Don't lose dignity. This is the clue to Brutus's pride before his fall. He didn't say he loved Caesar, he said Caesar loved him . . ."

"As he was fortunate, I rejoice at it . . ."

"Let your voice begin to rise toward the climax, and remember your breathing." Voice up and up . . .

"As he was valiant I honor him."

"Now. Drop your voice, you are angry, you are *RIGHT.*"

"As he was ambitious," voice down.

"Clench your fist. Show your CONTEMPT!"

"I SLEW HIM."

He taught me Hamlet's speech to the players, *"Speak the speech I pray you as I pronounce it to you, trippingly on the tongue . . ."*

Sometimes he let me be Prince Hal, and there I was, nine years old, meaning every word I let ROLLL off my tongue, down stage (we had both forgotten long since that we were in an attic at the Mason School of Music).

"Take the audience into your confidence. You are a rake, a devil with the ladies, a rebel, a wit, but underneath remember that you have a king in you."

"I know you all, and will awhile uphold the unyoked humor of your idleness, yet herein will I imitate the sun, who doth permit the base contagious clouds to smother up his beauty from the world, that, when he please to be again himself, being wanted he may be more wondered at." Prince Hal was the favorite private role of my childhood.

Mr. Drew never gave me a woman's part to play, I think it was because he only knew the men's parts. Maybe he had played them; maybe he had wanted to. But seventy-five years old, and nine, we were contemporaries, he and I and Hamlet the Dane, and sometimes Mercutio, *"She is the fairy's midwife, in shape no bigger than an agate stone . . ."*

Once he took us to his church to perform. It was large, red brick, and Methodist. It was on the West Side, a world away from the East Side and we who only went through the West Side to swim in the country-club pool on the hill beyond it wouldn't have been caught dead there. There were a lot of places like that that were branded into us as we grew, no reason, nothing to inform, except that they were places where you wouldn't be caught dead. I saw a lot of the town you wouldn't be caught dead in with Mr. Drew.

It was on a Sunday evening. I wore my Dutch costume, and Phillip his, to entertain for Mr. Drew at his church supper. It was in a half-basement. There was the smell of chicken and cake, and new-baked bread, and mayonnaise and green salad and cotton dresses, so it must have been summer.

I stepped out onto the small raised platform that was the stage. It had music stands on it, pushed back. There was a knock. Phillip had used one of the music stands for a door. It nearly fell over. It sounded tinny.

"Who iss dot?"

"I am de census taker."

"Yaaah? Vot you vant?"

We were a big hit. The audience kept on applauding the cute little children in their Dutch costumes. Mr. Drew had told me what you do when there is a lot of applause. You give what is called an encore.

I stepped forward and stood there alone. Phillip had obviously escaped. I can still feel the space all around me, the pool of silence, still smooth my hands on my Dutch apron, and wait.

Then I spoke.

"Romans, countrymen and lovers, hear me for my cause!" I could hear a murmur in the crowd, and I knew what to do with that. I let them have it, proud, imperious, *"And be silent that you may hear!"* The place was dead quiet.

But I knew as I went on what every actor, Act Tor, experiences. I was laying an egg. I had betrayed Mr. Drew and myself. I had gone public, come out of the attic, out of our secret shared world. At the end there was a little clapping here and there, and some smiles, and Mr. Drew took me home. He said I had been very brave. I cried in the car, but I stopped before my mother saw that.

I was rescued by Mr. Drew, over and over.

In the late twenties a bright outlet in small towns was the newly started Little Theater. At first it was wonderful. There was Shakespeare, and Shaw, and *The Importance of Being Earnest* and *Charlie's Aunt*. When Mr Ramon Savage, the director, called Mr. Drew and asked if he had a pupil who could be Robin a Page in *The Merry Wives of Windsor,* Mr. Drew sent me. So I followed Sir John Falstaff onto the stage, and sat down in the front left corner and played with a top. Behind me Mistress Page and Mistress Ford and Mistress Quickly flounced around the stage in beautiful antique rose and antique blue and antique green velveteen costumes with big dagged sleeves and trains. I wore a blue velveteen suit with a dagged hem, and tights, and a cap with a long tail.

But I heard the language of my Brutus and my Hal and my Hamlet. I sat in the corner of the stage and listened as to a lover, to William Shakespeare. I can't remember that I had any lines, but I found out then that if you sit down left, totally concentrated on what you are doing, no matter what words are flying over your head, you can steal the scene.

My parents tried to understand the passion for Shakespeare, but when I asked for the plays at Christmas when I was ten, they bought me Lamb's *Tales from Shakespeare* because they thought I was too young to understand the plays. I opened the book and saw that they were the wrong words, closed it, and never opened it again. My mother said I was hard to please. How could I have expected them to understand? It was not a part of the girl they were creating.

When I found I could get the plays from the library, I walked along the street in my first year at Roosevelt Junior High School when I was twelve, reading, while my friends imitated my walk and chanted their nickname for me—Shakespeare.

Sara Spencer graduated from Vassar where she had studied with Hallie Flannigan, who was the source of the new passion for Little Theaters all over the country. It was said that she would have gone far, whatever that meant, but she had had polio, and walked with a limp. I couldn't quite reconcile the explanation with the fact that she had come back "home" after going to Vassar, and seeing the world, even Europe, which was my Mecca and my hope. She started a Children's Theater in the same abandoned church that had been made into the Little Theater, the Kanawha Players.

Sara Spencer had huge eyes, a wonderful voice, the persistence of a devil and, as I found out, the patience of a saint. She tended to be a little spiritual, and cared for nothing lower than the angels—I couldn't, for instance, imagine her reading *Boots and her Buddies*.

When I was growing up, high-mindedness was derided in towns like mine, especially by "nice" people, and Sara Spencer was high-minded. She suffered for it. Her detractors, and sometime victims of an iron will and a true belief, said she could walk across the water of the Kanawha River. I loved her in a way that made me want to argue with her, bring her down to my own understanding. When she got too high-falutin' it drove me nuts.

I was twelve when she cast me in her first play. I stood on the empty stage of the church and Sara Spencer stood at the back of the dark house. It was a real stage that had ropes and flies and sandbags and wings. I was, that night, for her, a Chinese nurse. What the words were I don't remember. I remember being taught to bow like a servant. But the total recall is of standing there alone, with Sara Spencer's voice coming out of the darkness, "Again . . . again . . . No, Mary Lee, you are not a silly little girl in a costume. You are an *Amah,* a nurse. You are old and tired and responsible, and very very dignified. Show me all that. Again. Again."

It went on for an hour until it was dark outside and I forgot that I would catch hell when I got home. It was an unforgivable sin to "worry" my parents. "You've got to *be* her, not just *mouth* her," Sara Spencer called from the darkness.

Finally I, an aging, dignified Chinese *amah,* who was tired and responsible, spoke my lines and it was right, true pitch, and I knew it and she knew it. I went home on the streetcar after dark, completely happy. That night, with her voice coming out of the darkness, I learned that empathy, in writing or in acting, is what makes a fictional person ring true, and all the facts of life cannot replace it. I hear her voice still, "again, again."

It has taken a long time to thank the teachers who guided me for those years, not lost at all, no matter how much I tried to ignore them as I grew up, standing outside the gates of mediocrity, knocking to get in. Wisdom had no place in these triumphs and these yearnings, thank God. If I had been wise too early I might have become a critic.

But I had heard the voices and found the words, and found them outside myself. When the voices are shared, and a universal language is recognized in a small world, surrounded by people who don't hear the same words, or find the same possibilities in them, time doesn't matter. It is the same with me as it has always been, beyond taste into what is true, either in pitch or empathy or passion. I have been foolish over most of the decisions of my life, except for that. True pitch is true pitch whether you are twelve or eighty.

There have been later teachers, other times. But there are still the early voices, and I can call them back when I need them and I do, "A great big girl like you settin' down," "Speak the speech I pray you *trippingly* on the tongue," and the voice from the darkness, "Again . . . again . . ."

*M*y mother said Betty Coopey, my best friend then, had breasts before I did because she was a Yankee. Betty Coopey could play anything on the piano. We bought pink song sheets and sang, "I cover the waterfront, and look at the stars . . .," and "I've got a right to sing the blues, I've got a right to feel low-down, I've got a right to hang around, down around the river . . .," and "Willow weep for me, willow weep for me," in little high voices and wondered if the boys would ever like us.

Then I was getting breasts, too, like Betty Coopey's only not as big. I had changed from ballet, which I couldn't do, and tap dancing and acrobatics, at which I was a disaster. My father insisted that I learn ballroom dancing from a teacher that they said had been trained by Ned Weyburn. He told my mother men didn't like girls who couldn't follow. He also said that I should put a little perfume in my hair.

I was being prepared, but not by Addie or Aunt Myrtle or Mr. Drew and Sara Spencer any longer, or for anything either of them stood for or cared about. When Mr. Drew called to see if I were going to "take" elocution, my mother said I had other interests. I never even thanked him.

But, still, I was always in a play. In October of 1932, I was given the best part I had ever had. I was going to speak the words of my beloved Shakespeare as Titania in *A Midsummer Night's Dream*, *"The moon methinks looks with a watery eye, and when she weeps, weeps every little flower bemoaning her enforced chastity."* I looked up chastity. It was glorious. Not that other awful thing, that nasty word that one of my cousins had written in water from a puddle while we waited in our girl scout uniforms to be shown over the Governor's Mansion.

I knew I was going to be a great Shakespearean actress. I dreamed of it awake at night in those wonderful times of silence when I prayed for insomnia. I designed evening dresses to wear when I was allowed to go to dances. I swooped around with Fred Astaire, and I was rescued by Hamlet the Dane, who understood about a weary life. There is no wearier life than being fourteen. The year 1932 was only a special time for me when I was reading or shouting "Roosevelt Roosevelt, he's my man," or being Titania.

Then, on a Sunday morning in late November, when I was getting dressed for Sunday school, I leaned too close to the gas fire on the wall of the bathroom and my nightgown went up in flames. I can still see the flames flowing up toward my face, my eyes. I covered my face and screamed and screamed, and my father, who was reading the Sunday paper downstairs, heard the scream and knew at once, he said, what it was. "A scream like no other," he called it.

He rushed upstairs, grabbed my winter coat, flung it over me to put out the fire. Then he reached for mineral oil to put on my already reddening body. I ran. The bottle was like the rubbing alcohol that he usually said was the right thing to use for sores, and he ran after me, flinging the oil toward my body. The ivy covered wallpaper of my parents' bedroom was flecked with oil.

Finally he caught me and wrapped me in a sheet and put me in the car to go to the hospital while my mother called his cousin, Dr. Gott. I felt nothing. There were only red areas of my body.

Dr. Gott was waiting for us at the hospital. When the sheet was taken off I was covered, front and back, with huge balloon-like blisters of burned flesh. There was no pain. My surface nerves were dead.

There was no more Titania, no more smooth adolescent girl's body, only wounds that are still scars on my stomach, my back, my arm. My world changed forever. I grew up, both physically and mentally, in a hospital bed before Christmas of 1932. I was there for three weeks.

Addie never once came to see me, and it hurt my feelings. I learned only a year ago that she never went where she thought she would embarrass my mother. She told my cousin that she had always known my mother was ashamed of her. That was why she never spent a night in our house, wherever we were.

I lay under a tent with a sheet over it, and balanced a book, any book, on the rim. My leg muscles are still strong from having lifted myself inch by inch to separate my burned back from the bottom sheet. It took nearly an hour. I was taken then into a bichloride of mercury bath to soak, a burn cure that had been introduced during the World War. One day my mother came in and found six doctors sitting around the bath, discussing politics and burn cures. The nurse had put a little piece of gauze on my pubis, where there wasn't even any hair yet. I had thrown it off in disgust.

I read. I read as if it were going to save me. I had to have one book taken away from me because it made me laugh and that hurt too much. I remember reading an article in *Reader's Digest* about Berlin, a city so beaten down by depression that young men were going around the streets with sandwich boards that read, "I will do anything for money." From then on I followed what was going on in Europe as if it were happening close to me.

One day when Dr. Gott came in I said, "I don't think you ought to give me any more of that medicine." I had been having shots for nearly three weeks. "I don't think it is good for me. I wait for it." The medicine was morphine. I went through withdrawal after that, but neither I nor anybody else knew what was wrong. They thought I was "nervous." But I found that if someone read to me, if I could hear words, any words, it calmed me as I was lifting my back slowly from the bed.

Fourteen. Emaciated. I was not allowed to go back to school until February. But I was allowed to walk, and I have done it ever since, five, ten miles a day. It is a habit that has stayed with me all my life, when I have been in trouble, or thinking, or waiting for work problems to solve themselves, which they do if I let them alone, or finally stopping smoking. It all started then, when I was fourteen, too thin, too tall, scared and ashamed. I wandered around the school building, watching my friends in the windows. Solitary reading. The ever-present Shakespeare, Shaw, trash, but nothing in the middle. What my mother called "bessellers" bored me, and lied to me.

I distrust for the same reason the conventional high-minded memories of sensitive, talented children who only recall the first time they read *Alice in Wonderland,* or heard Mozart, or were first conscious of the high flights of angels made of wings and mist. They have forgotten that angels come in very earthy forms, angel neighbors, angel strangers, angel teachers, angels with other names. I suspect that they have forgotten that they, too, played doctor and nurse, squashed bugs, wet their pants, and talked dirty.

Every Sunday afternoon I went with my parents to the "club" where my father played golf, and my mother sat by the pool and gossiped, and I lay in the sun hoping for a tan that never came, only freckles. For six weeks I laid the suggestion carefully that we stop at friends of my parents on the way home. It was easy.

I had found Pierre Louÿs's *Aphrodite* in the closet of a bachelor brother, and when my mother asked what I was reading I said, "Greek myths." Anyway, that's how I learned more about Nazimova, and some other things like, curiously enough, the value of pearls, what you did to get them.

I was growing up and grasping at habits and mores that would make me accepted, the most important single goal for American girls from fourteen to, if they are lucky, eighteen. Some never get over it and make up the bulk of aging adolescents who become, in their turn, mothers.

By the time I could rejoin the Little Theater, things had changed for the worse. Mr. Ramon Savage had gone, and he was replaced by what I see now was the next stage, a faulty one, of the Little Theater movement. Unemployed actors and disappointed directors were taking the local jobs, and they brought with them their longings, their taste, and their failure. There was no more Shakespeare, no more Shaw; they were replaced by what they called "Broadway plays," as soon as they were released to be printed in French's little books, and we learned to say "sides" instead of "lines," and swanned and swooped and were sophisticated, which was the be all and end all in the early thirties. I knew, having never in my life been fooled about this, that what we were doing was second rate.

I was growing, without realizing it, a veneer of sophistication over innocence without a cushion of any wisdom at all. There was nobody to help me with that. Those years were arid years. But I could dance well, and I had grown tall, and when I left home people said I was "good-looking." I cut school to go to the picture show the week that Noël Coward in *The Scoundrel* was playing at the Rialto, a narrow theater where usually there were B movies. I went four times. I had three records that I played over and over until my parents cried for mercy: Nellie Lutcher, Flagstad and Melchior singing the *Liebestod*, and Hal Kemp.

I lay with my own "crowd" sun bathing at the country club pool and talked about love. We didn't admit, even to ourselves, that we were talking about sex. I tried over and over to do the dive called a half-gainer, like Dick Diver, later. When the voices of Addie or Mr. Drew or Sara Spencer or Aunt Myrtle intruded, I hated them; I was afraid of being caught listening. I wanted, not to be loved, I didn't see it that way—I wanted to be accepted. I longed to be mediocre and sat dreaming mediocre dreams in the white underwear that my mother said was acceptable, like not wearing your hat at a "cute" angle, or talking topics at a social gathering. But that was public, the self I presented as a present for anyone who would like it. There was another, growing, strengthening, still unfooled.

When I was sixteen I didn't go to New York City on the Chesapeake and Ohio railroad. I rose up into Pennsylvania Station from a long dark tunnel. It was like being reborn, at least for me when I saw it for the first time, saw beyond it into a dream I had had since I was ten and climbed the stairs to Mr. Drew's attic.

It was a school trip, two nights on the day coach, one night at the New Yorker hotel, two days in New York City, tours of the city, food, with responsible chaperons, all inclusive—Grant's Tomb, the Planetarium, the Metropolitan Museum, the automat, and a ride on the subway if everybody promised to stay together. I had other ideas.

My classmates rioted in the day coach, and the teacher chaperons finally gave up patrolling the aisles and retired into the restroom which smelt slightly of newly legal real whiskey when they came out. High school juniors spilled, sponged, clambered over the backs of the seats, held contests of strength, elbowing, pushing, flirting, wrestling, all the way the length of the car. The bolder boys, the ones who wouldn't have touched me with a barge pole, sneaked gin into their cokes and chose the girls they would neck when the lights went out. The girls they liked—love was not the word used—pretended not to see them. They were the "cute" girls, girls who wore wide sashes tight around their little waists and had breasts and unmothered hair, no correct way, just flying, girls who were five feet two, and had nicknames like Tooty and Diddie. I was not one of the chosen, ever, so I sat alone in the back of the car, leaning into the window and staring out, seeming to concentrate, above the nonsense, even when there was nothing to see, being, I hoped, languid, sophisticated. But now I see a gangly girl, dressed correctly, with the beginnings of small breasts, shining auburn marcelled hair, who was going to be handsome even beautiful sometime, but not then, not yet, and thinking, that long night with the darkness flowing past, not ever.

Somebody found out that the backs of the seats could be lifted off and laid flat to make beds. The lights went out. Gradually, the giggles and the whispers died down, the chaperons dozed, the bold boys chose the bold, small girls. Popular or unpopular, chosen or not, students slept across the seat backs, and I sat, alone, watching out of the window.

I was awake all night, every minute, every hour too important to lose in sleep. I watched the dark and listened to the wheels until I couldn't tell in the blackness whether we were going east or west, but I knew all the time that we were going east, east to New York City, three words like a song or a prayer.

I measured the time by the scatters of lights on isolated farms or all-night gas stations when the tracks were parallel with Route 60, passed the coke ovens, glowing in the night like witch fires, where they said there had been a plot to kill Mother Jones and burn her in one of them, but that had been a long time ago, long gathered into rumor and legends of the valley. Then the lights drew together into towns as the train pulled into stations, with their platform lights and the names of places I had never been, and the sleeping town beyond.

I watched station after station as the train slowed, stopped and sighed, nearer and nearer to New York City—Thurmond, Staunton, Charlottesville. In Washington the car was shunted and clanged into a coupling on the New York Central tracks. The teachers tried to get the sleepy students to wake up and glimpse the Washington monument in the dawn.

The stretched time of fatigue and sleeplessness made me too aware of the world, light grey outside, the junk yards of New Jersey, the dirty water of ocean beyond, the Pulaski Skyway; then—then the tunnel, the birthing, lights burning on me in Pennsylvania Station. I tried to act sophisticated, as if I weren't being herded like a sheep across the platform, up the wonderful wide regal stairs and out into the smell and sound, the taxis and the cars, the El shunt and rattle, the wind from the ocean that tore along the narrow streets between the high buildings, the carrier wave of the city in the morning.

In the lobby of the New Yorker Hotel, at least I remember it that way, there was a ticket booth for the plays—I did not even notice the feast of what we called Broadway plays. There were hits that season—Sherwood, the never ending Tobacco Road, others I have long forgotten.

I had bought a three-day-old New York Times the day before we left at the one place you could find it in Charleston, the newsstand near a shoe repair place on the way through the alley from Capitol Street to the Capitol Theater that had the Metro Goldwyn Mayer movies. I knew what I wanted, what I had longed for. I bought two tickets with the pocket money I had been given, husbanded carefully with lunch money—my father drove me to school on the way to work and gave me fifty cents each day to buy my lunch—so that I had saved enough to do what I had intended ever since I had persuaded my parents to let me go to see the Planetarium and go to the top of the new Empire State Building, and Grant's Tomb who was kin.

I bought two tickets. The first was to the Saturday matinee of Rostand's *L'Aiglon* with Eva LeGallienne playing Napoleon's son at Shönbrunn, and hoped it was better than *Cyrano*, which I hated. I asked to go to the bathroom when everybody was lined up making too much noise in the lobby of the New Yorker, shuffling and giggling onto a bus to take us to the Planetarium, and I never went back.

Sitting in a New York theatre, the slightly dusty spacious scent of it, the stretched darkness, the huge intimacy with the play, and Eva LeGallienne in a white uniform was enough to stun me with joy, even though all the time the imp within was whispering that I didn't like *L'Aiglon* much better than I had *Cyrano*. But the theatre itself was enough, real actors, the illusion of the play, more real for the time it lasted than any reality.

I remember staggering like a sleep walker along the street in the direction of the next play. I was afraid to try the Automat because I realized that if it didn't work right there was no way to get my money back. So I stopped at the restaurant with the only name I recognized—Child's—went inside as if I had done it before, and studied the menu, counted the money I had, and cried into a plate of spaghetti.

For the evening I had found a seat in the front of the first balcony to *Romeo and Juliet* with Catherine Cornell, Basil Rathbone, Brian Aherne, Edith Evans, and someone I had not heard of for Tybalt whose name was Orson Welles.

The house darkened, the greatest moment in any theatre, the curtains drew apart, and I was in Verona. Spellbound I mouthed, along with the actors, *"Do you bite your thumb at me, sir? . . . Nay, but I do bite my thumb, sir."* The little stage riot for one who was used to casts of thousands for such scenes in movies didn't matter; it was the words, and I knew almost all of them.

The meeting of the two at the masked ball is too subtle for my memory, but then it was dark on the stage that was no longer a stage, and I leaned forward and put my arms on the balcony front, heard Romeo say *"Hark what light is that at yonder window breaks?"* and I said with him, *"It is the east and Juliet is the sun."*

An old man sat beside me, listening, he told me at intermission to me and the actors together. When Catherine Cornell leaned over the balcony, her arm flowing down toward Basil Rathbone, and almost whispered, filling the theatre with that small sound, *"What's in a name?"* she leaned too far over and her rear end was too wide for that fourteen-year-old girl and she broke the spell and I started to cry. The old man patted me on the shoulder, knowing why, and whispered, "Don't look too closely, just listen to the words."

When Tybalt was killed he didn't stop breathing.

Brian Aherne was the most beautiful Mercutio in the world, and for years, his voice would come back, his arm flung out, a conjurer, *"She is the fairy's midwife, in shape no bigger than an agate stone,"* and then, as lightly, *"Not so deep as a well nor so wide as a church door, but t'will serve,"* and I cried again as if I had not known all the time he was going to be killed, as you cry at the right pitch.

I had just enough money left if I walked back to the hotel through Times Square to spend fifteen dollars at Macy's where I bought blue silk, very sophisticated lounging pajamas.

I had already been entered for Barnard, my choice of a college because it was in New York. But when my parents went to inspect the dormitory where I would be living my father saw a black student in one of the rooms and refused to let me go. He made the final choice. His daughter dream had to come true. He had invested so much in it, not only money, but dreams of the way nice girls had to be. I was sent to Sweet Briar.

Maybe Stendhal was right to say he would end his autobiography by his twentieth year, before he became a conscious observer. (He didn't.) After that, most of the events of his life, his crises, his lovers, his disappointments, were transmuted into fiction. Mine would be, too. I can trace the sources. But the lost recall, the fonts of those minutes that rang true, echoes of voices, things not seen consciously, but always remembered, have informed my work so much more deeply. What informed the largest work that I have done, *The Beulah Quintet*, lay so deep within, so early sown, so dependent on Addie, her voices, her world, that I was unconscious of it.

But at sixteen, seventeen, eighteen, I was not going to write anything. I was going to be a Shakespearean actress, not a nice girl at Sweet Briar. I had to face the fact that I was going to have to wait, maybe too long. I saw my life as drifting.

I cried a lot. But by myself. One of the times that my father showed complete sympathy was a night in summer after my first year at Sweet Briar when I lay crying in my tossled, hot bed and he heard me and came in to see what was the matter.

"Oh daddy I'm so ambitious," I told him.

"I know," he said, "so am I." He held my hand until I went to sleep.

One spring day in 1944, in wartime London, I walked through Hyde Park with Archibald MacLeish, who was in London for the American government. What his job was there I didn't know, but I did know that he was one of the poets I had learned about and who I honored, and also that he liked to walk as I did.

He had begun to take me seriously when I asked him about Eliot's translation of *Anabase,* the prose poem written by the French diplomat and poet Léger, whose pseudonym was St. John Perse. I had found the poem at Sweet Briar and had carried it with me to war, one of the few books I took with me when I went from Washington to England in 1942 by convoy to join the Women's Auxiliary Air Force, the WAAF, the women's section of the Royal Air Force. Later I was transferred to London and to the OWI, the Office of War Information. I was beginning to live a life that would be reflected consciously in work. I have written about my small corner of World War II in a memoir, *All the Brave Promises.* The unremembered would appear later in hundreds of autobiographical details it took years for me to recognize. I was conjuring them out of the deep unconscious past where Addie and the others who had taught me waited to be found again by other names, in other times.

That day in spring tulips bloomed in the borders of the park and the carts of the flower sellers. London was almost peaceful. We had learned to ignore the almost forgotten sandbags left to burst and flatten after the years of bombing. The buzz bombs and the V2s would come later, but that day we walked through the pale sun of a deceptive peace.

MacLeish told me what I wanted to know, that Léger had influenced his own *Conquistadors*, and we talked of rescues, Léger among them, who had escaped or were, like we were that day, set down in a wartime place far from what had gone before in our lives.

Whatever else we talked about that day is gone, except for one remark. He said, "You know, I have spent the rest of my life finding out that what I knew at eighteen was true." The remark stayed with me until it acted as the conscious impetus for a novel, *The Clamshell*, written in London during another war, in Viet Nam, which, with Nixon's election, I had left the United States to protest twenty-five years later.

In *The Clamshell* I went back to my own eighteenth year to find out what I did know. It is the most blatantly autobiographical of my novels. Originally it was meant to be a memoir. It soon grew into fiction. I needed to interpret what I had lived through, to resee the events beyond what I remembered as a victim, which was too one-sided. So *The Clamshell* is both factual and true. The attempted rape did happen. I did walk back through country darkness on a wet cold night in January escaping from a dangerous drunk, hoping for warmth, kindness and solace. I found them all from my close friends, but I was also faced with the trials I wrote about.

I was not believed. I was examined medically to see if I was still a virgin. A warmed rubber glove manipulated my virginity for the first time. I was put on trial by the student government, ostensibly for coming in late, but really to hear prurient details of an appalling experience in which I could have been killed. The scene between my mother and the president of the college, in all its brutal coziness and gentility, is true. My mother did react as I wrote that she did. And still today, when I walk in the gardens of the Palace in Williamsburg, I remember the pull of suicide that I left there.

But the novel flowed more gracefully than the raw memory, more ironically than the painful reactions to events at the time. It is true beyond the facts, as a novel must be. I wanted to rehear a man who had been the most important influence on me at Sweet Briar, and the most private. I also knew I had to construct him as a guide, because I hadn't known the real man well enough. My recall of him was only a series of fragments. His fictional reality is, I hope, what Joseph Dexter Bennett truly meant to me.

I had seen going away to college as a release from a growing up I wanted to shed like a snake sheds its skin in the spring. I flew toward it. It was there that I found the last teacher at the end of my childhood and the first teacher for a new way of speaking an already familiar private language. I thought I was free, but in my beloved Shakespeare's words, I was still poised, "looking before and after."

At Sweet Briar Mr. Bennett became my guide to choice. He was probably not aware of it, as I, since, have been unaware of my own influence on students. I had brought to my eighteenth year a yearning to grasp at the new like a person who has been starved, and not realized it. I knew nothing, although he never told me that. He simply took me to Wordsworth, to Keats, to daily interest in the world that was beyond what I was experiencing as an idyllic prison in a ten-thousand-acre setting for what was supposed to be a bucolic time of life. I lived partly in a secret place where Guernica was real, Madrid, John Cornford, a world away, a war away, but there within me.

Mr. Bennett was an unashamed lover of the Georgian poets who were already, although I didn't know it at the time, and I'm sure he didn't care, being rejected by the modern critics, the taste makers, who were as unimportant then as they are now. The first day I saw him, he marched into class and informed us that Wordsworth's "Whose dwelling is the light of setting suns" was the greatest line of poetry in the English language. The fact that his looks reminded me of Robert Benchley took some zest from the pronouncement.

I went to a seat by a window in an empty classroom where nobody would find me and read the rest of the poem to try to find out if what he said was true. So it was there that Wordsworth's *Lines Written a Few Miles Below Tintern Abbey* glowed around me, and I think that at that moment I was as happy as I have ever been in my life.

The first poem I wrote after I was ten was for Mr. Bennett. It was about Addie. After he read it he stopped me in the hall, and said, "Mary Lee, this isn't the right place for you. You are wasting time. You have talent. Go and use it and learn for yourself." Then, sadly, he said as he turned away to wander down the hall, letting me hear, "I wish somebody had told me that." He walked away, the first sad man of the generations of poets turned critics that I would know in the academic world, those who chose safety and thought it was safe.

It was Mr. Bennett who sent me to the unused, unsung corner of the library that I still see. I still raise my hand toward the clutch of little books, reading a language written, miraculously, in my own lifetime, that echoed so deeply within me. It was there in that corner that I found and heard for myself Eliot, Auden, Day-Lewis, MacNeice. They were young, and they were telling me in poetry what I had been born knowing, that the world was as deep in concrete and coal dust as sweet trees and country lanes. I found a question in Stephen Spender's *"Who live under the shadow of a war, what can we do that matters?"* and I hated him then for asking it. He seemed to me to be whining. I had come from a world where people had lived under the shadow of a kind of war all their lives. "Matters more!" I wanted to tell him, "Matters more."

I did not talk to anybody about these voices. I simply went on, publicly, and to my friends, being the girl they thought I was, a wild dancer. All the time that timeless place within me that never ages, never changes in spirit, began to grow toward finding redemption in work. So I walked in the beautiful Virginia spring, in what I saw as traps of pachysandra ground cover, under trees I didn't learn to name, reading about the Spanish war, and Hitler, chimney stacks and cigarettes, and lost, unemployed men standing on street corners in cities I had never seen. For the first time, I had found teachers that spoke to me from the printed page. I was as eager to follow their new language, their echoed reality, as I have ever been in my life. I began to break away from the vale of good taste that still tries to cling when I sleep, when I dream. I set out through a long apprenticeship, to join their ranks.

All the way from a corner of the library the voices called, louder than any voices that I heard at the time, remembered more than the boys I tried to impress, as I was trained to do, than the friends I had, than the other teachers who were sometimes kind and often stupid. I half listened. Waiting to get out. I did not go to Spain, but Melinda did, in *Choices*. I did not try to escape to the west, and fail, but Johnny Catlett did, in *Know Nothing*.

It was so slow a time. I even let myself be sent back for a sophomore year. Then, the summer that I was twenty, my mother made the worst mistake of her life as a parent, and the most blessed she ever made for me. She didn't like having me around. My books were dirty, my taste was acerbic, my mind was escaping. I rubbed their hopes for me the wrong way.

So she decided that it would be nice if I went as an apprentice to the Barter Theater in Abingdon, Virginia. She threw me into the briar patch. The Briar Patch, by the way, was the name of the school magazine at Sweet Briar, and where my first short story was published.

The Barter Theater had been established by Bob Porterfield. Quite literally, barter was accepted for theater tickets to help feed us all. Hams for hams was the joke, and the fact. By the simple journey to Abingdon, in the mountains, eighty miles away from Charleston, West Virginia, I went from being treated as raw material for a training I had not asked for, to being treated as a professional, for which I was totally unprepared.

A new play was being tried out at the Barter Theater that summer of 1938, Lula Volmer's *The Dunce Boy*, with a starring role for Porterfield which he hoped to take to Broadway in the fall. Lula Volmer had made a success on Broadway with a play about mountaineers called *Sun Up*.

Lula Volmer arrived. She was an old, fat, drunken mountain woman with dyed red hair who sat in the back of rehearsals, calling out criticisms of our work in her play. On Sundays she sat in the attic of the dormitory we lived in with her hair floating around her almost to the floor, a bottle of gin on one hand, and a Bible in the other, singing revivalist hymns at the top of her lungs. If I had ever wanted to write a cruel, dishonest parody of Addie, I would have used Lula Volmer as a model.

Bob Porterfield chose me to play the lead opposite him. I remember three things about our performance. First, Bob Porterfield could turn his upstage eye outward so that at our most dramatic scene when he knelt at my feet, he as the dunce in love, and me as the understanding teacher, he used his eye to try to break me up. Second, the climax of the last act, where Bob Porterfield rushes into the teeth of a sawmill, which was influenced strongly by *The Perils of Pauline*, was accompanied by the ever-rising music of Tchaikovsky's Second Piano Concerto, Da da da da da da DAH! Boom boom boom boom boom de boom. Third, we both knew that the play was a disaster.

The headiest thing I remember was the visit of a talent scout from David O. Selznick Studios. He asked me to read Scarlett O'Hara's prison scene from the movie script of *Gone with the Wind*. He set up an interview and test for me in New York in the fall, and sent me a ticket to get there.

Sweet Briar, the "club" in summer, nice girls, nice marriages, nice lives as someone else saw them, were very far away. Since after my ugly experience at Sweet Briar and my parents' almost obsessive fear that I would "go wrong," I realized then that they both concentrated far more on my virginity than my mind. So I gave my virginity away for a birthday present that summer, and went to New York in September.

*M*y mother wrote only a few times during my first year at Sweet Briar. She hated writing letters, but the ones she did write always carried news from Cedar Grove, as if it, as always, was the only real place in her mind. And, as always, it took me away from where I was, as if I were being commanded to enter the unchanging door, not wanting to.

Aunt Myrtle and Elsworth had gone on living at Cedar Grove with Addie. Elsworth had almost gotten rid of his cousins, but not quite. Uncle Preston and Aunt Mary brought their three boys, model airplanes, clothes, ambitions, and dreams back to one of the family houses in the valley of Cedar Grove. Uncle Preston's dreams of himself as the eldest son, the one who ought to be governor, were gone. He returned to his mother. She doted on him. She never saw any wrong or weakness in him.

Her family were gathering again in 1936, as they had in 1927, close to each other. Uncle Roger and Aunt Polly lived with their new and longed-for son, Roger, in the little turn-of-the-century barn-red house beside the Company Store.

Sometimes I kept my mother's letters in my pocket for several days before I let her intrude. In the new and more elegant world that had accepted me, I was a little bored with them and felt guilty about it. Dinner table disagreements seemed larger there than they were any-place else. The whole family spoke in political initials, NRA, PWA, WPA, making jokes and hating "that man" at the dinner table while my mother argued and I stayed quiet and wished that I were someplace else.

After all, it was one of President Roosevelt's initials that was lifting my parents out of the Depression. I thought it ungrateful of my father to join in the criticism when he was the civil engineer on project after project for the PWA. That money was sending me to Sweet Briar. They had the habit of saying they couldn't afford what they didn't want, which they were to keep all their lives, like so many who had been branded by the language of the Depression.

Elsworth painted everything that wasn't nailed down, asserting his place as what Aunt Myrtle called "the man of the house," which the rest of the family turned into a joke. I think that from the time he was a small child, he and his mother were afraid they would be asked to leave. He was the only one of the grandsons who did the repair work, fixed the fences, climbed the roofs, taking Addie's place when she had to stop.

When I read my mother's letter it had been in my pocket for a week. She began, as all Cedar Grove stories begin, a long way back in the past, with the young wounded miner, who had left his gun with Aunt Helen when she was a girl in 1923 and had never come back for it. It grew old, no longer fired, was covered with rust. Addie had long since seen that it was unloaded. It lay in the chifforobe drawer in the cyclone where years before I had watched the reflection of the moon and been so afraid that Miss Addie had caught the fear from the next room, her wonderful room, and had come in to comfort me.

Elsworth got the gun working again so he could use it, he said, to shoot the rats that were raiding the chicken house. It lay, once again, in the drawer where it had always been, carefully cleaned and wrapped in a towel. Elsworth was careful about things.

At the same time that I was half fulfilling my father's dreams, learning to be popular, a good dancer, and was on the way to becoming that most envied of girls, a "prom trotter," Uncle Preston had moved from his and Aunt Mary's house back to the cyclone where he had slept when he was a child, next to his mother's room. At six o'clock one morning in the fall of 1936, he shot himself in the head with the miner's gun. Addie rushed in and caught him as he fell.

The second of her children was dead. She did not share her sorrow, except that she drew close to Aunt Mary. It was the only concession she made. It was Aunt Mary who loved and cared for Addie more than all the rest. They sat together, talking, sometimes joking, always reminding each other of the past, in the parlor in winter in the twin mahogany armchairs with the needlework Addie had made, and in the summer in rocking chairs on Addie's porch, shaded by Addie's rambler roses, making a chorus of wood on wood as they went on talking and rocking for the rest of their lives together.

Miss Addie had something beyond a spirit that could be kept or lost. It was a rock, deep in the layers of her soul, old and hard, like people have who have been to war or stood up to blows so often that it has become a way of life. So even that death neither dulled nor diminished her.

But when I went back at Christmas she was an old woman. It had happened in the few months I was away. The cyclone had been changed. Miss Addie had chosen the new, bright rug and the paper with large red roses on the white walls.

I had been trained well by my new teachers. I had taken "the road not taken" because I knew already where the other one led. I had seen it; Fitzgerald's words, "so we beat on, boats against the current, borne back ceaselessly into the past," would be the dedication for *O Beulah Land*.

But every time an old woman speaks a language two hundred years nearer Shakespeare than mine, every time I go on the river, every time one of my fictional people, too real to me to be called characters, dreams of an adolescent stumble or fear that has long since been forgotten in their adult days, as the eighty-two year-old Melinda does in *Choices*, I am drawing, not on intelligent adulthood, but on my own deep past: what I saw and didn't know I saw, what I knew and didn't know I knew.

In *Choices*, Pineville, Kentucky, is there as clearly as when I was four; when Mrs. Hightower and Grandma Haycroft and Eulalie speak, the child I was who was there is there again.

In *Know Nothing*, the third volume of *The Beulah Quintet*, it is Johnny who is thrown into the river to learn to swim, as I threw myself. They are my strong, always living sources, portraits that were parts of my people that for years I would not have known consciously I was drawing.

But the greatest gift and burden has been the valley itself, Cedar Grove, the shape of the valley of Beulah that Hannah, in *O Beulah Land*, first saw when she was escaping from the Indians in 1756. I wrote it in the British Museum Reading Room in London in 1954.

She stopped in her tracks at the sight of a valley lying like an upturned hand between two hills across the river. The gentle place rested, with a creek like a lifeline running through it, as if God, sickened by the magnificence of the huge trees and the mountains, had lain down in mid-creation, and gone to sleep awhile. She could see from the river bank the grass-thick bottom near the creek; the flat, trodden yellow ground where the animals had come so long for water; the grove of cedars on the hill behind it; the first turning maple on the hillsides beyond.

That would be the living center of *The Beulah Quintet,* from wild valley to log fort, to mansion, to coal town, to money, to failure, to barricade again. The rest are shards of memory.

When I returned in 1941 from Canada at war my mother's family were all still at their own kinds of bitter and personal peace. They liked each other less, but grew closer at the same time, as if they knew but refused to recognize that they, too, would be at war.

For years I lived beyond the periphery of their world, but they would appear in a dream I had, a room where I worked, and when they did, my words seemed too diffuse, too bloodless, for the little while they were there. None of the generation of "the family" knew or cared about what I was doing, out there somewhere, writing books they could not be expected to read.

One day in the summer of 1945, when I had come back from war and was living in a furnished apartment on Seventieth Street, in New York, working as an editor at *Harper's Bazaar,* there was a knock on my door.

It was Uncle Bado, Addie's third son, the quietest of my uncles, looking more like Lincoln than ever, and speaking softly, low in his throat, so that I had always had to lean into what he said. Maybe you had to lean toward Lincoln to catch his humor, what he said half heard, as people half heard and forgot him at Gettysburg, his soft short address after the main eulogy was over, an afterthought. So Uncle Bado becomes an afterthought of this memorial, and turns into its victim and its essence.

He said, "Honey let me in and don't say anything."

He came in slowly and sat down at the kitchen table. He took off his hat and put it carefully in his lap. "Oh my God," he said, "why didn't they leave me alone?" The family had insisted on a cure for his deafness, and he had just been released from the hospital after an operation on his ears.

"How can people stand it? I can't stand it, the horns and the voices and the click of women's heels on the pavement. That's the worst, the click of women's heels."

He couldn't have known that I happened to be the one person he could come to who would know what he was talking about. I had come home from war only a few weeks before. I had been a ground-to-air signals operator in the flying control room of an RAF station. I had brought my own injury, signals shock, caused by hour after hour of listening through heavy enemy jamming, that had made my hearing so over-keen that it was sometimes a torture, and still is when I am tired.

So we sat there, two people who had a longing for silence in common, drinking coffee in the kitchen of a railroad flat in New York that had, that summer, become a place of refuge for many kinds of war.

I had always cared about my Uncle Bado. He had a keen, subtle wit, and he had stood up for himself through too many family attempts to keep him from being his quiet self. When he was young he had been sent to the Colorado School of Mines, but it was not what he wanted. He wanted to be home, and to go down the mines, and he retreated into deafness to get there and stay there. He had finally done what he had always wanted to do. He had become a coal miner. He was doing what so many children of mine owners were to do, going back underground where it had all come from, both the riches and the losses, as if they were trying to pay something back they didn't talk about.

I remember laughter at Uncle Bado and Aunt Violet's dinner table with their two children, my cousins. Uncle Bado had taught his son the name he had been called when he was a child—Grant Edward Sigsby Hipsom Slipsom Hopsom Sly Harry Proctor Henry Snyder Tommy Tinker Tompkins. Aunt Violet was a gentle woman, as quiet as he was, as slow to speak.

The last time I saw them was nearly thirty years later. Once again, I had come home from war, this time between Turkey and Cyprus. Little seemed changed at Cedar Grove. Perhaps I sought what I knew. Uncle Bado and Aunt Violet had moved into the pretty brick house on the hill overlooking the entry into Horse Mill Hollow that had once been Colonel Bannister's house. Colonel Bannister was buried in the family church yard.

Uncle Bado took me up Horse Mill Hollow to show me auger mining, where he was taking out the last of what coal he could find. We walked up the hollow past where Elsworth had shot the snake, and turned up toward the cliff. Halfway up the steep hill where the wild honeysuckle and the trees had clung so precariously, a level floor had been cut out, wide enough for trucks.

A long row of circular holes, like miniature caves, had been drilled into the hillside, where a twelve-inch seam of coal that had lain forgotten or neglected or protected for so long had been augered out and sold. All the way back down the hollow, Uncle Bado pointed out improvements he had made in Miss Addie's houses. He had cleaned up where he could, taking Elsworth's place to look after the "property." It was the last time I ever saw him.

Roger, one of my two nearest and dearest cousins, was living with his family at Cedar Grove. The house looked attractive. But the little street of corncribs and pigsties and the grape trellis was gone. It had become an ideal suburban property and my mother was frantic with delight.

Roger had been drawn back, as so many of the family, including myself, were drawn back over and over, to something I still can't name. A duty unfulfilled? A debt unpaid? Another coal seam to be found, more black gold? Roger's deepest dream had just begun to come true. He was the Democratic whip in the legislature. Before his last illness he would be Attorney General.

He had been a Rhodes Scholar, a full scholar at Yale Law School, had taken the accepted road to Sullivan and Cromwell, the law firm in New York. But he had been lonely, and he, like so many of the family, lived and breathed politics, so he had come back to be lord of the little broken manor.

I returned from living in Turkey, where I had finished the first volume of *The Beulah Quintet, Prisons,* one of the last written. I had begun to write *Blood Tie,* a novel I had set in Turkey. When war broke out over Cyprus, I, like so many other foreigners, had to leave the Aegean coast, which was being threatened by the Greek dictatorship of "the colonels," who were backing Samson, the would-be dictator of Cyprus. I had come back with nothing. No money. Not even any clothes. A refugee as so many from that volcanic world of the Aegean had been shunted back and forth, over and over through the centuries.

I was lucky. There was always, for me, Beulah. I came back to the big house, and tried to work there, but that, too, was an illusion. I did not yet know that I carried it with me, that the haven, the font, the tap root, was within myself.

I walked through the little town to Sunday dinner with my Aunt Mary, who, even in her age, and in her refusal to wear anything but blue jeans, a man's shirt, and a baseball cap, was beautiful. It was a lovely day that Sunday; I was home, I was safe, and I was trying to be happy.

My cousin Preston had tried to marry, but that had failed. He lived again at home. He had inherited his mother's beauty, his father's heavy name, which throughout his own life, God help him, had been changed to June Bug. Preston's life was over after Korea, the forgotten war, the forgotten veteran. For months he had stayed in the attic at Cedar Grove, guarded by an Army police dog he had brought back with him, refusing to let anyone near him. He stayed in the small end room that the family said the Confederate soldier had died in. He finally quit drinking.

As I got nearer their house, I saw that Preston had had the huge mill wheel from the old mill up Horse Mill Hollow wheeled into the front yard. On it he had painted in large white letters, "Though the mills of God grind slowly, yet they grind exceeding small." I thought he meant the Tompkins family then, but maybe he understood that it was all of us, and that it had gone back a million years.

There was too much past, too much family, for me to work in the valley. I took the train to Charlottesville, which had been my other haven for over forty years. My friends had lent me a room in their house to work in. As I walked into the house, the telephone rang. I answered it innocently.

It was Roger. "Come home," he said. His voice, I remember, was completely calm, as if he were holding it steady. "Uncle Bado has been murdered and Aunt Violet may die at any time. I need you."

How I got home I can't remember. I only know that I was holding a telephone in my hand in Charlottesville, and then I was there, at Beulah, at Cedar Grove, and Roger and I clung to each other in the hall where I had stood so long ago, a child refugee from the Florida boom.

The "tradition," the illusions, the pride, had come full circle and struck down the quietest of the sons. Two drugged local boys had decided that Uncle Bado had money in the house because he collected the rents from the "Tompkins Estate," mostly Addie's little houses. They broke in at three o'clock in the morning, and armed with two tomato stakes from Uncle Bado's garden, they began to beat them both in their beds.

Aunt Violet woke and at first, she said, she thought she was having a nightmare. They beat and beat Uncle Bado, long after he was dead. Blood splashed onto the walls, the ceiling, soaked his bed, and hers. They tied her down and tried to rape her, while she jeered at them and saved herself by saying, "Can't you find a young woman who will have you?"

They broke her jaw, her wrist, and finally left her unconscious, thinking she, too, was dead. They took Uncle Bado's car keys to his new Buick, and set out toward Ohio, their clothes still soaked in his and Aunt Violet's blood.

Roger's telephone had rung at 4:30 in the morning. It was Aunt Violet. He said that she sounded quite normal. She said, "Come up here, Roger. Bado's dead." Roger thought he had died of a heart attack.

He found her sitting in the easy chair she always sat in. The rope that she had finally loosened was still hanging from her broken wrist. She was in such deep shock that she didn't realize that her jaw was fractured.

"They've killed Bado," she kept saying, over and over, until the ambulance came.

Roger cleaned the blood-flung bedroom so nobody else would have to see it. He said the blood had become thick, like blood Jell-O. He never got over it. In his final illness the last thing he remembered were Uncle Bado's eyes.

So what was left of the family gathered once again at Cedar Grove. We sat, trying to speak and having nothing to say. We waited for something to happen that was never going to happen. Somebody kept making coffee.

On the day of Uncle Bado's funeral the telephone kept ringing, voters telling Roger to vote for the death penalty which was coming up in the House. He had been against it. He said little, just "We'll settle this later."

All day people from Cedar Grove came and brought flowers, casseroles, salads, until the huge dining room table was as laden as it had ever been even at Thanksgiving. When the bill to reinstate the death penalty came up, Roger, who had borne so much of the tragedy, the cleaning up, the comforting of Aunt Violet, the invasion of the family when he, too, was in shock, stood in the Legislature and spoke.

"Today we are called upon to decide whether people will live or die. Emotion and myth overwhelm us. We need to stop and think. 'The last temptation,' Thomas-a-Becket cries as he is about to die, 'is to do the right thing for the wrong reason.' We need to stop and think about our reasons. Because when you push that green button in front of you, you throw the switch that sends 2,000 volts of electricity through the body of a human being. There is still time to refuse to do that.... Those of you who have seen the victims of violence will, I think, remember the eyes. You will remember the pools of blood and the splattered brains and the torn and disfigured bodies, but most of all, you will remember the eyes ... On the night in which my father's brother was murdered, and my aunt was beaten, I grabbed a butcher knife. All I could feel was the lust to carve those boys into small pieces ... There is something in each of us that loves a killing. But we are not *animals and we KNOW it is wrong to take another's life. It is doubly wrong to take a life under color of law. Because we, as lawmakers, know that the promise of law is reason, and the expression of our finer instincts."*

The death penalty bill was defeated.

On the night of Uncle Bado's funeral I slept in the back bedroom where Addie had died, where Uncle Roger had lived for so long. The high carved back rose behind me, so I felt protected by its solidity from my own fears, the same as when I was a child, that someone would come up behind me, one of the house's ghosts.

I read for a long time that night, until I was aware that all the other lights in the house were out, and there was night emptiness in the garden beyond the window. Finally I, too, turned out the lamp beside the bed and tried to find sleep.

The lamp turned on again.

I thought the switch was defective and turned it off again, more carefully.

The lamp turned on again. I turned it off.

The lamp turned on a third time. I sat up. "Miss Addie," I said to the night, "I know you want to help us through this sinful earth. But don't worry. We will be all right. Please go in peace and let me go in peace."

Addie's death had been slow. She had finally let herself be moved out of the room she had lived in since her marriage, the births of her children, all the turmoil and work and years of holding together an inheritance my grandfather had entrusted to her, her life worth more to me than the ever-failing mine, the riches in *infernum*.

She had lain for months in the same place I lay in that night, in Uncle Roger's carved Victorian monumental bed in the back bedroom where she wouldn't have to climb the stairs. Aunt Mary was the one who sat beside her, sometimes held her hand, sometimes told her stories, sometimes helped her remember. Once Miss Addie squeezed Aunt Mary's hand and sighed. "Oh my God, Mary, how long does it take an old woman to die?"

She was eighty-three when she died in 1947. I was back in England.

I tried to find out what the funeral was like, but I had asked too late. Only two of my cousins remembered anything. One said it was hot as hell and the preacher talked too long; the other said he was drinking beer and shooting pool in the cyclone. Her funeral was a compromise. She was not buried from her own church, and nobody would have dared bury her from the Little Brick Church, so her funeral was held in the parlor. At least I found out that she lay in a closed casket on her quilting trestles in front of the preacher. The house was crowded with people from the town of Cedar Grove.

After the funeral, her family sat around the dining room table, for the last time Addie would ever tell them what to do. The will was read.

She had administered the estate as best she knew, and now it was time to turn it over to the children of her marriage to Mr. Tompkins.

The fragments of what had been the large farm were once again divided and divided like the pieces of a quilt, a few dollars' rent here, a sale there. Money mattered to all of them, except for the house and the three acres around it. There was cash, but the will itself was so opaque that then and even now, nobody knows quite which lot, which tendril of the past, divided and divided, were Miss Addie's illusions of riches, and which were real.

Years later, my mother lay in her turn, in the canopied bed where once she had cried because there was no money to pay a grocery bill, waiting to die and angry because she had planned to die at seventy and she was already nearing ninety. I sat in the green velvet rocking chair in the house that she and my father had copied from the Queen Anne houses at Williamsburg, the house my father and coal money had finally earned for her.

Her voice went sentimental, lilted as it did from time to time when she remembered a "lovely" thing that had happened or not happened, or wanted to advise me still, when I was in my sixties. It was the voice she had used for reading me stories when I was a child.

"I want you to tender me a solemn promise," she said, reaching out her hand to me. I took her hand, ready for the list I had heard so often, that began, "When I die . . .," and went on through the list of her house, her Staffordshire figures, her "early American" furniture, the bed she lay in, the clothes, the silver, the Duncan Phyfe card table, the Governor Winthrop desk, the bed that Jefferson Davis had slept in or had not slept in as a boy.

"Yes, ma'am," I said, as I had said for years, in the same place in the rocking chair, listening.

Then her voice went as hard as bedrock. *"Never never never,"* she rasped, "sell your share of Number Three Seam."

Number Three Seam was the last dream of riches. It was cannel coal. The seam lay under the Kanawha River, impossible to mine. She was clinging to the days when she was a child and cannel coal was the most valuable of all the seams. When my own mother's will was read, I sold my share of the "estate" including Number Three Seam to my cousin, Nancy, for ten dollars. I insisted on cash. The old habit I had had of checking my clothes, from the underwear out, for any connection with the coal face had finally ended. I was as free of it as we can ever be who have been born in that uneasy space in the coal fields between *ceolum* and *infernum*.

Addie had ended her will with the words, in her own strong handwriting "I want my daughter Myrtle to have the button scissors and the little pickout." They were the seamstress's tools she had brought with her to Cedar Grove. Then she had added, "This will may not please you all but you will haft to put up with it."

But her final words to her children were in a letter she had left to be read to them. She told them where they stood, the failures and the hopes, and she ended with, "I want you children to look after Myrtle. I know she can't have the little house in the back yard outright, but I want you to let her live in it for the rest of her life. She has been better to me than all you Tompkins children, and she is worth more than all of you put together because she has a good heart."

The next time I saw the house, it had been left empty for several years, while the family had decided on what to do with it. It had been left to all of them, the Tompkins "children." Uncle Roger and Aunt Polly had decided to buy the shares of the others and to live in it. My mother was ecstatic over what she called putting it back the way it had been in its early days, the correct way.

She drove me up to Cedar Grove over the road which the family had allowed the state to build in a ramp high over the house so that cars passing looked down on it, ignoring it and the town. The money from the condemnation rights had helped to pay for my parents' house, and buy Cedar Grove from the heirs. She wanted to show me what she and Uncle Roger intended, not allowing my Aunt Polly, his wife, a part in her decision. "After all," she explained, as she had so often, "She is an in-law. She wouldn't know."

We crossed Miss Addie's sagging porch and went into the hollow hall. The house seemed small and frail to me when it had always been so solid, dependable, and in a way, grand. It smelled of damp and pigeon shit and dust. The stairs creaked more loudly than they ever had. There were tearstains of rain down some of the wall paper. The rooms were nearly empty. The family had taken out of it what they had agreed should "go to" each of them, the furniture, the hangings, the china, the linens, the piles after piles of quilts made by Addie and Aunt Myrtle.

Once again it had all been divided, as it had when my great-grandmother died, when what was left of the fortune of that newly rich man, Mr. William Tompkins, the furniture, the linens, the silver made from coins from his first sale of salt in Cincinnati, had spread over the valley. In the dining room, the great table, the side board, all the things that had been there "Before the War" were gone.

The floor to ceiling gilt mirror in the parlor, which showed the 1861 flood five feet up across its reflection of the room, had gone to Uncle Bado and Aunt Violet in the house that had been left them by Miss Addie, the house on the hill with its view of the valley and the roof of the big house. One of the Duncan Phyfe card tables was at my parents' house, the other at Uncle Roger's. My mother had "grandmother's" sewing table beside her bed.

Where there had been so much life for me in the kitchen, it was cold, even in summer. A green stain that Aunt Myrtle never would have stood for crossed the sink from a leaky tap. The only sound was the soft churl of the doves in the attic. They had not left. "There must be a window open up there," my mother said, but neither of us went up the frightening attic stairs to find out.

My mother was seeing the house as it had been before her life began and was going to be again. "We are going to restore the mantels the way they ought to be, and the *porte cochere* at the front door instead of that awful porch, which never was" she said it before I could shut her mouth "apropos."

The "we" changed to "I."

"I have found perfectly lovely old mantels for the parlor and the library to replace those ugly brick ones." There was the little hiccup in her voice that told me she was going to lie or dream a new past. "The mantels I found were designed by Thomas Jefferson for Sweet Springs."

Addie was being removed from the house.

All the closet doors hung ajar, empty, except in Addie's room. There, on the floor like a discarded rag, lay the Joseph coat I had loved. Nobody had bothered to take it. It was still intact, only a little worn in places where some of the fragments of my grandfather's silk ties had rotted. The beautiful black feather stitching that held the pieces of her memory together had not faded. I picked it up. The one thing I would have wanted had been left for me. My mother grinned. "You would want that old thing . . ."

It hangs behind me as I write, Addie's Joseph coat her daughters hadn't bothered to pick up off the floor.

Forrest Hull, who had been my mother's sweetheart and read poetry with her when she was a girl, still lived in the little house at Cedar Grove across from the company store. He was the town's poet and its painter and its chronicler. Forrest recalled everything, told some of it, kept much to himself, and was there for my handsome cousin Preston, to sit with him beside the railroad and share a wide-mouth jar of bourbon and ice when he finally came down from the attic after Korea.

Forrest was still there to chronicle the "renovation" of the house, the porch gone, the new correct *porte cochere*, the mantels, a little too wide for the space they occupied, the Williamsburg blue, Williamsburg green, Williamsburg wallpaper on early Victorian walls which had been dark red in 1844, because it was "the latest thing."

In 1955, my mother, my father, and I went to the centenary of what we had always called the little brick church. She was trying to have it named *Virginia's Chapel* for the Historic Register. I did not know until I saw the plaque that day that it stood on the sight of the first fort, built by William Morris. It was summer. Heat and speeches hummed in the little church. The preacher was an eighty-year-old circuit-riding Methodist, who told us that he had preached his first sermon in the church. Behind him, Forest Hull's mural showed Christ the Shepherd with three sheep under a tree, a lamb in his arms that looked like a kitten, and behind him a turning river, beyond it a valley, like the valley of my Beulah, that the first Hannah had seen from far off. In the background he had painted low mountains that were the end of the Alleghenies as they lowered toward the Ohio valley, down the Kanawha.

We could see the family graves beyond the window as we sat there listening to the old preacher, fanning ourselves with paper fans that advertised the funeral home.

His first words were, "You might as well put away your Waterburys.

I am an old fashioned preacher, and I don't just talk for fifteen minutes like these young ones." He didn't. He covered the biblical history of the valley, which, as Addie would have known, was very different from the secular one. She, too, knew who had been saved, who had seen angels, who had talked to the devil, who had prayed like old Aunt Essie so the mountain would be moved that kept her garden from getting enough sun, because the Bible said faith would move mountains. She prayed all night, and then, in the morning, when the mountain was still there, she said, "Hell, I knowed the damned thing wasn't gonna move nohow."

After him the mayor of Charleston, who had been a boy in the valley, spoke. He talked about having been in love. He took us in our spirits out into the graveyard that surrounded the church, inside the wrought-iron fence, across the path away from the rest of the family, as the slaves had been buried in a place of their own behind the church. He called out to a woman as if she could still hear him.

"And over there beyond the Tompkins family, a Morris, child of the first people who settled this valley, the most beautiful woman I ever saw in my life. Minnie."

After the ceremony the women of the town set out a picnic on a long table in front of my grandparents' vault, nearly touching the wrought-iron railing. There were classic bowls of potato salad, fried chicken, fresh tomatoes, pickles, cakes, pies, all labeled with the name of the woman who had brought them. There, in the graveyard that usually smelled of wild flowers and cut grass, a Methodist picnic scented the summer with its own kind of incense.

Forrest drew me over to the vault.

"Honey," he told me, "I came up here when they opened the vault for your grandmother. They was a big flat rock over the stone steps, and when they lifted it aside, there were two benches like beds for the coffins. A shaft of sun lit your grandfather's face for the first time since he was killed. His coffin had rotted and his skeleton was just laying there, his arm hung down like he flung it in his sleep. He still wore part of his white shirt and his collar, and the great big red tie your grandmother had dressed him in the day he was put down there. They's only two shelves, no room for anybody else. They laid her right there beside him and then they closed up the vault, I guess forever."

Requiem

We sat under a canopy in the near darkness of the 16th of November, 1997. The first snow of the year drifted onto our hands and our hair. Up the hill beyond the discreet canvas, it floated across the windows of Virginia's Chapel. The wrought-iron railing around Addie and grandfather's Etruscan vault was dim beyond the veil of snow and evening. The brick of the chapel, the memorial to the fort, the naked trees, had lost color in the near darkness.

Roger's casket lay on clean steel rods to hold it above the grave where it would be lowered into the ground as soon as we had gone away and left him in the darkness. Only a triangle covered with plastic against the weather lay on its surface. A man took it to Roger's widow and laid it in her hands. It was an American flag. His best friend since the first grade read, *"I will lift up mine eyes unto the hills from whence cometh my strength."* His voice fell around us as quiet as the snow.

We had driven in a long, long line of cars, their funeral lights catching the snow's frail indifferent fall, on the same route that grandfather and Addie took from Charleston upriver, slowly past the river houses, past the Capitol, along the river where a tiny opened space had been left to make a park, and where the Ruffner house, one of the oldest and most beautiful on what was then Kanawha Street, where I had grown up as a neighbor, had been denuded of its clapboard and its graceful wings, and only its earliest form, a log cabin, had been saved. In the same park a house where my great aunt's Patten family had lived had been moved,

233

too, to preserve it and make way in the city for more important buildings.

We passed Belle, the little town named for some girl I had forgotten or never knew, long buried under the great Dupont plant. Every place in the narrow valley where a house could be built or a trailer could be set, was full. Only in the narrows where the hills came down nearly to the road was there the clean sweep of the river beyond trees, as it had been once, or nearly been, or might have been.

We passed pyramids of coal as high as small hills, tracks where coal cars waited, a bridge condemned, no longer needed, its road bed rusted, as frail as steel lace. In the industrial places not one single corporate owner had cleaned up its leavings—the abandoned buildings, the old tracks, the fallen stores. Not one tree, not one clearing, not one playground.

Only the people left there, seduced so long ago by jobs, had stayed because the valley had become their homes, and had tried, with small houses, and small gardens that still, in November, showed the marks of care, to make the valley decent again.

Cedar Grove had gone back as nearly to its hills as it could. There was still the scar up the hillside between the puny third growth timber where the tipple had been. The red brick Company Store, with its fine Georgian dentils, had fallen into the road one day and the bricks had been hauled away. Only the little house where Uncle Roger and Aunt Polly had lived when they were first married was left, empty. The houses built so long ago for the mine superintendents had been razed.

Railroad tracks were gone. There were a few cedar trees that had outlasted what was an ended tenancy for us of the valley. The procession passed the Narrows, passed the little hollow that had been one of the property lines as the "Estate" had shrunk and shrunk to nothing, crossed the ramp where the family had sold *coelum* as condemnation rights to the road commission and used the money to pay for building Queen Anne imitations in Charleston.

Not even the roof could be seen from the ramp as cars swept by. Below it, half forgotten, the Big House had become small and frail, unwanted, uncared for, the new correct *porte cochere* my mother had insisted on now old, falling, forgotten. Abandoned machinery that the last tenant had not moved littered the back lawn. Thieves had backed a pick-up truck into the yard and emptied the house of what was left—Uncle Roger's bed, the mahogany chairs, even the old kitchen table.

Roger had been the last to live there, with his own son, the fifth generation. He and his family had left after my Uncle Bado's death. For a long time his family opened it for Thanksgiving. Roger had called it the last "ceremony of innocence."

His curse, beyond land, beyond pride, beyond any strength the hills may have brought him, had been in the genes of his mother. From her he had inherited the tendency toward premature Alzheimer's disease that killed them both. He was brilliant, his humor more legendary than his father's. At his large funeral, his wife had asked his oldest friends to tell stories about him. There were sweeps of laughter in the polite Episcopal church.

It was said when he was tested for the disease that it may have been triggered so early by his uncle's death. The last time I saw him, when most of what was left of his brain was his humor, and when he still looked as handsome as ever, he said, "I remember his eyes," and Patty, his wonderful strong young wife, who would tend him as in the word tender as in tender mercy, as he drifted from husband to child to a blind and speechless body, reached over and touched his hand and kept hers there until his face cleared and we talked about other things, funny things that made him happy again.

The cars drew to a stop along the road by "Virginia's Chapel." There were two plaques, one for the "historic" church, one for the Morris fort that had preceded it. That was our heritage, all that was left.

Far enough downhill so that the little brick church rose above it, etched against the dark sky, a large square had been closed with chain link fencing. We sat over the graves of almost all of the people I have remembered in this book—Aunt Helen, Aunt Violet, Uncle Bado, Uncle Roger, Aunt Polly, Aunt Myrtle, Elsworth, his wife Loretta. There seemed to be only enough room left for Roger. The graves were neat, their gravestones white, and they were in rows as if they had been at one of the Sunday dinners waiting for Addie to finish her prayer.

The graveside ceremony was over. We stood and wished we were warmer, trying not to cry. We hugged each other and promised to call and promised to meet. I wanted to stay to drift a handful of earth over his casket when he was lowered down. I wanted to say goodbye, as a recognition of the earth we came from and that I wanted to give back, if only what I could hold in my hand. But the pile of earth had been hidden by a tarpaulin, earth hidden, death hidden. The funeral staff, no longer professionally grave, blew on their cold hands and waited for us to leave.

I walked uphill through the dusk and the snow past the wrought-iron fence where Uncle Preston, Aunt Mary, and June Bug lay, to say goodbye to Addie. Someone had moved both of the stone urns made by the Italian stone masons into the grass above the vault. My cousin's son had put red geraniums there; he said he and his mother did it every year. Through the dark of the new winter we saw that one of the flowers was still in bloom. That single brave color, in the snow of that cold place, was the only thing that made me begin to cry.

My husband and I drove east through the valley, stripped of trees that in the summer and in my memory gave it a sheen of beauty. He was a stranger to the valley. I saw it at last, a cleansing terrible vision, through his eyes, the raped neglected greed-diminished place as it is in winter, bare and cold, the skeleton of it exposed like the body of an old forgotten woman.

Where Uncle John's farm had been, and the fine cattle and the horses grazed, the pylons of an Appalachian Power plant stretched steel cat's cradles of wire against the sky like Indian Towers of Darkness.

We drove the road I had ridden every morning on the school bus when I was nine to Montgomery to school, past Glasgow, past London, named by some homesick Englishman who had come in early in this century to seek his fortune. And gone away again, as we were doing, out of the raped valley, the darkness.

At Smithers, where my Uncle Bado and Aunt Violet had once lived, the coal camp houses were gone. There were small, attractive houses, cared for, as if to defy the valley's past. Only the board and batten building was left of the old coal company, where meetings had once been held—I had been taken to a square dance there. It looked like it was waiting for the wind to take it away and bury it.

We drove past the Alloy plant, land that had once been Aaron

Stockton's, where some of the buildings looked abandoned, but where nobody had bothered to tear down what was no longer needed, and make a landscape of the broken ground. We had gone all the way up the valley to where it all began for me, at the Falls of the Kanawha, where Aaron Stockton had built his house , and by 1810 was welcoming strangers with money to the valley.

We passed the island where my parents had met but it was too dark to see the falls, only I could hear them, softly, far away. We spent the night at Aaron Stockton's inn, on the top floor. Out of the window I could see the falls, tamed by a dam I hadn't ever known was there, built to harness water power. The rusted ruin of the old plant still squatted over the river. Nobody had bothered to remove it and give at least some imitation of the view there had once been. It had been, and still was, in the summer and in my memory, so beautiful.

High fat white columns had been set around three sides of the inn years ago, when it had been made into a club house for the nice young men who came there to work in the plant, or at the Rinehart and Dennis Company who were building the tunnel through Gauley Mountain to harness more power from the New River to run more turbines. It was where the tunnel workers had caught silicosis, where my father was an inspector, and where he, too, may have breathed in the microscopic silicon shards that finally helped to kill him.

It was only as we were leaving in the morning that I could see what remained of the original house, sheltered and almost hidden under the new pitched roof of the inn, its slave-made bricks the red of Cedar Grove.

DATE DUE			

#47-0108 Peel Off Pressure Sensitive